THE
NEW AGE
OF
FINANCIAL
SERVICES
MARKETING

A Hands-on Applications Guide to Harnessing the Power of Database Marketing

**Edited by
Arthur F. Holtman
and Donald C. Mann**

FINANCIAL SOURCEBOOKS

NAPERVILLE, ILLINOIS

Published by:

Financial Sourcebooks

A Division of Sourcebooks, Inc.
P.O. Box 313
Naperville, Illinois, 60566
(708) 961-2161
FAX: 708-961-2168

Proofreading: Joyce Petersen
Design: Monica Paxson
Production: The Print Group
Cover Design: Concialdi Design

This publication is designed to provide accurate and authoritative information in regard to the subject matter covered. It is sold with the understanding that the publisher is not engaged in rendering legal, accounting, or other professional service. If legal advice or other expert assistance is required, the services of a competent professional person should be sought.

From a Declaration of Principles Jointly Adopted by a Committee of the American Bar Association and a Committee of Publishers and Associations

Library of Congress Cataloging-in-Publication Data

The New age financial services marketing : database marketing for
  financial institutions : a hands-on appication guide / edited by
  Arthur F. Holtman & Donald C. Mann.
      p.   cm.
   ISBN 0-942061-15-2
   1. Bank Marketing. 2. Data base marketing. 3. Data base
management. 4. Financial services industry. I. Holtman, Arthur F.
II. Mann, Donald C.
HG1616.M3N48 1991
332.1'068'8--dc20   90-28739
                                                                       CIP

Printed and bound in the United States of America.
10 9 8 7 6 5 4 3 2 1

TABLE OF CONTENTS

FOREWORD

Donald Mann
FUSION Marketing Group

In the early spring of 1990, I wrote an article that appeared in the August issue of *Bank Marketing* entitled "Database Marketing, How It's Changing Your Business." Here are the opening four paragraphs of that article:

"Financial services marketing isn't the warm and cozy place it used to be.

"Accountability is the new watchword. Senior management is increasingly demanding cost/benefit analyses of marketing and media programs to use for planning and future budget allocations. Ideally, the Marketing Department will be the 'initiator' of moves toward bottom line oriented marketing accountability.

"The combined pressures of increasing competition and regulatory change are beginning to have a profound impact on the ways financial institutions market products and communicate with customers and prospects. The Marketing Customer Information File (MCIF) has become the *starting point* in the race to develop effective competitive and relationship building strategies.

"Here's the problem: the technology and its marketing applications are so new that the financial services database marketing 'book' is years away from being published. Yet the industry is rapidly adopting this new technology . . . and wondering what to do with it."

I was wrong in my prediction in the last paragraph. You have the book on financial services database marketing in your hands, several years sooner than I thought. While the technology and its applications continue to evolve at a dizzying rate, this book presents the "state of the art," as reported by the users who are driving that evolution. To have worked in this area for two years or longer marks one as a "pioneer," and there are a number of these represented in the chapters that follow.

We have to go back to the early 1980s to see the beginnings of what has become a revolution in the financial services industry. It was then that the MCIF had developed from concept to reality inside a handful of institutions and through two major service bureaus, Alcon and Urban Data. These initial systems were primarily research tools, capable of producing tons of reports examining an institution's householded customer base from every conceivable perspective. The operative idea here is the creation of a "householded" customer base. This is the heart of the revolution that followed because, for the first time, an institution could look at the *total* business a customer brought with it. All of a sudden, the term "relationship" began to creep into marketing discussions.

The ultimate effect of this new perspective on financial services marketing has been a marked increase in the momentum to shift from product-driven strategies to customer- or segment-driven marketing. The fact that the customer is the ultimate source of an institution's profitability is so obvious it hardly bears mentioning, but the importance of the MCIF is that it gave financial marketers the ability to *apply* this fact to the development of marketing strategies. Financial institutions are unique in the amount and history of customer transaction behavior they capture and store. It is this behavior that the MCIF consolidates and reports through the householding process, and this is the most powerful marketing information it is possible to possess. It is safe to say that this information, and your access to and use of it, will drive the retail side of your business in the future.

By the middle of the decade, a number of financial institutions had begun to use the data provided by the MCIF in the planning and execution of direct mail programs. These pioneers experienced no small degree of difficulty because they were trying to use a research system for marketing applications that it was not designed to support.

The early MCIF software had no tracking capabilities beyond the "by guess and by gosh" methodology of comparing cross-sell reports from different updates. The primary contribution of the early MCIFs to direct marketing programs was the ability to define, identify, and extract mailing lists from key customer segments based on household relationships. This was a giant leap forward in sophistication for financial marketing—it was just a little awkward in application.

The second generation of MCIF-driven financial services marketing was based on the work of one company, Customer Development Corporation (CDC). In the mid-'80s, CDC began refining database marketing concepts in its work for national finance companies. It developed a proprietary MCIF system that was designed specifically to make possible the execution, management, and tracking of complex direct mail programs targeted to existing customers, based on the purchase behavior and activity of those customers. CDC christened this service "Matrix Mail" and expanded the concept to financial institutions.

CDC was the first marketer to harness the power of the purchase behavior of customers to predict future buying behavior. For years, direct marketers had paid lip service to the maxim that the Recency, Frequency, and Amount of a customer's purchase activity can be used to predict the propensity to purchase additional products. That was why these marketers happily paid additional list rental costs for "Hotline" (recent) buyers and "Multibuyers"—they respond at higher rates than other names from the same list. CDC created an MCIF that was designed to identify and segment customers based on their product usage and purchase recency, among other criteria. CDC then executed direct mail programs in which the offer made to a specific customer was determined by these criteria. These direct mail programs were driven "automatically," from monthly updates of the clients' customer activity. CDC called the recency of activity criteria "Event Triggers" and generated millions of dollars in profitable business for its clients. Virtually everything that has followed in the evolution of financial services database marketing is based on the innovations pioneered by CDC. Tom Lund, CDC's founder, discusses these developments in the introduction that follows.

The year 1987 was pivotal for the development and applications of MCIF systems because the "third generation," or new PC-based, systems first became widely available that year. Before this development, all of the MCIF systems were housed on mainframe computers in service bureaus. The only direct contact the financial institution users had with these systems was through the reports they generated. These would arrive in crates that often reached to the ceiling of the hapless Marketing Director's office, where they usually stayed until being moved to someone else's office. The information, though valuable, was so overwhelming that it was not used to the extent it could have been. Add to that the cost and difficulty of securing special reports and mailing tapes and you can see why several groups of entrepreneurs recognized an opportunity of tremendous proportions.

The result was the PC-based MCIF, which placed the householded customer database on a desk in the Marketing Department with built-in utilities to generate reports and, ultimately, mailing tapes and tracking files. Among the most influential new companies providing these systems were Customer Insight Corporation, Datapol, Infoshare, Marketing Profiles, and OKRA Marketing.

Many of these early innovations consented to share their experiences in this book. The early PC-based systems were more oriented toward research applications, giving their users increased flexibility in running, formatting, and updating reports. However, they also offered powerful marketing segmentation and direct marketing execution potential, placing this power, for the first time, in financial marketers' hands.

The development of these systems was driven by their users, many of whom had several years of experience with the service bureau MCIFs and, as a result, pushed the vendors to add flexibility and utility to the systems. These users had sensed the power of the data that the MCIF provided; now they had a tool to apply that power to their marketing programs. Interestingly, many of the early adopters of the new technology were small to medium-size thrifts and banks. In part, this was due to the data storage and processing limitations of the PC at that point in time. It was also strongly influenced by financial considerations—the PC-based systems brought the price of an MCIF down to levels that broadened the potential market considerably. The result was an ironic twist of fate: the smaller institutions had a head start on their larger competitors in climbing up the database marketing learning curve.

The past three years have been a period of rapid evolution, both for the MCIF systems and for the marketing applications of those systems. Compared to the early days of the "first generation" service bureau systems, costs have fallen so dramatically that almost any institution can afford to have a state-of-the-art MCIF sitting on a desk in the Marketing Department. Self-contained householding software, which permits an institution to update the MCIF database on the PC, has been available for several years. These systems are getting faster and friendlier to use. Some systems offer incredibly sophisticated address standardization and file scrubbing routines, which strip off unwanted phrases from the name and address fields to prepare a file for mailing and genderize the names so that a personal salutation can be used in a letter. Both household-specific appended demographic data and geodemographic cluster coding are supported by many of the systems. These enhancements expand the MCIF's ability to target specific customer profiles for mailing purposes and make it possible to use the MCIF for marketing and site location geographic studies.

Perhaps the primary benefit of using an MCIF for direct marketing is its tracking capabilities. That's because one of the key advantages of properly executed direct marketing programs is their accountability. Through accurate tracking, the marketer can determine what worked, what didn't, and how to fix it for the next time. That translates to increasing cost efficiency over time. A reliable tracking report is the most powerful weapon in the budget battle, because management can see the actual returns on their marketing investments.

The problems experienced by the thrift industry will have profound impact on the entire financial services industry, perhaps as profound as those caused by deregulation. The marketplace will still grow more competitive and the competition keener, more sophisticated. If you don't have an MCIF system in your institution now, here's a chilling thought—your competition probably does. Do whatever it takes to get one soon because without it, you're simply no longer a viable player in the increasingly competitive financial services marketing game.

August 18, 1991
Memphis, Tennessee

PART 1

IN THE BEGINNING

1

AN INTRODUCTION TO DATABASE MARKETING

Thomas C. Lund
Customer Development Corporation

W hen I was asked to write the opening chapter of this book, I was both pleased and honored to have the opportunity. I'm certain that the book will be an important addition to the literature available on the subject of database marketing.

But I couldn't help thinking about the day one of my pre-teen children described to me, with great enthusiasm, what it felt like to be in love for the first time. She honestly believed that she was the very first person in history who had ever felt that way. She had made an absolutely unique discovery of monumental significance, and she was so excited that she had to tell me about it immediately.

"Database marketing" is the hottest catch-phrase in financial services. Every day, I read a new article or hear another speech on the subject, written or given by someone who has just embraced this incredible new concept. It's almost as if an entire industry just fell in love for the first time, and all those people think that this is a brand-new discovery.

I can understand why. I remember what it was like to encounter the idea for the first time. I fell in love with it, too.

In 1969, I gave up a sales career with IBM to take over and run a small ad agency. The agency had been doing some work for State Farm Insurance, and I reasoned that a quick way to increase billings would be to see what other kinds of assignments I could get from State Farm.

At about the same time, I managed to establish a relationship with a major consumer finance company, which was looking for the solution to a marketing problem that had plagued them for years—how to provide some meaningful marketing support to their branches.

Both companies had the same objectives. Both of them had a very large customer list, and they wanted to sell more to those customers. Both of them had national field organizations that were at the heart of their delivery systems, and both wanted to set up a system that would drive a constant flow of business into the field organization.

They were tired of the "feast or famine" effect created by periodic advertising and promotion pushes to produce traffic, and the field representatives were complaining loudly that they were getting no benefit from the mass media advertising the companies were doing. The field wanted promotion that would have an immediate impact on business.

It was the synthesis of the assignments from those two clients that led me to a concept that would change my career—and my life—forever.

After some initial research and field interviews, we discovered that what really drove the business of these two far-flung organizations was the high-touch service that their best agents and branch managers were providing. The perception of personal service from the local representative of the company was important to the customers.

How the best field representatives were creating that perception was by constantly staying in touch with their best customers, using a combination of highly personalized direct mail and telephone calls. The problem was, only 10% to 20% of the field representatives were doing that job well, and the rest weren't doing it at all.

We hit on the idea of building a computer system that would mechanize the sales and service techniques employed by the best agents and managers, so that those techniques could be replicated throughout the organization. Both clients told us that no one had ever tried to do that before, and we soon found out why — the technology required simply did not exist.

From our initial field interviews, we had learned a great deal about customer behavior, and had even developed some theories about how we might predict which customer might buy a specific product next. We thought we would be able to test those theories using the accounting files maintained on our clients' mainframe computers. Since I had sold for IBM, I knew what the computer was capable of, and knew that it could be done.

But when we asked for the data, we hit the first obstacle to implementation. There was no way to get the information out of the computer in a way that was usable for marketing. One of the objectives was cross-selling, but the data centers couldn't even determine who had purchased more than one product. We were told by one of the client's data centers that what we wanted would require 10 years' work and $40 million in programming.

We didn't even have a computer; ad agencies in the late sixties didn't need them. And we couldn't find a service bureau that could create the system we wanted to build. So, we bought a computer and went into the database business. That was in the days when computers were very expensive, and the decision represented a major commitment for us.

Our clients wanted much more than research. They also wanted a direct mail program, because the field wanted traffic, and direct mail was what the best managers were doing to create it.

From what we had seen, the most effective direct mail was mail that had been prepared and mailed by the field force itself. The good managers seemed to instinctively know which customers should get mail. Because they had built personal relationships with their customers, the mailings enjoyed extremely high readership. And because they knew they couldn't work hundreds of leads at a time, they sent out smaller mailings more often.

The problem was, most of the managers didn't have time to do their own mailings, and the home office had no control over whether or not the mailings were even legally correct. Without the mail being centralized, all the mail was going out with first-class postage, and there was virtually no way to determine how much money was actually being spent. Plus, there was the question of how to constantly improve the efficiency and effectiveness of a program that had no centralized control.

The answer seemed obvious. Once we built a computer system that would allow us to find the right customers to mail to, we would simply implement the program the way the top 20% of the managers did. The objective, of course, was to raise the other 80% of the branches to the same level of proficiency and consistency. That's when we hit the second major obstacle.

Since the objective was personalized service, the mail had to be personalized, to a degree that no one had ever tried before.

- The mailings had to look as if they came from the local office, and the offices had to know whom we had mailed to so they could follow up. There were literally thousands of offices and branches, and there wasn't even a computerized list of them. We had to build one, then figure out how to keep it updated and match it up with the right customer when the mail was produced. Plus, the mail somehow had to look local.

- The field organization had figured out the fact that different customers responded to different communications at different times. As a result, we had discovered dozens of creative approaches that were working in the field. They all had to be implemented simultaneously, every month, in order to ensure an even flow of traffic.

- Combined with branch variables, we were generating hundreds of different lettershop lots every month. When we tried to find a lettershop to handle the project, they looked at us as if we were crazy. So, we set up a lettershop.

- The mailings that worked best were letters, followed up by phone calls and personal contact. There were a few people experimenting with computer letters at the time, produced by impact printers on pin-fed, continuous form stock. We had the same problem finding someone who could handle small, complicated lots as we had with finding a lettershop. We had to start producing computer letters ourselves.

- Letters had to be signed. Remember, in those days there was no such thing as laser imaging and digitizing, so we had to go into the hand-signing business. We ultimately were signing more than a million letters each month, making Peoria, Illinois, the world capital for writer's cramp.

- The most difficult problem to solve was inventing a way to make the system *interactive*. The best agents and managers told us that if you asked a customer to buy something, and he did, you should recognize that fact and talk to him differently next time. Plus, the computer had to remember everything it had said to an individual customer to keep from repeating itself. There was no software available anywhere that would handle that kind of history. We had to hire programmers so that we could write our own.

- In order to mimic the way good managers and agents were selecting customers to sell, we borrowed a segmentation concept known as RFA analysis from the mail-order industry. Customers were selected on the basis of recency, frequency, and amount. Our research soon proved that RFA was the perfect starting point.

  The more recently a customer had bought something, the more likely he was to buy again in the near future. Even though it was easy to put together a logical scenario in which it made sense to wait awhile to solicit a recent buyer for additional business, the facts told us otherwise.

  The more frequently a customer had bought, the more likely they were to buy. Our clients had a natural inclination to want to move every single-service household to a second service, but it was simply more cost-effective to sell a fifth service to a four-service household, or a fourth service to a three-service household. The only time it made sense to try to sell a single-service household was when that household had bought a high-dollar product very recently. The higher the dollar amount the customer had borrowed or invested, the easier they were to sell again.

- The idea was so revolutionary that no one would buy it on faith. We had to develop tracking procedures that would allow us to measure all those complicated mailings incrementally—isolating the mail as a single variable in a proactive selling environment. So, we created a history-based continuous "control group," to measure the difference in product purchases and dollar gain from customers who were a part of the mail program, compared to a statistically selected sample of those who had been held out to establish a baseline measurement.

Within a year, we had evolved a continuous traffic generation program for the branches that could only be described by laying it out on a grid. It actually worked in three dimensions, since the grid layout could be altered each month if the client wanted to change the product mix being promoted. We coined the term "matrix mail" to describe it.

I wasn't running an ad agency anymore. In fact, we had very painfully become a company unlike any other, with a unique combination of services all under one roof. I didn't even know what to call us. In a management presentation for one of our clients, I described us as a database marketing agency, and the name stuck.

In retrospect, all the capabilities we had to invent to start the database marketing business look very primitive. But given the technology available at the time, we had accomplished something really remarkable. By trying to solve a field sales problem, we had accidentally built the first database marketing system.

Best of all, it worked. In fact, it worked so well that I had clients literally changing the way they did business in order to take maximum advantage of the system. We had created a *selling system*, and we had made heroes of the people who had believed in us. And that was the most rewarding experience of all.

Database marketing is a powerful concept. It is now used across a wide range of industries to sell a wide variety of products. But to best understand the technique as it applies specifically to financial services, it is necessary to put the banking business into a historical perspective, as well.

The Marketing Services Evolution

In simpler times, bankers were database marketers in the purest sense of the word. If you've ever seen that great old James Stewart movie, *It's a Wonderful Life*, you'll remember that the customers of the Bailey Building and Loan were treated like very special people.

George Bailey knew every depositor by name. He knew their kids' names, too, and he knew where each and every one of them lived, because he had personally approved the loans that had bought their homes. He knew his customers—his database—and he used what he knew about them to build his business. The service was not just personalized, it was *personal*.

Banking really did work that way once, but not anymore. The financial services business is entirely too large, complex, and far-flung. Times have changed. Just look at what happened to the industry in the 1970s and 1980s.

The financial services industry, forced to adapt to the deregulation thrust upon it by the government, went through a series of critically important "growth stages" on its way to maturity. Figure 1 illustrates the stages in the industry's evolution.

In the beginning, banks had parity, because the government regulated what products were to be sold, and at what price. With the advent of deregulation, the industry began learning to compete in the open marketplace.

The first stage of that learning process was a tremendous proliferation in the number of products offered, as banks took advantage of their newfound freedom to innovate. Some product strategies made good sense; others didn't. Consumers quickly became bewildered by all the various "versions" of what were basically still checking, savings, time deposit, and credit-related products.

When having the latest, greatest product idea didn't provide the "key" to competing in a deregulated world, the industry moved to price competition. That wasn't the total answer either, and in some markets the strategy degenerated into highly unproductive price wars.

At about the same time, computer technology had advanced to the stage where automation could be used to enhance certain products and to make others more efficient and therefore more profitable. Although automation helped, it wasn't the total key to competing, either.

9

Figure 1

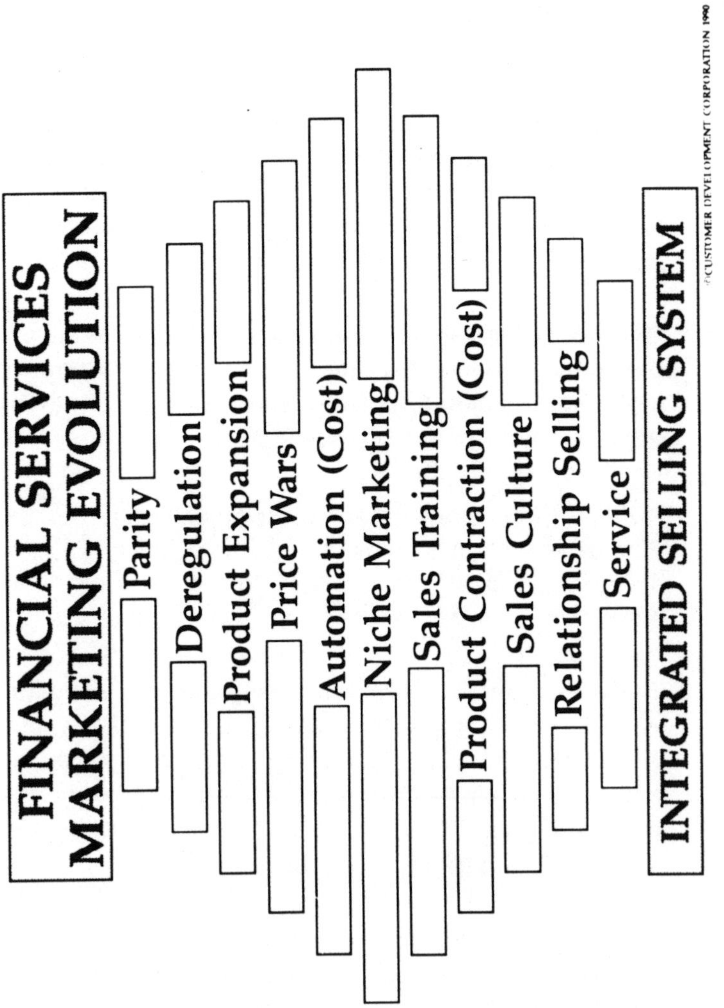

FINANCIAL SERVICES MARKETING EVOLUTION

- Parity
- Deregulation
- Product Expansion
- Price Wars
- Automation (Cost)
- Niche Marketing
- Sales Training
- Product Contraction (Cost)
- Sales Culture
- Relationship Selling
- Service

INTEGRATED SELLING SYSTEM

©CUSTOMER DEVELOPMENT CORPORATION 1990

Some institutions quickly became very good at niche marketing by determining what they were best at and capitalizing on those skills. Most concentrated on sales training and the development of a sales culture to bring nonsales employees in step with the realities of the new marketplace.

Ultimately, after more than a decade and a half of turmoil in which banking grew to maturity much faster than any business should have to, the industry relearned an old truth: the bank's relationship with its best customers was what actually drove the business. And what mattered most to those customers was service quality.

What really happened during those years? With the advantage of hindsight, it seems clear that most banks were searching for one single strategy that would make them successful in a deregulated world. After each industry shift, enthusiasm was quickly followed by disappointment because they had not found what they sought.

In actual fact, the key wasn't new products, lower prices, automation, niche marketing, sales training, or the development of a sales culture. It was *all* of those things, coupled with the ability to deliver quality service to the bank's best customers.

The Role of Service Quality

How service is delivered is an important element in the overall development of a selling system, and is therefore a key part of any strategy that includes database marketing.

Think for a moment about the companies most people think of as the "best" companies. Firms like IBM, Xerox, and Daimler-Benz all have one thing in common. They are known to provide superior service.

The interesting thing about service is that it's largely a *perception*. If someone is ignored by a clerk in a favorite department store, they might complain that the store is mistreating a long-term, loyal customer who has spent thousands of dollars in the store over the years. But in all likelihood, the clerk did not know those things about the customer. A single thoughtless act by a single employee can destroy a carefully crafted reputation for service.

Similarly, in the companies that treat customers right, it's the small things that make up the perception of service. How enthusiastically and helpfully a doorman greets a guest at a hotel can speak volumes about the way the hotel is run, in the same way that a personal thank you note for opening an account says a lot about a financial institution's service.

The people in a bank's branches are its "front line" in the competition for good customers. How those customers *perceive* the service they get from branch personnel is what really matters.

Every time the bank communicates with a customer it should be saying something meaningful to that individual. If it does, the customer will feel better served.

A database marketing program designed to strengthen and build on the relationship between the managers and their best customers can actually increase the perception of service that the institution offers. At the same time, it can provide a lower cost per sale than any other advertising medium.

But no amount of marketing expertise will overcome a badly executed "back room" operation.

The Four Stages of Database Marketing

The real objective of database marketing is to use the power of the database to sell financial products and services more efficiently.

- The basic tool required to start is the *MCIF*, or Marketing Central Information File.

- Since customers buy on their own timetable, *database research* is using the MCIF to discover what those timetables are. It's knowing who to sell, what to sell them, and when.

- *Implementation* is using the research to make the right offers for the right products to the right customers at the right time.

- Closing those sales through the institution's available distribution system is *database selling*.

All four of those stages have to be tied together into a database marketing system and executed in sequence, if an institution is going to take full advantage of the opportunity in its customer file.

Imagine that you are a mountain climber, like the one in Figure 2. Your objective is to get across the mountain range that you can see from your vantage point at the foot of the first mountain.

From your perspective before you begin your climb, you can see not four but only one mountain. Unless you already know that there are a total of four mountains to cross before getting to the other side of the range, there's a high likelihood that you will underestimate the difficulty of the climb ahead of you and the time required to complete it. When that kind of miscalculation happens to an organization, the resulting embarrassment and discouragement may kill the whole idea.

Building the Database

The last mountain to climb is creating the database. For anyone who has continually fought the battle of trying in vain to get a clean, usable customer list from the data center, it is easy to understand why the creation of a database may seem to be the only really significant hurdle to be overcome. Getting the right information from the customer file can seem so stupefyingly difficult that everything else must pale by comparison.

Fortunately, today the database is far and away the easiest mountain to climb, if only because there are so many options in the marketplace to pick from.

Because of rapid advances in personal computer technology in the last few years, the power of the MCIF is now within the reach of virtually any institution that wants it. The basic criteria that must be met are speed, enough data fields to handle a virtual avalanche of information, flexible reports, and built-in graphics capabilities.

Another criterion that is becoming increasingly important is the relative simplicity of the user interface. More and more, there is a trend

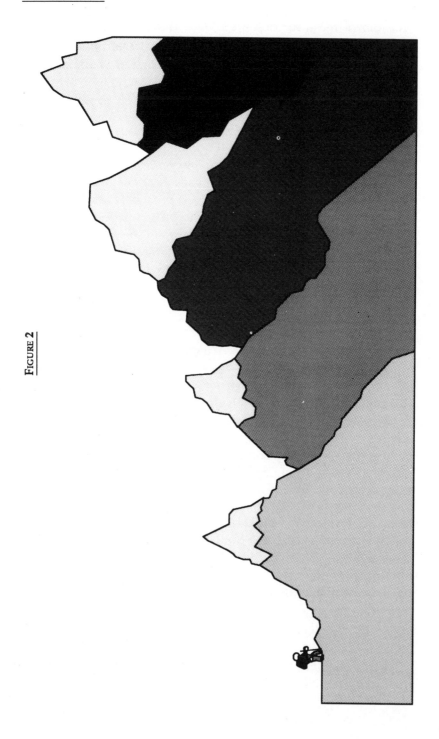

FIGURE 2

toward placing the MCIF in field offices, regional headquarters, and even in branches. As the locations proliferate, the technical expertise of the average user decreases. A system that doesn't require programming skills or laborious training is quickly becoming a necessity.

Database Research

The second "mountain" to be scaled is doing the basic research. As this stage of the process unfolds, the research department becomes very knowledgeable about the customer file, and begins the process of defining the high-priority customer segments and selling opportunities within the database.

Over the years, the validity of segmentation using recency, frequency, and amount has been proven over and over again. The most successful database marketers have searched the file monthly for the fleeting (and perishable) sales opportunities that RFA reveals.

The RFA technique can be improved dramatically by adding age segmentation. As people move through the major stages of their lives, they turn from borrowers into investors, then into savers. All of these major behavioral shifts can be predicted using date of birth, which can be appended to the file when it's not available in the bank's accounting records.

With the availability of larger and more complex databases, segmentation technology has literally exploded. We've discovered that there are many more predictors of behavior, and they usually fall into three categories:

1. Behavioral information, for example, actual product/service purchases.

2. Attitudinal information, such as life-style shifts.

3. Compiled demographic information (generally census-based).

With long experience, we have found behavioral and attitudinal information to be more predictive in building models than compiled information. We believe it's because compiled information tends to generalize by geographic area, while behavioral and attitudinal information tends to be more household specific.

As an illustration, here is a list of just some of the MCIF data fields that are usually required to do an effective job of segmentation for general advertising, direct mail, telemarketing, or personal selling purposes in a banking environment. Note that much of this information is not resident in the bank's account files, so it must be added to the database from external sources.

Buying Index by Product
Household ID Number
Life-style Code
Employment Category
No. of Accounts in Household
No. of Individuals in Household
Highest Deposit Level Ever
Inquiry by Product
Prospect List Source Code
Current Household Deposits
Current Household Loans
Street Address (1)
Street Address (2)
City
State
County
Zip Code
MSA
Census Tract
Census Block
Telephone Number
Tax Number
Mail Code
Birthdate/Age
Household Branch
Number of Children
Account Sequence Indicator
Gender Code
Mail Responsiveness
Historical Buying Patterns
Primary Language
Employee Code

Length of Residence
Home Value
Income
Marital Status
Individual ID Number
First Name (1)
Last Name (1)
Commercial Account Indicator
First Name (2)
Last Name (2)
High Priority Zip
Past Period Household Deposits
Past Period Household Loans
Interest Rate
Current Account Balance
Past Period Account Balance
Average Account Balance
Account Open Date
Account Maturity Date
Primary Account Type
Secondary Account Type
Closed Account Code
ATM Indicator
Homeowner Code
Account Branch
Last Change of Address
Education Level
Courtesy Title
Profitability

...and the list goes on from there.

In addition to data from the bank's files and information available from external sources, there are also opportunities to add other attitudinal and behavioral information. Suppose, for example, an institution had surveyed its best customers regarding their banking and financial services habits, and wanted to capture and use the survey information for segmentation. It might include:

Primary Bank	Secondary Bank
Total Household Deposits	Total Household Equities
Specific Competitor Codes	Level of Affinity
Account Categories Used	Account Categories Not Used
Branch Preference	Service Perception
Saving/Investment Attitudes	Life-style Indicators

...and that's just the beginning.

For some types of trend analysis, it is necessary to keep track of each household's total deposits and loan levels every month for 24 consecutive months for each product. That information alone will require the addition of hundreds of dedicated fields to the database.

The need for all of this information begins to create two problems for researchers.

First, much of the work on an MCIF is what I like to call "conversational analysis," a process in which the researcher and the PC actually appear to be having a dialogue. During the exploratory phases of the initial research, questions are much more likely to generate additional questions than clear-cut answers.

The researcher poses a question. The MCIF provides a report that proves only that the question should have been asked another way. The researcher reframes the query and asks again. The next report reveals the need to study a subset of the data. The process goes on and on, sometimes through hundreds of queries and reports. In technical terms, it is an iterative process.

Imagine what it would be like to have a conversation in which there were extended periods of silence between the two parties trying to communicate. If the objective was to have a conversation with the database, the enforced waiting time would be extremely frustrating.

Unfortunately, until now there has been a direct correlation between the number of fields in a database and the processing speed of a PC. The more fields there are, the slower the system runs. A slow system makes the concept of a conversation with the database impossible.

In the near future, all PC-based research systems will have to carry literally hundreds of fields of data, as the need for information increases, without a corresponding degradation of speed.

The second problem created by all those predictors in the database is synthesis. There are so many data elements that the only way to effectively manage the process is to build predictive models for every customer behavior that the institution wants to either enhance or retard.

Some of the modeling technology is extremely complex. One of the most fascinating concepts we regularly use at CDC is called "neural networking," in which a computer is literally taught to use the same data manipulation techniques employed by the human brain to recognize patterns in a database.

We use that technique, along with a variety of other artificial intelligence and expert systems, to produce a "Household Potential Index," in which every household in the MCIF is given a series of scores that represent the likelihood that the household will buy individual asset and liability products. We can also use the same systems to predict undesirable behavior, such as the likelihood of account runoff.

The indexing technique has proved to be unerringly accurate in its ability to predict purchase behavior. In fact, if a household scores high enough for certain products, we have discovered that there is sometimes no real need to mail an offer—the household is so likely to buy that no outside pressure is needed to cause the purchase action.

In a relatively volatile environment like banking, predictive models have to be reconfigured at least twice a year, or when major competitive changes take place in a market. But the database information has to be run through the model on a monthly basis at the minimum in order to accurately find perishable selling opportunities that the competition doesn't know about.

As an example, our research shows that 20% to 30% of the households that score as being highly likely to open a line of credit in a given month will not score high for that product the next month. This phenomenon happens at least partly because many of the high-scoring households satisfy their need for credit elsewhere, and that's why the opportunities revealed by predictive modeling must be viewed as perishable.

To put it another way, the technique requires monthly updates. It simply won't work as well on a database that is updated only quarterly or semiannually.

Traditional database research can provide a profile of the characteristics common to recent buyers of a specific product. But only a small percentage of the people who fit that profile actually buy in that same time period. Predictive models allow the researcher to get much closer to being able to pick specific buyers out of a database in advance.

Implementation

The third "mountain" is the stage of the process where people usually start to become frustrated. The researchers *know* that the opportunities are there, and that those opportunities are fleeting and perishable. But they don't see much happening. It's as if they've provided the combination to the lock, but no one seems to know how to use it to open the safe.

When an institution mails a product offer to nearly all of its customers, it is not doing database marketing. It is using mass advertising techniques inappropriately, in a medium designed for targeting.

The ideal implementation of a database marketing system starts with the monthly use of predictive modeling to index each customer on its likelihood to buy every product and service that the institution has to offer.

The next step is to make appropriate offers of the products that the institution wants to sell to the customers that score as being most likely to buy those products.

In other words, the goal is to make the right offer for the right product to the right customer at the right time.

Because mailings work best when they are localized, they must be designed to appear as if they were generated by the branch or calling officer with whom the customer does business.

And finally, because the institution wants to sell most of its products all of the time, the ideal system must be designed to make many small mailings selling many products with different creative approaches, simultaneously.

The key word in this process is "system."

Figure 3 is a simplified example of the ultimate system for the implementation of a database marketing program for financial institutions. It is called *matrix mail*.

Although the matrix illustrated differs dramatically in execution and sophistication from the original and from the indexed systems we use today, it has its foundations in the same concept we used to implement our first database marketing programs in 1969.

The basic premise behind such an approach is to determine how the top 20% proactive salespeople in the organization communicate with their best customers, then to mechanize that method so that every other branch, agent, or salesperson in the organization can be brought to the same level of proficiency.

When it's appropriate, the matrix can be either supplemented or overridden to maximize "event marketing" opportunities, such as new product introductions. At all times, special behavioral triggers such as address changes and major balance shifts are handled with secondary matrix schedules designed to take advantage of them. And it also includes the implementation of special mailings on demand for branches or regions, to react to special situations.

A good example of "special situation" mail is a loan offer dropped immediately after a natural disaster in a market area.

Using a matrix is a profoundly logical thing to do, but it's certainly not easy. More often than not, institutions without the appropriate inter-

FIGURE 3

Month After Account Purchase

Subgroup	1	2	3	4	5	6	7	8	9	10	11	12	13	14	15	16	17	18	19	20	21	22	23	24
Core HH $50K+	CKG	MP	RA	CD	INV	CKG	RA	MP	CDD	CKG	INV	CD	RA	IL	MP	CKG	CRA	RCD	IL	INV	CKG	CCD	MP	IL
Multi-Svc $15K+	CD	CKG		RA	CD		MP	IL	CDD	RA	CKG	CD	CDD	MP		RA	INV	RCD	CD					
Single Svc $25K+	IL		RA		CKG		RA		CD															
New HH	MP		CKG	CD	CC	RA	INV	CD	MP	IL	RA	RA												
Rcncy HH	MP	CKG		IL	LNS		IL		CD		RA													
Loan Buyers	CC	CHK	IL	RA		IL	CHK	INV		IL		CHK		CC										

© CUSTOMER DEVELOPMENT CORPORATION 1990

21

nal resources will gravitate back to the use of the database as if it were little more than just another mass advertising medium.

And that's a terrible waste of a very powerful tool.

A Fully Integrated Selling System

The fourth and final "mountain" that financial marketers have to scale is to force the the field sales and service organization to use the information. This challenge requires more than technology; it requires some political expertise as well.

Figure 4 is an example of a true *Integrated Selling System*; one that takes full advantage of the power of database marketing throughout the organization's service delivery system.

The first step, shown at the top of the illustration, is the development of a Marketing Central Information File.

Note that the MCIF can be expanded with the addition of prospects, as well as customers. Creating a database of purchased prospect lists is not too unusual, but most institutions never get to the level of asking proactive calling officers to add their own hand-compiled prospects to the file. When they do, the officer-compiled lists are almost always much more effective than purchased lists.

The center part of the illustration shows the process required to implement a centralized marketing program. Most bank database marketing programs stop there.

The next generation of Selling Systems will also encompass the techniques shown on the left and right.

The database marketing program is taken to the branch level, illustrated on the right, allowing the institution to "laser in" on special problems and opportunities that exist within the effective marketing radius of specific offices. This approach will necessarily complicate the process because of the higher degree of segmentation employed. But the results are invariably worth it, particularly in organizations that operate in widely dissimilar markets.

FIGURE 4

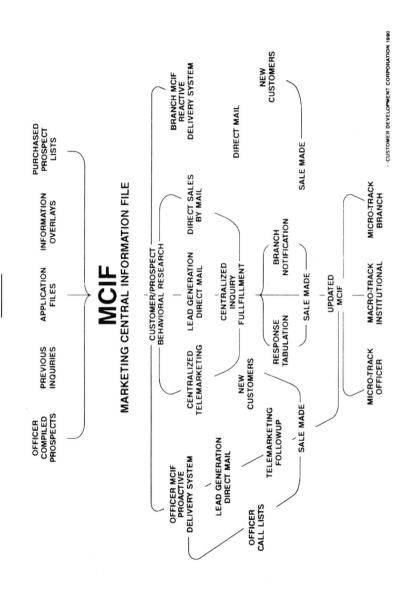

And finally, the marketing path shown on the left side of the illustration represents the ultimate "micromarketing" opportunity. The power of database marketing is used to assist a single calling officer, platform salesperson, or customer service representative.

The most sophisticated application of this idea is to provide the institution's best salespeople with their own database, coupled with centralized marketing support for their selling efforts. That support includes indexing to prioritize the customers for each product, lead generation direct mail that can be ordered on an "as needed" basis, and the ability to upload information that the salesperson collects for future use in sales calls, segmentation, and modeling.

A Journey, Not a Destination

Discovering this concept has been an enriching and enlightening experience. The whole field of database marketing has continued to evolve in very exciting ways. The technology has changed, but the core idea hasn't changed that much:

- Selling strategies work best when they are localized and personalized.

- The marketing effort has to work with the way a field organization runs its day-to-day business.

- The program must provide the lowest possible cost per sale at the same time it creates a strong perception of personal service.

- Customers buy on their own timetable, not the bank's. Thus at any given moment in time, some customers are ready to buy, and others are not. Marketing dollars should be spent talking to the ones who are ready.

Built properly, this system will allow any institution to become truly market driven—evolving as the marketplace changes.

If there is one fact that is very clear to me, it is that successful database marketing is an evolutionary process. The techniques we employ today were not even dreamed of just a few years ago, and it's highly likely that within the next few years we'll be doing things we can't imagine today.

And that's why it's so much fun.

2

Definition of Terms and Applications

Glossary of Common Terms

Address Standardization
Computerized process that standardizes upper-case and lower case letters, punctuation, and street name abbreviations on a mailing list to facilitate further processing (data appending, genderization, merge-purge).

Appended Demographic Data
Household specific demographic information like age, marital status, length of residence, etc., that can be appended and retained in a customer file for the purposes of segmentation and profile modeling.

Artificial Intelligence (AI)
The emulation of human reasoning and perception by a computer system. Some MCIF systems use AI techniques now, more will in the future.

Command-Driven
A software system that responds to queries or instructions in a specific format that the user must use. (See menu-driven)

Customer Profile
A data profile of the customer's relationship to a bank or to a particular product, service, geographic area, or branch.

Data Compression
Method of reducing the amount of space a data file uses without destroying any information. Also called compaction.

Demographics   Characteristics describing an individual, household, or market, including such variables as age,
sex, income, occupation, education, and marital
status.

Deposit Centile   1% of the deposit customer base.

Depth of   The number and types of accounts a customer has
Relationship   with an institution, often thought to represent the
customer's level of involvement with the institu-
tion.

Download   Transfer of a file or program from a mainframe to
a terminal or PC-system.

Encoding   Coding the elements of a file, sometimes used as a
security measure designed to prevent unautho-
rized access. (See encryption)

Encryption   Scrambling/encoding of files typically used to
prevent unauthorized access.

Event Trigger   An action by a customer that can be identified by
the MCIF and used to "trigger" a mailing—exam-
ple: a welcome letter is sent to a new mortgage
customer offering a free checking account.

Expert System   Artificial intelligence systems that draw on a
knowledge base and decision rules developed
from studies of human experts.

External   Offsite or outside an institution's routine data
processing operations.

Genderization   Computerized process that identifies gender of
mail recipient in order to assign courtesy title for
personal salutation (Mr. or Ms.). This is a sensitive
area in which the options and pitfalls should be
clearly understood by Marketing.

Geocoding   The assignment of a geographic code to an address. Typical levels of geocodes include:
- block-level: Smallest geographic area of U.S.
Census data. Generally a city block.
- blockgroup-level: Multiple block groupings all
beginning with the same numeric codes.

- census tract-level: Census unit that shows relatively homogeneous population profiles and housing characteristics. Contains roughly 1,400 households and 4,000 inhabitants.

Geo-Demographic Cluster Demographic and life-style coding routines that aggregate households by census or postal geographic definitions for the purpose of assigning a cluster code. Examples are VISION and PRISM.

Household All persons occupying a housing unit, whether related or not.

Householding The process of aggregating all data records for a household (see scrubbing files).This is the heart of any MCIF system. It is a computerized process that first assigns accounts at the individual customer level and then attempts to identify and bring together all customers who make up a household. This procedure is the method by which the MCIF database is created.

Interactive Describes a process in which a computer responds in real time to a user.

Internal In-house, or within an institution's routine data processing operations.

Local Area Network (LAN) A data communications system that enables users on a number of different machines to share programs, information, and equipment.

Macro Generator A software feature that allows a user to develop macros, or multiple commands reduced to a few keystrokes, to simplify and speed up operations. Useful for report generation as well as data entry.

Mailing Select The definition, in terms the MCIF system can use for selection, of the segment(s) to be mailed a specific offer. An example would be: CD customers with aggregate deposit balances greater than $50,000 and liquid funds of less than $10,000 and CD maturities not earlier than 11/15/93. An MCIF system would search for customers matching this

27

select and set up a file that could be output to tape for a mailing.

Management Information System (MIS)
Software system, often running on a micro, designed to allow data analysis for management decision making; usually by extracting information from central operating files and reformatting information into more accessible, higher-level format.

Market Segmentation
The dividing of a market into subgroups, or market segments, with similar demographic or psychographic characteristics.

Marketing Central or Marketing Customer Information File (MCIF)
A database designed for marketing purposes containing information about each customer and her/his usage/purchasing relationships that is periodically updated to reflect changes occurring in customer accounts. Database can be maintained in-house (internal), or by an outside vendor (external); it can be online or offline. Some terms sometimes used synonymously include:

- MIS: Marketing Information System
- CIF: Central Information File (usually refers to operational system)
- CMF: Central Marketing File
- CIS: Customer Information System

Marketing Decision Support System (MDSS)
A system of computer-based procedures and methods that regularly store, generate, analyze, and report information relevant to marketing decision making. The global term for MCIF, it is marketing's version of an MIS.

Matrix Mail
A form of database-driven direct mail that involves a multicycle set of letters that are sent to a customer, based on actions that can be identified by an MCIF (see event triggers). In this form of mailing, any offer can be mailed at any time a customer makes a targeted transaction.

Menu-Driven
Software feature allowing the user to select one option after another through a series of menus.

Merge-Purge A computerized process that merges several mailing files and eliminates duplicate names from the final mailing list. It is usually used to eliminate customers from a noncustomer mailing list, because the householding function of the MCIF renders this operation redundant on customer files.

Offline For MCIFs, an offline system is one that is not directly connected to the operational CIF, and hence offers periodic rather than immediate updates.

Online Direct communication between user and computer in an interactive mode.

1) An MCIF user can be online with a vendor's mainframe; or

2) An MCIF can be online to the operational CIF and would offer immediate updating whenever there is a change in any customer account.

Psychographics The analysis of consumers' activities, interests, and opinions (as in psychological profile). Sometimes called life-style analysis.

Real-Time The actual time in which an event occurs. For an MCIF, this typically refers to online updating.

Relationship Marketing Marketing that is focused on establishing, maintaining, and enhancing customer relationships.

Scrubbing Files The process of examining the records in a database to standardize the information and eliminate duplicate or erroneous information, in preparation for aggregating all accounts belonging to a household.

Serial Mail A form of database-driven direct mail that targets specific product offers to specific customer segments, based on their propensity and capacity to respond to the specific offer. It is, thus, a planned series of communications to a defined target market on a specific schedule.

Update   To add new data and change old data from file or database. For MCIFs, updating refers to integrating all customer account changes (new accounts, new households, and closed accounts) that have occurred since the last update to the database.

Outlining Some Common Applications of MCIF Systems*

---

*Developed from materials provided by Urban Data Processing

Each type of application is designed to help you understand your customers and potential customers better, and the relationships or opportunities that exist with them. Thus, an MCIF is often perceived as the foundation of relationship marketing. The applications listed below are simply a checklist to highlight the myriad of ways in which understanding of that relationship can enhance your business.

Management Reporting

- Trend Analysis
  - Cross-sell performance
  - Opportunity analysis
  - Product mix
  - Open/closed activity
- Overview of Total Bank Status
  - Users vs. providers of funds
  - Highlight of strengths and weaknesses
  - Product profitability/value
  - Strategic planning

Bank/Branch Administration

- Identify Most Profitable Customers
- Establish Goals for Growth
- Develop Cross-sell Programs

- Evaluate Performance

  - Products

  - Promotions

  - Cross-selling

  - Management, sales personnel

  - Delivery systems — ATM, branch, telephone bill paying

Site Location Analysis

- Geographic Distribution of Prospects, **Customers, Services**

- Area Penetration

- Identify Areas by Profit Potential

- Strategic Planning of Branch/ATM Network

  - Analysis of unprofitable branches

  - Consolidation of overlap areas

  - Expansion into new markets

Target Marketing/Segmentation Studies

- Identify "Preferred" Customers

- Relationship Analysis

- Customer/Potential Customer Profiling

- Segmentation by Product, Geography, Demography

- Reach Target Markets

  - Direct mail/telemarketing

  - Customer/potential customer profiling

  - Sampling for surveys

  - Lists of prospects

- Track Results of Marketing Programs

  - Track dollars and accounts

Product Development

- Evaluation of New Products

  - Define target audience

  - Pricing structure

- Product introduction and tracking
- Existing Product Lines and Mix
  - Value-added by-product
- Packaging and Promotion

Pricing

- Relationship Pricing
- Fee Income
- Assess Risk in Repricing

Profitability

- Individual Account
- Service Type(s)
- Customer Household

Calling Officer/Personal Banker Programs

- Generate Prospects
- Monitor Response, Performance

Corporate MCIF

- Development of Commercial Services
- Cross-sell
- Prospecting
- Analysis by Industry, Product, Sales Volume

Closed Account Analysis

- Identify Appropriate Customers for Exit

Interview

- Evaluate Trends

Mergers & Acquistions

- Customer Notification
- Branch and Service Consolidation

Mapping/Graphics

Community Reinvestment Act

3

MCIF SELECTION CRITERIA

FUSION Marketing Group

The following outline is designed to assist an institution to organize a Marketing Customer Information File (MCIF) vendor review. It was developed in consultation with our clients over a 3-year period (1988-1991).

Note: For this exercise to be meaningful, you must rely on input from users for a number of items. It is critical to interview (and, ideally, visit) several users of each MCIF system you're considering. Vendors should be as anxious as you are to get you together with their users.

Suggestions on how to use this outline:

1. Start with a clear understanding of how your institution will use an MCIF: research, direct mail, sales tracking, pricing models, telemarketing, etc.

2. Rank each of the 23 items on the outline relative to your objectives —assign a value from 1-5 to each item. You may choose not to use any items in the scoring depending on your objectives/priorities. You may also want to add some items for your specific objectives. This ranking provides you with a weight for how important or useful the item is vis-a-vis your objectives.

3. Score each vendor for all applicable items; assign a grade from 1-5 to each item. The higher the number, the more that system provided this item to your satisfaction.

4. Multiply item rank value by vendor item score for each item (i.e., a Flexibility value of 2 × a vendor flexibility score of 4 = 8 points).

5. The vendor receiving the highest number of points should be providing more of the items you need, and therefore should come closest to meeting your needs.

I. Householding

   A. Methodology and implications (e.g., understand step-by-step process, which data items are used for match, how tight does data item match have to be, is the short name for each application file created, etc.)

   B. Flexibility in tailoring householding algorithm

   C. How is "match key" created—Full name/short name/address/Social Security number?

   D. Assignment of household to branch (i.e., flexibility)

   E. Assignment of mailing address to household

   F. Internal scrubbing—address standardizing/exception phase suppress

   G. What is procedure for verifying database?

   H. Is a "constant keycode" created and what could cause that key to change?

II. Updating

   A. PC based or mainframe or both

   B. Speed

   C. How often

   D. Cost

   E. What history is kept on the household?

   F. Ancillary services provided as part of update (i.e., geocoding/data appending)

III. Standard Report Capabilities

   A. Comprehensiveness of standard report package

   B. User-friendliness of reports

C. Automatic census tract penetration report

D. Standard decile reports

E. Cross-sell by segment in addition to total base

F. Availability of custom report generator—ease of use/flexibility

IV. PC Access to Database

A. Limitations of selection criteria for standard reports

B. Capability to design special reports

C. Name and address on file (i.e., provide lists/tapes of customers for mailing/telemarketing)

D. If list/tapes can be provided, simplicity of selects

E. Ability to queue research and list selects

F. Processing time of research/list selects

V. Mainframe Access to Database

A. Costs/timeliness of special reports

B. Costs/timeliness of customer list/tapes

C. Can mainframe be used as a backup for PC processing?

VI. Direct Mail Support

A. Internal letter production/word processing interfaces (if it is decided that in-house production of letters is important)

B. What information can be printed to tape for mailing or galley listing of those mailed (e.g., account balance, household balance, "friendly" salutation, other special information, etc.)

C. Automatic serial/event trigger mailing support

D. Capabilities of capturing letter history

E. Ability to mail to account/customer/household at different addresses

F. Flexibility in salutations (friendly/formal salutation)

G. Titles picked up from application file and passed along to MCIF

      H. Gendercoding available (if so, how much flexibility)

      I. Ease of selects

      J. Standardization of addresses on MCIF file

      K. Ability to create one letter tape with letter codes appended to households to receive different letters

      L. Can select be done at household level but mailed to specific individual?

      M. Do not solicit flag passed from update to update

      N. Tracking (see VII for more detail)

VII. Direct Mail Tracking

      A. Procedure

      B. How is match key created/used to find household from update to update (constant keycode)?

      C. Implication of account changes on match key and how it affects tracking

      D. Flexibility (ability to move tracking window)

      E. Data available/format of reports

      F. Segmented results analysis

      G. Additional costs (if mainframe support)

      H. Maintenance of control group (for one mailing vs. indefinitely)

      I. Experience

VIII. Data Appending

      A. Procedure: internal/external

      B. Any limitations on data items captured/appended

      C. Costs

      D. Data appended to MCIF database vs. reappending at each update

      E. Experience

IX. Sales Tracking

    A. Procedure (does it "fit" data carried on mainframe)

    B. Reports

X. Telemarketing Support

    A. Procedures for sorting and generation galley listing

XI. Noncustomer Database Support

    A. Procedure to create/maintain noncustomer database

    B. Size limitations

    C. Implications on processing time

    D. Tracking procedure (finding prospect that becomes customer)

    E. Ability to integrate inquiries into database

    F. Experience

XII. Multiuser Access

    A. Availability

    B. System requirements: hardware/software

XII. Users Group

    A. Size, experience levels, involvement

XIV. Hardware/Software Compatability with Existing Systems

    A. Operating system

    B. Compatibility with spreadsheet, mapping, word processing, modeling software

XV. Profitability Module

    A. Availability

    B. Real-world application (comprehensive/simplistic)

XVI. Experience

    A. How many installations

    B. Type of installations

XVII. Customer Service

    A. Responsiveness

    B. Type of installations

XVIII. Startup/Implementation

    A. Timing

    B. Availability of detailed plan/critical path

    C. Training

    D. Field support (user references)

    E. Review users manual

    F. Experience of "trainers"

XIX. Internal Data Processing Support Needed for Startup

    A. File conversion requirements

    B. Support to provide file conversion (rather than have internal data processing department provide extracts)

XX. Development of System Enhancements for Existing Users

    A. Creativity

    B. Distribution schedule/costs

    C. Responsiveness to user requests

XXI. Responsiveness to Client Special Needs/Requests

    A. Support/availability of unique applications as opposed to system enhancements

XXII. Flexibility

    A. Extent to which system can be tailored/adapted by/for user

XXIII. Costs

    A. Startup

    B. Ongoing (e.g., annual fee, monthly maintenance, account management, reports, etc.)

4

MCIFs—
A GUIDE TO DECISION MAKING

Art Holtman
FUSION Marketing Group

The following guide is designed to spark discussion concerning the uses and applications of a Marketing Customer Information File (MCIF) system. Ideally this outline would be used during the planning phases of acquiring an MCIF system.

I. USES OF A MARKETING CUSTOMER INFORMATION FILE: Research vs. Communication/Implementation—Find the Optimum Blend for Your Institution

  A. Research Applications

    1. Household analysis
    2. Product penetration
    3. Balance distribution by account
    4. Deposit/loan decile analysis
    5. Service cross-sell
    6. Services per household measurement
    7. Single-service analysis
    8. Customer segmentation
    9. Sales tracking
    10. Relationship pricing

      11. Trend analysis

      12. New household analysis

      13. Profitability analysis

      14. Services combination reports

      15. Deposit distribution

      16. New product development

      17. Location analysis

      18. Branch performance

      19. Telemarketing

      20. Direct mail tracking

B. Communication/Implementation

    1. Database marketing plan

    2. Direct mail

    3. Telemarketing

C. Implications for Planning

    1. "Without doubt, marketing CIF systems have been used to create more unused reports than any other bank information system. Once the household database is built, the temptation is nearly irresistible to generate esoteric cross tabulations. This creates a flood of fascinating reports."

        Marketing CIF Systems, Council on Financial Competition.

    2. "It is easier and less threatening to generate reports than it is to generate results."

        FUSION Marketing Group

    3. The MCIF system is a source of strategic information, to be utilized at the highest management level for strategic planning.

    4. A fully utilized MCIF may shift organization structure from "Product Managers" to "Market Segment Managers."

    5. The new MCIFs now offer tracking capabilities. Marketing can now become more measurable and could become a profit center.

II. USING AN MCIF TO INCREASE SALES

A. Direct Marketing—key elements.

   1. List

   2. Offer

   3. Creative

B. Target Marketing: Projecting results through segmentation and selection.

C. Database Marketing: Predicting results and managing the sales process.

III. STRATEGIC APPROACHES

A. Product Driven Strategy

   1. Product developed to meet needs of targeted market segment.

   2. Profile of most likely buyers of the product is defined in criteria that can be used for selection of prospects within the customer base (and outside). *The definition must be actionable* in terms of selecting prospects from available list resources.

   3. Develop position and creative approach of package to appeal to target market.

   4. Limitations

      a. This strategy restricts objectives of promotion to product goals rather than longer term multiple sales and relationship building goals.

      b. Product goals result in potential conflict within organization (i.e., Tax Deferred Annuities vs Certificates and Credit Card vs Home Equity Loan).

B. Customer Driven

   1. Products don't produce profits — customers do.

   2. MCIFs make possible the identification of smaller and smaller segments. Each customer becomes a segment with an "individualized" strategy.

   3. The most efficient way to sell more product is to match the product to the best prospect.

4. Creating a Database Marketing Plan

    a. Identify customer segments with which your institution wants to do business.

    b. Determine their existing products with your institution (from your MCIF).

    c. Determine their total financial service usage and potential service usage.

    d. Identify "product holes" for new product development if needed.

    e. Develop prioritized Product Offers for each targeted segment.

    f. Develop effective Relationship Building Offers.

    g. Establish systematic communication *plan* to targeted segments. Integrate both types of offers in communication plans.

        (1) Consumers don't buy financial services. They don't generalize. They want specifics.

        (2) People want to do business with people they know.

    h. Establish agreed-upon objectives prior to implementation of plan.

    i. Tracking/results analysis and ongoing refinement of plan.

5. Limitations

    a. Complicated to implement.

    b. MCIF system may limit flexibility.

    c. Need for more frequent updates.

C. Major Differences Between Product and Customer Driven Strategies:

1. Timing

    a. Customers receiving an offer may not respond because they did not have need for the product or did not have capacity to purchase the product at the time they received the solicitation.

    b. Nonresponse is not an indication that they did not like the institution or the offer. Perhaps simply not the right time.

    c. Customers/prospects buy financial services on personal timetables—not those of the financial institution.

    d. Difficult to create a need for a financial service.

  2. Sales Channels

    a. Most product-driven mailings attempt to create next day sales (usually through mail).

    b. Customer-driven strategies may attempt to drive customers into branches for the sale or may sell directly through the mail.

  3. Relationship Objectives

    a. Most product mailings do not attempt to build relationship with a customer/prospect.

    b. One-on-one relationship between branch manager and prospect is not developed.

    c. Subsequent/ongoing sales not measured.

IV. SEGMENTATION STRATEGIES FOR YOUR CUSTOMER BASE

  A. Key to either product-driven or customer-driven strategies

    1. Previous buying behavior is the most effective segmentation.

    2. You have household specific information.

    3. Technology gives you a predictor of behavior.

    4. Affinity/Frequency/Recency/Amount.

    5. Segmentation obviously affects List *but* also affects Offer.

  B. Deposit segmentation

    1. 20%/80% Rule (20% of retail customers hold 80% of retail deposits)

      a. Bread and butter customers.

      b. Greatest potential for additional deposits.

      c. Not a homogeneous segment! Further segmentation and product usage analysis is needed.

    2. 1%/20% Rule (1% of customers hold 20% of deposits)

      a. Implication: Grovel Marketing.

      b. You can't do too much for this customer.

    3. 10%/10% Rule

      a. This is the average retail banking customer.

       b. Good deposit potential from subsegments within this decile.

   4. Bottom 70%

       a. Little potential for additional deposits.

       b. Some "nuggets" for deposits may exist within this segment, hard to find.

       c. Can generate additional lower balance Savings and Checking Accounts.

       d. Targeted potential for credit products.

C. Product segmentation

   1. Product cross-sell grid can identify opportunities.

   2. Certificate of Deposit cross-sell shows potential segmentation strategies.

   3. Checking cross-sell can define most profitable customers to target.

   4. Mortgage loan cross-sell.

       a. Easier to sell additional credit products.

       b. Limited deposit potential.

       c. Most active deposit products will be Checking Accounts and Savings Accounts.

       d. Easier to find deposit nuggets in the loan customer segment because of additional selects on database.

   5. Combination product segmentation

       a. Credit cards: credit card/other loan combination increases average balance; credit card deposit combination decreases average balance.

       b. Examine impact of deposit product usage on checking balances.

D. Recency segmentation

   1. New household analysis.

       a. Initial product mix.

       b. Product cross-sell.

   2. Aging analysis

E. Further segmentation analysis to help develop a database marketing plan

   1. Product usage by deposit segment.

  2. Deposit level impacts: Product usage impacts magnitude of average deposit

F. Enhancements to database for further segmentation

  1. Household specific demographic data.

   a. Useful for asset and nontraditional product offers.

   b. Permits going deeper into the deposit base than product usage data allows—find your competition's best customers.

V. CASE STUDIES—Following are applications (and results) of many of the principles presented in this overview, specifically:

A. Product Mailing: Credit Cards

B. Serial Mail: Deposit Products

C. Product Mailing: Home Equity Loans

D. Serial Mail: Deposit Products

E. Demarketing: Low Balance Checking Accounts

PRODUCT MAILING: Credit Cards

Situation: This institution has assets of $1 billion with offices in three market areas. It is the dominant institution in one of these markets. This program involved introducing a credit card to its customer base. The card offered an interest rate almost 200 Basis Points below the competition.

Strategy: Test rollout of low interest rate credit card to determine most cost effective customer segments as defined by product usage for ongoing, more cost effective solicitations.

Strategic Implications: This is a perfect example of the hypothesis that existing product usage can be used to predict the propensity to purchase other products. All customers were assigned to product segments, based on a prioritized product listing. While these results represent an extremely successful campaign based on a highly aggressive product offer, the differences in magnitude of response by product category are generally instructive. To examine the extremes—Loan customers responded to the offer of an asset product at a level 509% greater than Certificate customers (27.5% vs 5.4%). This illustrates the increases in marketing cost-efficiency that result from careful segmentation testing in the early phases of a campaign.

Results:

Prime Account	Qty. Mailed	Number of Applications	%	Cost	Cost/ Application
Checking	9,865	2,511	25.5	$ 6,314	$ 2.51
Money Market	3,235	307	9.5	2,070	6.74
Regular Savings	11,019	1,664	15.1	7,052	4.24
Certificates	5,632	304	5.4	3,604	11.86
Loans	4,316	1,188	27.5	2,762	2.32
Mortgages	12,447	1,621	13.0	7,966	4.91
	46,514	7,595	16.3	$29,768	$ 3.92

Even the lowest responding cells in this example generated cards at an attractive acquisition cost. The cost/application will, in ideal circumstances, be less than the annual fee. In that case, the program is self-funding and all cells meeting or exceeding that threshold should be included in future mailings. An aggressive institution would include all cells whose cumulative cost/application is less than the annual fee.

SERIAL MAIL: Deposit Products

Situation: This $1.5 billion institution implemented a serial mailing program designed to track and reassure the productivity of deposit households segmented by deposit level product usage.

Strategy: Test productivity of two segment selects and measure comparative deposit acquisition activity and new account activity.

Strategic Implications: This example illustrates the 80/20 Rule in generating sales. Although High Deposit Customers generated

Results:

New Account Activity Comparison:

	High Deposit Hshlds $20,000+ Number Mailed: 9,226				Core Service Deposit Hshlds Deposit Product & ATM Card Number Mailed: 9,448			
	New	Activity	Total	Average	New	Activity	Total	Average
Regular Savings	85	0.9%	$ 581,053	$ 6,836	209	2.2%	$658,148	$3,149
Money Market	39	0.4	665,010	17,052	4	0.3	14,518	3,630
Certificates Retirement	169	1.8	6,137,873	36,319	12	0.1	89,945	7,495
Accounts	73	0.8	834,123	11,426	9	0.1	32,123	3,569
Checking	85	0.9	316,544	3,724	116	1.2	80,591	695
Total	451	7.5%	$8,534,603	$16,016	350	4.0%	$875,325	$2,442

Cost Efficiency Comparison:

	Cost	Cost/ New Account	Basis Point Acquisition Cost
• High Deposit HH	$5,443	$ 7.90	050
• Core Serv. Deposit HH	$5,574	$14.63	600

new accounts at roughly half the cost of Core Deposit Customers—look at the results when related to deposit balances: a difference of 1200% (50 Basis Pts. vs 600 Basis Pts. acquisition cost). Also note the difference in account types opened within each segment. High Deposit customers opened Short and Medium Term CDs while Core customers opened Regular Savings and Checking accounts. Finally, note the difference in the average balance for each type of account opened between the two segments and you'll realize that the Activity Rate (Response) only tells part of the profitability story for this type of campaign.

PRODUCT MAILING: Home Equity Loans

Case Study: Promote home equity credit line, with no mortgage customers included in the database.

Strategy: Use total loan balances and credit lines to select for home equity loan solicitation. Assumption is that heavy credit users are more likely future borrowers.

Results:

- VIP Loan Customers: $10,000+ in total lines/outstandings
  Number Mailed: 3,443

Balances	Total #	Activity %	Balances	Average
Installment Loans	70	2.0	$ 631,963	$ 9,028
Equity Line	49	1.4	1,070,635	21,850
Equity Loans	89	2.6	1,982,858	22,279
Total Loans	208	6.0	$3,685,456	$17,719

- Core Borrowers: $2,000–$10,000 in total lines/outstandings
  Number Mailed: 5,670

Balances	Total #	Activity %	Balances	Average
Installment Loans	74	1.3	$ 397,637	$ 5,373
Equity Line	17	0.3	296,598	17,447
Equity Loans	117	2.3	713,286	6,096
Total Loans	208	3.7	$1,407,521	$ 6,767

Comparative Cost Efficiency	Cost	Cost/ Loan	Cost/ Equity Loan	Basis Point Acquisition
• VIP Loan Customers $10,000+	$2,031	$ 9.76	$14.72	55
• Core Borrowers $2,000–$10,000	$3,345	$16.08	$24.96	238

Strategic

Implications: The 80/20 Rule works for asset products, too. The "VIP" segment delivers new loan balances at one quarter of the basis point cost of the "core " segment. You'll note that the VIP segment responded at almost twice the level of the core segment (6.0% vs 3.7%) and generated average balances almost three times as great ($17,719 vs $6,767). Caution: Although one segment significantly outperformed the other, both campaigns may prove to be cost effective once the acquisition costs are amortized over the average life of the loan.

SERIAL MAIL: Deposit Products

Situation: This is a $600 million institution in a medium-size city with 9 offices. The objective of the serial mailing program is to generate additional deposits. The results for this program, which is ongoing, cover a period in which two mailings were tracked. Only new deposits are reported.

Strategy: Implement Serial Mailing to selected deposit segments to test productivity of selected customer segments.

Results:

Segment	Mailed	# of Responses	Activity Rate	Total Deposits ($ M)	Average Balance
High Deposit HH	6,919	1,149	16.6%	$42.1	$36,631
Mid Deposit HH	4,555	498	10.9	7.0	14,051
Low Deposit	1,195	127	10.6	0.8	6,393
Mortgage Loan	3,216	193	0.6	0.5	2,385
Total	15,885	1,967	12.4%	$50.4	$25,623

Cost Efficiency:

	Cost*	Cost/ New Acct.	Basis Point Acquisition Cost
High Deposit	$7,611	$ 6.62	18
Mid Deposit	5,011	$10.60	72
Low Deposit	1,315	$10.35	164
Mortgage Loan	3,538	$18.33	708
* Two mailings made during tracking period.			

Strategic Implications: The "Cost Efficiency" chart above is self-explanatory: high deposit customers generate higher deposits at lower acquisition cost than other customers. An institution armed with this data can generate predictable levels of deposits at anticipated levels of cost.

In this case, looking at cost per new account actually understates the magnitude of the differences in productivity. Comparing the High and Low Deposit cells, the cost per new account was $6.62 vs. $10.35 (a difference of 64%). Now take a look at Total Deposits and Average Balances.

Within the Deposit Segments, the High Deposit cell produced 52.6 times the total deposits of the Low Deposit cell and has an average balance approximately 6 times as great as the Low Deposit cell. It is clear that the mortgage cell should not be included in future mailings.

DEMARKETING: Low Balance Checking Accounts

Situation: This $3 billion institution has 66 offices in a major metropolitan market. This campaign involved raising the minimum balance required for free checking and increasing monthly service fees on checking in an attempt to increase the profitability of this product portfolio.

Strategy: Drive away low balance checking account customers and increase service fee revenue while maintaining/increasing checking account penetration among high deposit households through selective communication—notify low balance checking accounts of increases while aggressively promoting relationship priced checking accounts to high deposit households.

Results:

Total HH Deposit Segment	Point in Time A				Point in Time B (6 months later)			
	Total HH's	Chkg HH's	%	Avg Bal	Total HH's	Chkg HH's	%	Avg Bal
$50,000+	6,570	1,979	30	$7,453	7,140	2,231	31	$8,174
$20,000–$49,999	8,811	2,585	29	4,867	9,130	2,909	32	5,177
$10,000–$19,999	7,631	2,216	29	3,555	7,485	2,525	34	4,083
$5,000–$9,999	6,925	2,335	34	2,938	6,494	2,660	41	3,280
$2,500–$4,999	6,795	2,599	38	2,100	6,836	3,334	49	2,283
<$2,500	40,940	18,603	45	897	30,341	14,341	47	683
Total Deposit Households	77,672	30,317	39	$2,117	67,426	28,000	42	$2,491
						<2,317>	<8>	
Total Checking Balances		$64,181,000				$69,753,000 +$ 5,572,000	+9%	

Strategic Implications: Many institutions have justified, at least in part, the purchase of an MCIF system based on its applications for pricing/demarketing. Here's an illustration of the results of one such application. Between June and December, Checking Households declined by 8% but during the same time average balances increased 18% and total balances increased 9%. The decline in accounts took place only in the <$2,500 deposit segment while the greatest increase in accounts was in the $2,500–$4,999 segment. While some customers closed their checking accounts in response to the fee increase, others increased balances in the account to avoid the service fee and/or took advantage of the no fee checking account for deposit relationship. Very importantly, these changes were implemented without driving off any High Deposit customers. In fact, both households and checking balances actually increased in all households exceeding $20,000 in total deposits.

5

THE MCIF START-UP PROCESS

Charles Roach
Roosevelt Bank, FSB

Due to the variety and intensity of internal circumstances, there is no one formula to be applied to the Marketing Customer Information File (MCIF) start-up process. Whatever approach works becomes the right one. We can identify, however, common denominator type environmental conditions, which, when recognized and addressed early, will greatly facilitate matters. Consequently, this chapter focuses first on recognition and strategy in dealing with internal circumstances. Following that, we'll look at the MCIF technology start-up, encompassing software selection and database construction. In different ways, environment and technology are crucial elements in developing an MCIF that performs to objectives. The environment must be controllable to be permissive, at least, to the investigative routine. And the MCIF manager must have periods of uncompromised focus available to master the technology and create the MCIF.

Since my experience has been with financial services marketing, we'll consider the MCIF in that general environment. The chapter further assumes that a novice manager is responsible for the MCIF, to include design/implementation and, eventually, daily operation.

At the outset, let's establish that the name of our database has four letters, not three. The MCIF is an established marketing tool and marketing responsibility for it is reinforced through verbalization of the title "MARKETING CUSTOMER INFORMATION FILE." The need for internal marketing is always present though it may not always be apparent. It is important to note that MCIF concepts are uniquely marketing-based, and beneficial output must originate from a timely, marketing-sensitive operation. Financial and operations departments within the company, as well as management overall, have needs for credible and utilitarian management information. Translated, this means they want report information that is familiar and applicable to their needs.

If you are to be the MCIF manager and you have start-up responsibilities, ask yourself, "What kind of MCIF environment exists in my organization?" Here are some common issues to examine. The answers to these questions and what you do about them greatly influence the MCIF environment:

- Who wants the MCIF and for what purpose?
- Have specific features been identified for which the MCIF is to be used or are people just interested in the reports? If specifics don't develop, "Ho-Hums" will develop down the line.
- Is anyone (really) "enthusiastic" about it? (An indicator of long-term success.)
- Does interest go beyond the marketing people? (Indicates company marketing orientation.)
- Are nonmarketing people nervous about the costs? (Indicates that people need more information to understand the benefits.)
- Is adequate time allocated for vendor reviews? Has time been allocated for the MCIF manager to move up the learning curve? (Indicates future time constraints.)
- Are MCIF objectives realistic? Clear? Practical? (A subjective assessment, but can be strong indicator of fulfilled/unfulfilled management expectations to come.)

We aren't far off the mark if we assume that every one of these conditions is a problem. Each leads to poor decisions and the waste of company resources. There are situations, for example, where the

MCIF was purchased for the wrong reason or for no apparent reason at all. Many systems never really got integrated into the organization. Several were abandoned within a year of purchase. These unfortunate case studies were the direct result of management inability to identify and resolve fundamental issues. The MCIF manager will most effectively influence internal circumstances by developing pragmatic approaches and sustaining a positive attitude.

Most active MCIF managers will acknowledge some degree of effectiveness with their MCIF program despite a less than ideal environment, provided they've been sensitive to their surroundings. In the early stages, it's easy to ignore or overlook these broad environmental problem areas due to the intense preoccupation with details going on at the same time. The risk is high, however, that the resulting alienation from influential people will diminish chances of achieving an effective and efficient MCIF operation. In other words, the ultimate effectiveness of the MCIF is largely conditional on, first, how effectively internal conditions are recognized and addressed and, second, how well the MCIF performs in addressing the needs that give rise to it.

The vendor review process generally provides the stage on which internal dramas debut. This is good because issues get out in the open. Hopefully, when the time comes to select the vendor, these issues will have surfaced and been recognized and addressed so that the process goes forward.

Who Does the Processing?

Who will crunch data and how will it be retrieved? This issue must be resolved before final selection of the vendor and, naturally, before serious work on the database can begin. It's a strategic question beyond the scope of this chapter. But because it is an issue that is sensitive to the internal forces that are potential problems, a few ideas in that vein are appropriate.

Costs, MCIF objectives, and planned utility are the primary issues in deciding the means and manner by which MCIF data is accessed and output. For example, Is a PC based system required? Vendor mainframe? Perhaps a combination of the two? Should an intermediary manage the database off site? Minimally, the MCIF manager's responsibility is to weigh the internal processing sentiment against the planned utility of the database and try to keep the two on parallel tracks.

Unfortunately, the processing issue is all too often decided on the basis of cost. Perceived cost is always too high and perceived need is much less understood. Cost considerations don't necessarily prevent the basic purchase decision, but they may prevent the correct marketing decision for the organization. The role of the MCIF manager is to fairly represent the alternative costs for each option under consideration. The largest impediment to doing this is having enough technical knowledge early enough to evaluate and price the options.

An absolute no-win situation is managing an MCIF with a system that is at cross purposes with planned utility. If the cost issue can't be influenced, then the only productive effort is to concentrate on establishing MCIF goals and expectations that complement the system to be purchased.

Vendor Selection

The vendor review process is covered thoroughly in another chapter but it is important enough to the initial start-up process to deserve a few comments. Vendor review is an excellent opportunity to learn MCIF principles and applications. Vendors will invest considerable effort to win your business and you can and should learn a lot from them.

Important Points in Vendor Review

First, determine which firms or vendors are to bid. Active MCIF users are probably the most available resource to obtain references. They are usually good sources of information, particularly if they have time to talk. Talk to enough users to understand the key distinguishing characteristics.

Decide on three vendors. More than three generally provides non-compensating incremental benefit. Fewer than three yields insufficient information and learning opportunity. Also, when only two vendors knowingly compete, their bids can become attacks on each other.

Handle vendor presentations profitably. Ask questions, questions, and more questions. Set up hypothetical situations. Be persistent and detailed. Develop specific points of product comparison over a broad range of features and mechanics. Take detailed notes. The reward? . . . Product weaknesses become evident, product differentiation occurs, product comfort levels are established, choice of product is easy. The price paid is the expenditure of personal time and effort. If you don't get enough information, don't blame the vendor.

Vendor review shouldn't be a unilateral effort. The varied interests to be included within the company would fall into three groups:

- Data processing (DP) people.
- Senior management.
- Others who will be the direct beneficiaries and users of MCIF information.

Representatives of all three groups should attend the formal presentations dealing with product overview. In the event DP people hang back, they should be encouraged to get interested in the technical side. Informal follow-up should occur to make sure all questions get answered and that everyone's concerns not adequately dealt with by the vendor get addressed.

Persistence and patience are needed to successfully address initial start-up problems. The attitudes and opinions of others aren't changed easily, even in the best of circumstances. The initial process has a dual objective. First, to control and smooth environmental conditions where possible; second, to discern MCIF marketing principles and applications. Appropriate design and construction will then occur with the vendor of choice.

Preliminaries to Database Construction

At the beginning of the chapter, technology was identified as a crucial element in meeting MCIF objectives. If technological mistakes are made during the start-up phase, an MCIF may be culpable rather than capable at some later date. To avoid this, the MCIF manager must understand the logic of the access and retrieval software before completing the design and loading of the database.

Let's start by examining several basic MCIF features as examples. We'll look closely to demonstrate the possibilities of investigative effort. A good understanding of these and other fundamental MCIF features is necessary before you can adequately conceptualize the content and design of the database.

- Householding—Forever after, the MCIF manager will need to explain and justify the householding routine. This requires a pretty thorough understanding of the householding algorithm. Obtaining this in full from the vendor requires persistence during the vendor review. Other relevant information includes knowing the basis on which householding decisions are made, such as how much name/address information is considered in the matching program. It will become evident that you are asking the right questions when the vendors switch from quick, mechanical responses to replies made with more reflection and consideration. The right questions are specific, hypothetical situations involving the effects on householding of address changes, file errors, file scrubbing, dissimilar names within the household, record matching criteria, social security matching, etc. Determine what holds the household together. CIF key? Constant key? What conditions create new households? Understand the answers and evaluate them carefully.

- Reports —Thoroughly review the standard report and nonstandard report possibilities. Comparison of vendor reports is a decidedly objective opportunity. Don't overlook the meaning or significance of any statistic. It's not unusual to be unhappy with one aspect or another. Focus first on report substance rather than format. If the software permits data output to dBASE, then reports can be formatted in that program. Some MCIFs feature a custom report writing option in the software. Make sure that any special information wanted is easily available, such as a simple query to obtain deposit (only) households. Once familiar with the reports, ask about the possibilities for customizing. Depending on the request, you might be accommodated.

Understanding the vendor's software logic for each standard report can save embarrassment and disappointment later on. For example, let's use the Decile Report. Vendors can define decile two ways, by dollars and by household. Personally, I see little marketing purpose for deciling of households, and with that attitude, I would have had an unpleasant surprise had we purchased that software. Another deciling logic I disagree with on standard reports is the individual deciling of branches. My preference is for branch deciles to be based on total Bank decile because the sum of the branches then equals the Bank Decile Report. My deciling preferences aren't important. What's important is that the statistics and style of MCIF standard reports match expectations. Don't assume they do, ask.

- Database Structure—Ascertain which data items are routinely carried in the vendor's software. For example, services per household is a standard item but accounts per household may not be. The ultimate structure and organization of the database can be better visualized by first identifying all of the vendor's standard data items carried for your products. For example, is rate carried for checking accounts as well as CDs? Then, you'll need to know what data are in your own files. An old-fashioned way to build and conceptualize the structure is to watch it take shape in front of you. Draw a grid to keep track of the structure or skeleton and another to allocate data items. Starting with the structure grid, list basic services along the top horizontally and the product types or classes in columns underneath each service. Organization notwithstanding, this grid enables you to visualize how you will eventually segment the database by service and product type in a manner important to goals and objectives. It's obvious, for example, that different types of checking accounts would be listed under the "checking" service. But you may want to think a bit about how to organize CDs. They're usually segmented by term, but conditions may exist to segment them by type. Even if term is a clear winner, how specific can you be? Are short-, medium-, and long-term segments okay? Do you want to be more exact?

A second grid for data items would list the basic services vertically along the left margin with rows extending horizontally listing applicable data items. Number the data items across the top of the grid. List the vendor's standard data items, such as balance, rate, open date, first from left to right. List the optional data items from your files next. Among these might be an obscure source code, but more common are value items to be calculated by the vendor from your file data: average number of checks cleared, total fees, number, location of window transactions. Recognize that all items won't apply to each product type within the basic service.

- Branch assignment—The assignment of households to branches must be accomplished in a way that can be accepted in the organization and also makes marketing sense. What are the options?

  - Propagation of households?

  An old-fashioned method whereby the complete household is assigned to every branch with an account in the household. This makes branch totals look impressive, but accurate totals derived from branch reports are impossible because of the multiple counting of households. This adds unnecessary complexity and is not recommended.

  - Hierarchy of criteria?

  The most effective range of possibilities lies here. The choices are to accept the vendor's assignment scheme, request extensive customizing, or reach a compromise with the vendor. In our case, we customized extensively to create a window-transaction-based assignment, which pulls the household to the branch where a majority of window transactions occur. This method was accepted logically in the organization and has been very satisfactory for marketing.

  Vendor assignments based on most recently opened accounts are reliable but would seem not to be as responsive to branch reassignment of movers within the database. The branch assignment decision depends on the situation—many vs. few branches; geographical vastness; market penetration; etc. Vendors may resist the transaction-based scheme due to the amount of customized programming required.

  - Direct Mail

  Event-triggered mailing capability is an important feature for many MCIFs. If this feature must satisfy a known MCIF objective, many questions are necessary, especially those with recency and frequency implications. Don't stop with vendor questions; internal files must be intensely scrutinized.

As examples, do your files have "valid" account open dates? Are updates going to be frequent enough to provide lists?

- Other direct mail questions . . .

Are you satisfied with the quality of gender coding and your ability to modify it? How will the database be geo-coded? Extra cost? What are the specifics relating to mail-merge (titles, salutation, variables)? How do the tracking files work? Determining exactly how the tracking feature works from update to update requires the same thorough questioning as was necessary to learn the vendor's householding routines and standard report logic.

Designing and Constructing the Database

How much data to load? How should the data be organized? Through these questions, we can look at most of the critical issues.

Load refers to the amount of accessible data. The question of how much to load will come up again and again if the process is being approached correctly. Professional opinion comes down on both sides of the issue with some advocating a small database while others recommend capturing the maximum or loading up.

Obviously, the answer is related to the planned usage of the MCIF, but don't neglect "unplanned" usage! At first, MCIF technology will produce astonishing impressions to the uninitiated from even the most inane database. Typically, as MCIF culture grows within an organization, so will demand and expectation for more sophisticated programs. Which is why I recommend "loading up." An opposing argument says "Add it later if you want it." While this is possible, valuable trend information can be lost. If an internal PC-system is being considered, the vendor will tell you what the processing speed implications are with a "loaded up" database.

All MCIF vendors provide a householding feature and standard data items like household balance and number of services. Loading only the standard items requires minimal effort and, as just mentioned, still provides new and exciting information. Full utility of the MCIF, however, depends on the amount and type of data included and requires intense inquiry of not only the vendor but also of internal DP people to determine what can be captured from your own files.

Here are some basic data item and design questions to ask about your own DP files.

Re: Direct Mail

1. Will your database structure be compatible with your software so that all data items and all combinations of data can be queried?

2. Do you want more than one name per account carried on the MCIF?

3. Are "account open dates" valid?

4. Are your files updated for changes, new accounts, no mails, etc., in a timely manner prior to producing MCIF update tapes?

5. How are classes and types of accounts that don't receive mail identified?

6. Are employees, including directors, identified?

7. How are closed accounts identified?

8. Is "date of last transaction" valid?

9. Can loan accounts be identified and segmented as prospects for various insurance products?

10. Have you identified every product file item on which you would ever want to base a mailing list?

Re: Branch Performance

1. Is the way your DP files carry "branch opened" the way you want it on the database?

2. Can you capture account transaction and transaction location information?

3. If you want to customize the household branch assignment routine, can you capture the required data from the DP files?

4. How are accounts with bogus branch numbers identified? How do you want them assigned?

5. Do the DP files track customer transaction activity at employee level (for sales tracking)?

Re: Market Research

1. Can age and telephone number be stored in your DP files? Getting this information may be another issue.

2. How much closed account data can be captured? That is, "date closed" and "amount closed" plus related data items prior to closing.

3. Do special purpose codes exist, or is there the capacity for them, that designate specific types of activity such as "source of funds," "VIP"?

Re: Profitability

1. Will vendor capture fees, service charges at account level?

2. Is "average balance" a DP file item? If not, can it be calculated from available data?

3. Can "window transactions" be tallied at account level?

4. Can checks cleared be identified? tallied?

5. Are all products and services offered in your files?

6. Can loan payment status be determined and captured?

7. Is rate captured on all products?

Perhaps the purpose of the grids as organizing and design aids is now clearer.

Data Processing

No treatise on the art of MCIF making would be complete without reference to the role of the DP provider. In-house systems and DP service bureaus exhibit differing attitudes toward the end user but don't necessarily command differing approaches. Having had experience with both, I would consider using the same approach to obtaining MCIF support.

Our MCIF startup was supported by an in-house DP system. Our people were cooperative with me and with the vendor. Unfortunately, that may not always be the case.

I made many reference check telephone calls to active MCIF users throughout our start-up process. I always inquired about the relationship between the vendor and DP. I received a lot of insight from these users that was invaluable in developing a DP "Not to Do List." Occasionally, vendors would provide advance intelligence about certain installations before I called and, indeed, there were some unfortunate conflicts. Worse, a residue of hard feelings affected the ongoing MCIF.

Some of the underlying reasons for problems with DP may be:

1. "Didn't feel part of the process"— A valid DP concern considering the implications of having a new database around they don't control.

2. "Felt threatened by perceived competition"— DP staff will sense an implied criticism of their existing system and performance when the ooh's and aah's start over the MCIF's snappy new information.

3. "Resent doing more work just for marketing"—What DP section doesn't already have enough to do? Then those crazy marketing people want their own database?

4. "Balk at working with the vendor"—For a fact there is strong resentment if the vendor is peremptorily turned over to DP to "work out the details." Too well, DP knows about file dumps. An all too common prescription for conflict with DP is to let the vendor and DP design and construct the database between them. Even under ideal circumstances, DP staff will tend to be professionally suspicious and distrustful of MCIF vendors.

If these potential DP problems are neutralized, it should assure willingness and good faith from DP staff. The first three situations are communication problems, but the last one requires special effort and attention. I found that becoming an ongoing intermediary between our vendor and our DP staff was an effective cushion. Plus, the commitment of my time dispelled the "crazy marketer" attitude to a degree. Detailed, important vendor/DP meetings must initially take place for the vendor to learn the client's files. I was present during these meetings and, commensurate with my level of understanding at the time, made a significant contribution by just listening. Thereafter, it was necessary on relatively few occasions to refer vendor programmers directly to DP. When it did happen, I remained involved. The downside of this approach is the potential to over control.

There was major payback on my investment of time as intermediary. I didn't overlook anything on our files for inclusion in the database. In fact, I even discovered fields that made some data items possible.

Summary

If there is anything so profound as a philosophy running through this chapter, it advocates that the MCIF manager stay close to every phase of the process; learn it, smooth it, do it, whatever it takes. The environment and technology issues vary from operation to operation. But whatever they are, they are best resolved person to person. One of those persons must always be the MCIF manager.

This level of personal involvement may run counter to managerial theory that measures effectiveness through delegation. But during the start-up phase, I didn't observe a single MCIF manager that had the resources to delegate. Does this mean that there is a direct relationship between effort put forth and MCIF quality? You bet!

6

DEVELOPING A DATABASE ANALYSIS AND MARKETING PLAN

**Donald Mann
and Art Holtman**
FUSION Marketing Group

The Marketing Customer Information File (MCIF) can make your marketing programs like guided missiles with sophisticated homing devices. You can use it to unerringly target the best prospects for a specific product in your customer base. But you have to learn *how* to tell it what you want. This chapter will summarize the "whys" and "hows" of database analysis and planning (including the impact of tracking on the plan). Both of these steps are key preconditions to a successful database marketing program. Without them, you are simply using your MCIF to generate mailing lists in a more effective manner. That's an admirable application all by itself; but it does not hint at the marketing power you can apply through Database Marketing.

Conceptual Framework for Analysis

The goal of Database Marketing is to impose a structure on your direct marketing programs that applies the data resources you have within your MCIF in a methodical fashion. This methodology enables the marketer to continually refine targeting strategies and to match products and offers with the most responsive prospects. It creates an environment in which almost every variable in your direct marketing program is easily and accurately tested and tracked.

The starting point for developing this methodology is to examine and understand the particular submarkets that exist within your customer base. These are identified through SEGMENTATION STRATEGIES and PRODUCT/PROSPECT PROFILE DEFINITIONS. These are derived from an analysis of your database, coupled with an understanding of the factors that motivate the need or desire for a specific financial service. For many years, direct marketers have known that prior purchase history is the most reliable predictor of future purchase behavior. Translated to financial services, this means that existing product usage and balance levels are the most powerful predictors of future product usage, especially for liability products. That's precisely the kind of information you have on your MCIF.

The fact that it is the customer, not the product, who is the ultimate source of revenue and profitability is so obvious it hardly bears mentioning. The clear implication is that the way to maximize profits is to focus on the customer. This is resulting in a shift from product-driven strategies toward customer or market-driven strategies. To the extent that an understanding of customer wants and needs drives the marketing planning process, the potential success of these plans is greatly enhanced. A few farsighted institutions are already contemplating the next step: replacing the current Product Manager system with Market or Segment Managers.

These managers will base their plans on a comprehensive understanding of the purchase behavior and projected needs of the market or segment that they manage. The foundation of that understanding is built upon an analysis of the product usage, purchase frequencies, and balances maintained by the customers in that segment. That's where the MCIF comes in.

The value of an MCIF is in its use as a resource to aggregate and summarize this data at the account or household level, so you can use the data to gain a better understanding of the identifiable segments within your customer base. At that point you can begin to derive "best prospect profiles" for specific products using what you've learned from your segmentation analysis. These segments can be identified and quantified using the principles of AFRA:

AFFINITY: prior product usage is the best predictor of future product needs. For example, high deposit customers are terrible prospects for most loans.

FREQUENCY: the more business a household has done with you, the more it is likely to do. It's easier (and, more importantly, more cost effective) to sell the sixth product to a customer than the second.

RECENCY: likelihood to purchase can decline as length of time since previous purchase increases. This is particularly true in cross-selling programs in which you are attempting to expand the relationship through additional product sales.

AMOUNT: the more they've got with you, the more they'll give you. It's easier to get an extra $25,000 from a high deposit household than $5,000 from an average deposit household. Remember, high deposit customers rarely keep all their funds in one institution, so they typically have more to bring.

The precise definition of your best potential segments is ideally based on a comparison of the make-up and product usage/penetration of your customer base with national normative statistics. That enables you to derive specific answers to questions like: "Is a 34.6% checking account penetration of my $50,000-plus deposit segment good? How much further penetration could I reasonably set as an objective?"

If you don't have access to reliable normative data, or really want to do the job in detail, you'll need to derive profitability measures for each type of account. Using these measures, you can determine acceptable acquisition costs for each product, taking into account the balance levels required to make the account profitable. An analysis of the existing customers who maintain profitable relationships with you will prove invaluable in deriving a best prospect profile for a specific product.

To accomplish this, you would examine the total product usage and balance levels (and demographics, if available) of customers who are, for example, "profitable" Checking Account customers. You would then search for other customers who match that profile but don't have a checking account with your institution. If you have demographics appended to your base, your search potential is greatly increased because you can go beyond product usage profiles. There will be a percentage of customers in your base who are your competition's most profitable customers. That means you can't identify them through product usage profiling (because they do the bulk of their business across the street). An extensive set of appended demographic data will provide you with the additional points of identification to "mine" these potential gems from within your base or to dramatically increase the accuracy of your noncustomer list selects.

You will *never* have justifiable reasons to market to your entire customer base. The most profitable strategy is to mail as *few* pieces as possible to reach your objective. This will depend upon the purchasing potential of your top deposit and loan segments and the sales goals you've set for specific products. With very few special exceptions, you should never mail deeper than 30% into your base. As mentioned above, if your database has been enhanced through appended data, you have additional segmentation options open to you. Household specific demographic enhancement is particularly useful in identifying those customers who are not currently in your top 20% to 30%, but have the potential to be. If you're serious about database marketing, you *must* enhance your database.

Enhancing the Database

Appending a customer base with actionable enhancements is one of the smartest moves an aggressive marketer can make. It is a critical first step in expanding and refining your segmentation strategies and is a precondition for developing a usable noncustomer database. The question is "Which data to append?"

The first issue is differentiating between *geodemographic cluster* data and *household specific* data. If your applications are research oriented—market and penetration studies, branch location analyses, etc.—the cluster products like Micro-Vision and Prizm can be very useful. Their output is easily understood by all levels of management because they aggregate census level data under descriptive titles (Furs, Station Wagons, etc.). They also integrate with mapping programs, which is great for market penetration and branch site analysis studies.

If, however, you plan to use your appended data for defining direct mail list selects forget about cluster data. In brief, it won't work for those applications. The reason is simple: you don't send mail to a census block or a zip+4 postal area, you send it to a household. And cluster programs assume that all households in a geographic cluster are homogeneous. Think of your own neighbors for a moment and you'll realize that's not true. Some have kids, some don't. Some aren't married. Others are retired. They're not all the same.

So you *must* use household specific data for direct mail selects. The most useful demographic data items to append are those that let you determine the household's Family Life Cycle position (age, marital status, home ownership, children, etc.). After product usage and balance levels, which you already have on your MCIF, this is the most powerful segmentation tool you have to predict propensity to purchase specific financial services, because the need for specific financial services is related to the household's Family Life Cycle position.

Here are the critical demographics to append (in order of importance):

- Age of head of household (2-year ranges are okay)
- Income (usually inferred, see below)
- Home ownership (*not* dwelling type)
- Length of residence at current address
- Marital status
- Presence of children
- Dwelling type (single-family vs. multifamily)
- Type of automobile
- Automobile value

These data elements will dramatically expand your ability to apply meaningful segmentation strategies to your database. Beyond this basic set of demographics, additional data can be added that further

expand your ability to identify and target productive prospect profiles. A good example is motor vehicle registration data. The types and
values of vehicles owned by a household can give you accurate insight
into its life-style, self-image, and financial position. In fact, because
motor vehicle registration data is household-specific, it can be a more
accurate indicator of wealth than most income data, which uses an
algorithm to *infer* the income of a household.

Analyzing the Database

Once the database has been built, the key first step is to examine what
you have before starting to plan how to use it.The purpose of analyzing your database is to identify where your base is strong, where it's
weak, and what windows of opportunity it contains. Here's an outline
of the contents of a Database Analysis:

Product Usage—Start with the basics by examining your product-
penetration and average balances for the total institution. Then look at
the same measures for your deposit product customers and your asset
product customers separately. This is where normative data can be
very useful, as it allows you to put the raw statistics into perspective
to begin to gauge the relative strengths and weaknesses of your base.
Spend some time looking at single-product vs. multiproduct customers and the ways that their product usage differs (balance levels,
length of relationship, etc.). Do the same with your cross-sell reports.
This is where you can start to identify specific problems and opportunities within your base.

Deposit Stratification—See how you compare to the 80/20 Rule and
you'll discover that you're amazingly close (in over 25 analyses for
institutions ranging in size from $350 million to over $25 billion, we've
seen variations of no greater than 5%). Interestingly, however, we
have seen substantial variations in the aggregate deposit cutoff point
for membership in the top 20% of an institution. The cutoff point range
has extended from less than $7,000 to over $24,000 in aggregate
deposits. This strongly suggests that the 80/20 Rule not be universally
applied as a segmentation technique, because of the lack of homogeneity
of households meeting that criterion across different institutions.
Typically, the most effective method for establishing your initial
segment definitions is based on aggregate deposit levels for liability

product customers and a combination of product usage and appended life-cycle data for asset and investment product customers.

Segment Analysis—Once you've defined your segments, you'll want to treat each segment like a mini-customer-base (which it is) and analyze product usage, balance levels by product, and cross-sell ratios. This is where you can really home in on the most potential productive markets within your base for specific products. It's at this point that you would apply your profitability measures to back into acceptable acquisition costs for each product/balance combination. From this information, in combination with your product sales objectives, you can put together your Database Marketing Plan. The output of this analysis should be definitions of your most potentially productive segments for each product. These "prospect profiles" will be used to define the test cells in your Database Marketing Plan (see below).

The key benefit of a database analysis is that it tells you where you are now and what sales potential exists in your customer base for growth in deposits, loans, checking accounts, and other products. In other words, it defines the extent to which you can expect to reach each of your marketing goals through sales to existing customers vs. new customers.

Database Marketing Plan

Trying to implement database marketing without a plan is like trying to make a souffle without a recipe: the results may not be what you expected.

At the same time, because of the dynamic nature of database marketing, the plan must be flexible enough to accommodate changes in tactics and the results of tracking analysis during its execution. One of the primary advantages of database marketing is the ability to identify what worked, what didn't, and how to improve future efforts. The plan, therefore, provides a framework, in terms of mutually agreed-upon strategies, with tactical specifics to be revised and updated based on results.

The goal of the Database Marketing Plan is to capitalize on what Stan Rapp and Tom Collins identified as "Individualized Marketing" in their book, *The Great Marketing Turnaround* (Prentice-Hall, 1990). Their book, which is subtitled "The Age of the Individual—and How to Profit from It," traces the development of marketing over the past three decades, concluding that the great marketing success stories in the '90s will be about "Individualized Marketing," which they define as "a very personal form of marketing that recognizes, acknowledges, appreciates and serves the interests and needs of selected groups of consumers whose individual identities and marketing profiles are or become known to the advertiser."

The MCIF gives you the tools to identify and select the groups of customers to target. It's important to recognize that you have a finite number of good prospects in your customer base for additional deposit, loan, or investment product sales. These customers are identified in a Database Analysis. A Database Marketing Plan coordinates the communication schedule to these prospects so you can obtain the required tracking data to refine your prospect or segment selects in order to maximize the total cost-effectiveness of your marketing plan.

The foundation of a Database Marketing Plan is the same as for your total marketing plan:

- establishing current marketing objectives
- identifying target markets (mailing selects)
- focusing on product sales goals

Depending upon the sales goals for each product, the plan should contain a calendar of solo product mailings targeted within and outside your customer base and serial (matrix) mailing programs that target specific customer and prospect segments. It should also address opportunities for testing new products and refining segmentation strategies and creative approaches to improve marketing cost-efficiencies.

Although it's difficult to create a need for a financial service, you can motivate customers with latent needs to *act now*. In developing your schedule of mailings, you should vary not only the offer but the strength of the offer to different segments, based on the profitability of the business they are likely to bring you. For example, you should be willing to pay more for a checking account with a $7,500 average balance than one with a $750 average balance. Other offer variations can involve combining products or offering pricing incentives. Bear in mind that you can afford to be much more aggressive in serial mail than in media because your offer is limited to your best customers or prospects.

The ultimate importance of the plan is that it forces agreement on the key objectives of the program and outlines the steps to reach those objectives. The specific timing and sequence of offers and mailings will doubtless change during the implementation phase. That's not of great importance, as long as the plan contains a comprehensive listing of the bases to be covered *at some point* in the program. Changes in the competitive environment and the results of your tracking analysis virtually guarantee that your plan will be a dynamic, as opposed to static, document. In the final analysis, then, a Database Marketing Plan is not a document — it's a *process* that is driven by the structure of your execution and the tracking data that is produced as a result of that structure.

How Tracking Affects Plan Execution

The primary benefit of properly executed direct marketing programs is ACCOUNTABILITY. Through accurate tracking, you can determine what worked, what didn't, and how to fix it for the next time. That translates to increasing cost efficiency over time. A reliable tracking report is your most powerful weapon in the budget battle, because you can show management the actual returns for their marketing investments.

A key advantage of tracking through your MCIF is the ability to measure TOTAL activity of the response group, not simply the sales of the specific product offered. This is critical in a serial mail program because the intent is to build cumulative response over the course of the campaign through a planned series of related communications to defined segments. Customers who are targeted in such programs will purchase a range of products, dictated by their needs, *in addition to* the specific products you're offering to that specific segment. Your tracking needs to capture the total activity of each segment. That's where your MCIF proves invaluable, because of its ability to report all activity within the response group during the tracking window. The old method of "counting coupons" only captures a fraction of the purchase behavior within the targeted segment.

Your customers will also purchase some products with no communication at all. Ideally, you want to look at the *incremental* sales that result from your marketing communications to accurately gauge the effect of your program. To do this, you need to set up a control group who receive no mail. This group's purchase activity establishes a baseline for response analysis. A control group is a two-edged sword, however. Improperly used, it can kill your program. Here's how:

> There are very few institutions that are large enough to set up control groups for every segment in a serial mail program. A control group that is too small will magnify the effects of any activity that occurs within the group, relative to the segment. In one instance a single $200,000 deposit by a member of a control group resulted in a tracking report that concluded that the control group outperformed its total serial mail segment for a 6-month period. It turned out that the control group had fewer than 90 households, so a single transaction had huge impact.

To be reliable a control group should generate a minimum of 100 product transactions during a tracking period. If you assume a 2% average activity rate within the tracking period, you need 5,000 households for a control group. Many institutions can set up a control group for all deposit customers, rather than each segment of deposit customers. This way, you can track the performance of the deposit mail group against its control group and the performance of each segment within the deposit mail group against the other segments. Because of the low activity rates experienced for asset products and investment products, it's almost impossible to set up reliable control groups for these.

Your tracking reports need to measure both account and balance activity for each individual segment in your serial mail program, as well as for each response group for solo product mailings that are selected using your MCIF. The reason is that response, measured by activity, is not the only measure you look at. It's vital to compute the basis point acquisition cost to see the true economic effects of your program. Without this final step in the analysis, a $250 transaction has the same weight as a $25,000 transaction.

In addition, the analysis should measure the total new account activity (number and balances) of each segment mailed. An examination of the types of services purchased by each segment will expose buying patterns, which are used to revise the offer sequences in the serial mail plan. The performance of each segment will be used to refine the plan and, perhaps, adjust the frequency and schedule of mailings to specific segments.

This is the single most important step of any Database Marketing program. Through your MCIF, you have access to all the information you need to not only measure but to improve the effectiveness and efficiency of your marketing efforts on an ongoing basis.

This is what Database Marketing is about. It is already changing the way financial services are marketed by permitting large and complex organizations to identify and respond to their customers' individual needs. Basically, the technology has made possible a giant step backward to the time when a banker knew his customers and was able to advise them based on that knowledge of their individual circumstances. The result is both an actual and a perceived increase in service quality, which strengthens the relationship with the customer and results in truly enormous increases in marketing cost efficiencies.

7

DATA APPENDING

Jordan Modell
Chemical Bank

Ｉf your company has installed a Marketing Customer Information File (MCIF) system, you work for one of the lucky companies that actually knows the depth and breadth of the different account relationships it has with its customers. With this information, your company can embark on capturing sales history by customer, test different customer segmentation strategies, assess true profitability for every customer and much more.

What is the next step? This chapter addresses how such a company can be in the top 1% of marketers—that select group that has the ability to, as the Boston Consulting Group puts it, "market to a segment of one."

How does a company achieve a one-on-one relationship with a customer? Just as people do with acquaintances. If you meet someone you like at a function, you might tend to discuss where they live, their families and kids, what kinds of cars they drive, what kinds of recreational activities they like, magazines they like to read, etc. While we might learn this information in a first meeting, we learn more about our friends over time.

Data appending is very much like learning about new friends. Enormous databases have been constructed in the United States over the past 10 years that have all of the above information and much more. When direct marketing was in its infancy 20 and 30 years ago, the most you could find out about individuals was what magazines they read. (The most popular mailing lists available were the *Reader's Digest* and *Life Magazine* lists.) The strides in technology in the 1980s brought forth a wealth of consumer information that can now be appended to files for use in segmenting the files for various offers.

In this chapter, *data appending* is defined as the process of adding information—individual, household, or general—to an individual's name.

Types of Data Available

The data available for appending ranges from specific information regarding an individual (age, marital status) to household (real estate owned/registered motor vehicles) and general (geo-demographic income, education) data. Some of the most reliable data available comes from public records. Accuracy is increased dramatically if for example, consumers have to submit birth certificates to get driver's licenses, provide accurate addresses for telephone service, and procure notarized statements when they purchase a home. Public record information includes:

> Driver's license files
>
> Motor vehicle registrations
>
> Voter registration files [1]
>
> Birth records
>
> Marriage licenses
>
> Divorce records
>
> County real estate files

Not all of the information is available in every state and/or county. Some localities restrict the access to public records under the "right to privacy." The recent murder of a television actress has instigated the restriction of files, so that addresses are not given out except to organizations that can show that the information will be used properly.

---

[1] Voter registration files can only be used for purposes defined by the Election Reform Act as related to political or initiative campaigns.

In addition to the above public record files, there has been an explosion of private files that contain a myriad of data. These files include:

> Phone numbers
>
> Catalog buyers
>
> Registration of consumer purchases
>
> Magazine subscriptions
>
> Market research survey files

Finally, the federal government has developed excellent data from its decennial census count—data that includes:

> Educational attainment
>
> Family composition
>
> Occupation
>
> Housing information
>
> Ethnic identification

This data is developed on a variety of levels—state, county, city zip code, census tract, and census block. Much of the data is used by city planners and political parties for redistricting of legislative boundaries, but a multimillion-dollar industry has developed from fine-tuning the information and putting it into the hands of business. Besides providing census data, several companies have developed proprietary segmentation tools for using general census data and creating clusters of households with similar characteristics. These companies also provide update information to the census file so their clients are not restricted to using outdated information.

Operating Processing

Now that we have reviewed the types of data available, how is data appending done? There are a number of companies that can append the above information to your customer records. Following is a list of the major companies involved in data appending:

> Metromail Corporation
>
> R. L. Polk
>
> Donnelley

SmartNames

Infobase Services

National Decision Systems/Equifax

Claritas Corporation

TRW

Each of these companies has its particular specialty: for example, Polk, auto registration; Donnelley, phone numbers; SmartNames, real estate files. They also have access to much of the other data available.

After you supply your customer list (with names, street addresses, cities, states, and zipcodes) to the appending companies, the processing includes a number of operations. To facilitate the transfer of data from millions of records, they will convert your records to the same format as their base files. Depending on the data to be appended, they will then geocode your customer records, assigning the addresses to particular census tracts and blocks.

The next step involves parsing each name and address into an algorithm that allows the computer to compare each name with names in the file. When data is appended, the computer does not do this on an exact full-name-and-address match. A common appending process takes only a portion of the name and address (a specific number of consonants and vowels) and compares it with the records on file. Certain fields require an exact match—zipcode, for instance.

As the computer finds matches, it will "append" or add the data to the end of the customer record. In the case of specific individual data, the file looks for individual names. For other data, the computer does the match based on the census tract and/or census block. Much census data is "indirectly inferred," based on the data received from all households in an area, and is normally expressed in percentage form—presence of children, occupation, etc.

Costs for Data Appending

Costs for data appending vary by company but follow several industry practices. In cases where all data elements are being appended, companies often charge on all records being submitted to processing. Charges are expressed in costs per thousand records processed—e.g., $40 per thousand (M), or $40/M, records submitted. If only a few data elements are being requested (e.g., exact age, phone number, home-ownership) most companies will charge a processing fee for all records submitted and then charge for all successfully matched records. Average charges for matched data elements are

Phone numbers	$20/M
Exact age	$20/M
Age ranges	$14/M
Homeowners	$10/M
Value of home	$35/M
Car values	$12/M

Applications for Using Appended Data

A word of caution. When confronted with the variety of data available for appending to records, it is easy to get carried away and get more data than is necessary for your specific purposes. Some data items are more accurate than others. You should work closely with your supplier to assess appended data for each data item. Too much data on your customer files will make your entire MCIF system run slower. As data changes at a rapid pace, information that sits for 6 months can quickly become outmoded. Work closely with your data-appending company by describing how you will use the data and what results you expect from the data.

Now that you have added all of this information to your file, what do you do with it? Below are a number of financial services campaigns and data elements frequently used to segment customer files to increase responses.

Product	Data Elements
Home equity lines	Home ownership, income, age, presence of children
CDs	Income, age, survey data on services used

Product	Data Elements
Annuities	Age, income
Mortgage refinance	Age, Homeownership, income
Auto loans	Income, motor vehicles owned
Credit cards	Income, age, credit history [2]
Branch openings	Census block, income

With the data appended to your customer file, you can now ask research questions of your file to learn what kind of households have your checking accounts, annuities, and home equity lines. Then you can look for other households within your customer file (and non-customer prospect file) that share certain characteristics with your current customers for that product and then mail solicitations.

Caveats About Data Appending

Short of making a market research firm very rich by calling each of your customers individually, the only way to know how old a customer is, how much a household earns or how many kids they have is via data appending. Whereas the data is not always 100% accurate and you cannot get full coverage on all data items for every household, data appending is an economical means of obtaining the data and avoiding the risks of asking personal questions of customers such as What is your income? How many children do you have? And so on.

As previously stated the accuracy of data appending varies. It is directly related to the source of information and how "compulsory" the data is. Specifically, voter registration will be more accurate than warranty card responses to age questions. It is imperative that you run a "sanity check" of each data item. A way of doing this is to publish an internal document listing cross-tabs for all of your customers by data item.

---

[2] Recent rulings by the Federal Trade Commission under the Fair Credit Reporting Act have seriously restricted the use of credit data or information on credit usage. Consult your legal department on appropriate uses of this information.

Consumers have become very concerned with the amount of data available concerning their lives and are reluctant to share it with anyone unless they have a clear picture of how and why the information will be used. A good example of this is the recent household database program that was proposed by Lotus: "The Consumer Marketplace."

Lotus was going to provide small businesses with files of households in specific areas, along with specific information on those households. The files were proposed as ideal for small businesses or, for example, for insurance salesmen to use in lead generation. There was such an uproar over the release of the data on such a wide scale (more than 70,000 complaints were registered with the company in the 2 weeks after the product announcement) that the company suspended the introduction of the product.

Eight Advantages of Data Appending

---

1. Reduces market research costs

Let me assure all my friends in Market Research that I do not say that data appending *eliminates* market research costs but, rather, that it *reduces* market research costs—it allows research budgets to be allocated more efficiently. At its most basic level, data appending can eliminate the need to design questionnaires to elicit information you already have on file.

Data appending can also eliminate some of these kinds of research decisions: "Let's just do a quick study with a questionnaire to find out how many of our customers have *x* attribute." These types of quick questionnaires, used primarily in preparation for a new marketing campaign, can cost thousands or, in some cases, hundreds of thousands of dollars a year. These questions can now be answered quicker, and certainly cheaper at the touch of a button.

2. Builds relationships by tailoring the right offer to the right people

Chemical Bank has taught me that good direct marketing doesn't "sell" anything—it fulfills customers' needs. If you offer the *correct* product, service, and/or information to the *right*, receptive, audience, the customer actually looks forward to your message.

By knowing more about your customer, you can actually avoid serious customer relations problems. Have you ever gotten a credit card solicitation from a bank with whom you already have a card? How about a Christmas card from your stockbroker of 20 years, only you're Jewish? How about the cashier at a 7-11 store who gets a Jumbo CD solicitation? Or the renter who receives a never-ending stream of home equity offers?

On the packaged-goods side—Young married couples receiving special offers to buy property at the Lawrence Welk Villas. Single males getting coupons for 50 cents off purchases of Midol. Females solicited for Brut aftershave. Low-income couples being told how affordable it is to lease a Mercedes.

In all of these cases, at best the customer will feel that "My bank/credit card issuer/package-goods distributor or whatever, doesn't really know and/or understand me!" The worst case will have them muttering, "If after all these years (and all the dollars I spent with them) they still don't know me from my sister Kate, then I'll move my next purchase/business elsewhere!"

Not only have you wasted time and money mailing to the wrong person but you also have annoyed and possibly permanently alienated your own customer. The problem is compounded when you use special personalization and/or expensive layouts: "They spend all this money on these colorful photos and even sign it with my banker's name, and they still know nothing about me, one of their best customers."

By using appended data correctly and addressing the needs and desires of customers, direct marketing can actually cement existing relationships and leave customers feeling that you are looking out for them, rather than milking and intruding on them.

If your file has some of the standard data elements appended—age, income, home ownership, car ownership—you can spend a lot of time pricing your IRAs and mail a slick personalized package telling high-income homeowners who have expensive cars how they can retire as millionaires in 25 years. And your customers will say, "Now there is an institution that is really looking after *my* interests!"

3. Helps target direct mail through focused segment mailing

The days of mass, blanket mailings are over. With rising postal costs and the overburdened mailbox, mailing packages to every household in an area is no longer cost-efficient. This is the age of segmented mailing—taking the right offer to the right people—as opposed to a generic offer to everybody.

The trick is finding out who are the right people. David Ogilvy, the great sage of advertising, once said, "I know that 50% of my advertising is being wasted . . . I just don't know which 50%." Well David, we are getting closer. Now you can mail to just your wealthiest customers or to your customers with foreign cars or to high-income households without home equity credit lines.

By cross referencing fields that have been data appended, you can now go even further. You can mail Tide coupons to just those families in suburban areas who have kids under 10 and only one working parent. You could offer great trade-in values to households with 3-year-old foreign cars. With a little imagination (and your ever-present MCIF), the possibilities are endless.

4. Allows you to create better test cells in a mailing

As was just discussed, data appending can reduce mailing costs by targeting your mail. But you don't have to stop there. Once you have established the *theme* of your mailing, data appending can aid you in defining your test cells to improve response rates.

If the mailing is to middle-income families with children, you may wish to set up test cells like those that follow to see which target segment gives you the best return for your time and effort:

1. Lower middle income without kids

2. Lower middle income with kids

3. Lower middle income with kids under 10

4. Lower middle income with kids 10 to 17

5. Lower middle income with girl(s) under 10

6. Lower middle income with boy(s) under 10

7. Lower middle income with only girl(s) 10 to 17

8. Lower middle income with only boy(s) 10 to 17

9. Lower middle income with only girl(s) under 10

10. Lower middle income with only boy(s) under 10

As you can see, the segmentation possibilities increase almost geometrically in direct proportion to how complicated the mailing is. Now you can have test cells by age bracket, income, car type, or whatever else your product manager requires. *Now you can offer your product managers a choice of high-quality small target mailings or loosen the criteria and enlarge the target segments.*

5. Helps back-end analysis of previous and current mailings

All of this data allows much easier back-end analysis to see how well/ poorly you did on a mailing. Once you get the results back from your test mailing, you can easily tell by test cell how well your efforts succeeded. But what happens to mailings without test cells? What happened to mailings that you did in the prehistoric days before you appended data to your file?

Are these mailings consigned to single-digit success rates? Is their success or failure summed up in one word . . . either "Yes" or "No"? Actually, by applying enriched data to the files of previously mailed-to customers, you can look at the true results of a mailing at any time.

Just take the response file from the mailing and append data. You can ask whatever questions you want, just as if the respondents were standing in your office. "What do most of you have in common? " Most are homeowners, with upper-middle-class incomes. "What about cars?" The majority bought a new car in the past year? Ask away, as long as you have those elements coded you can talk with these people on file.

This brings me to my last point on this advantage: Not only will your respondent file yield you a treasure trove of good information but your nonrespondent file can be a treasure chest of information for your next mailing.

6. Is critical to proper modeling

Predictive modeling is perhaps the hottest topic in direct mail marketing today. Companies like American Express, and Reader's Digest, are putting money, time, and effort into building statistical models. By predicting what type of consumer will respond best to a specific offer, a well-built model can have a great impact on response rate and mailing costs. With the price of mail rising at many times the rate of inflation, it has become as important to know who *not to mail to* as to whom you should mail.

In just a short time after you have data appended to your MCIF, you will have the ability to build predictive models. As you mail more, continue to refine each model with sophisticated response analysis. Finally, for general purposes, develop a suppression file of those customers least likely to respond to a particular type of mailing.

Data appending is essential to correct modeling because it helps profile both respondents and nonrespondents. Without having to call up customers and ask why they didn't respond to a certain mailing, you can look for similarities among nonrespondents and differences between them and respondents by simply asking your database to do the work for you.

7. Reduces telemarketing costs

By appending data to your customer file, you will be able to know the best time of day to call prospects and customers. It costs a lot to call a customer or prospect, and your risk of losing them by annoying them is much greater than with any other medium. In a high-risk, high-reward situation the more and the better information you can get on a customer, the greater the chances of success.

Data appending is a key to one-to-one customer contact. It can tell you more than just what product your customers purchase from you, it can tell you something about them:

Are they likely to be home with the kids?

Is it best to try a free gourmet hook with them because they are DINKS (Dual Income, No Kids) or a discount on a cruise because they are RENS (retired empty nesters)?

8. Reduces attrition by helping design antiattrition campaigns based on customers' real vs. perceived needs

Unless you know about customers' true economic and social situations, you will never really know why they are leaving your company.

It is far too easy to say, "They just have low balances, they are not a problem." They may have had the capacity to be some of your best customers but let their accounts/purchases dwindle because of some perceived slight.

On the other hand, people who have large balances may have characteristics that should alert you that they are rate shoppers and are likely to disappear if you adjust your pricing strategy.

Conclusions

As discussed above, there are a variety of data elements available for appending to your customer file and dozens of ways that the data can be used to make your programs more cost-efficient. Take the time to research the projects you are planning over the next year and determine how appended data can assist in segmenting the file for the mailings and tracking the results. You will find that the time is well worth the effort.

8

MODELING

Scott Wisner
Infobase Services

Anyone who has worked in direct marketing has probably puzzled over the fact that the response rate for a typical direct mail campaign is somewhere in the neighborhood of 2%. After all, that's one response for every 50 pieces mailed. Since 2% respond, it must be that there is a need for the product; so the solution to the puzzle must be that the response to the mailing can be increased by identifying the unique characteristics of those who responded and selecting future mailing lists based on these unique characteristics.

Segmentation and Modeling

Segmentation and modeling are statistical analysis techniques for identifying the characteristics that distinguish responders from non-responders.

Before discussing how to perform and evaluate different segmentation and modeling techniques, it is important to understand some of the basic difficulties in distinguishing responders from nonresponders. Primary among these difficulties is basic human nature—no two individuals will always make the same decision, regardless of how similar the individuals are. Furthermore, even the same individual may make different decisions when faced with the same situation at two different times. Another difficulty is that it is difficult for direct marketers to measure all of the factors that may affect the decision to respond to a direct mail solicitation. In summary, there is no way to predict exactly how an individual will respond to a direct mail solicitation, even if you know everything about them, and there is no way to know everything about the person to whom you will be mailing a solicitation.

The practical consequence of not knowing exactly how any individual will respond is that direct marketers must work in terms of response rates and probabilities. Therefore, the first part of this chapter discusses a framework for evaluating alternatives with different response rates.

The second part of the chapter discusses information about prospects, which has generally been useful in predicting the types of individuals who are most likely to respond. Data discussed include internal data, such as purchase data and previous response data, survey data, and commercially available enhancement data that can be applied to customer files.

The final part of the chapter discusses technical aspects of modeling and segmentation. Modeling techniques that are discussed include regression and logistic regression, two of the most popular techniques. Segmentation techniques include Automatic Interaction Detector (AID), Chi-square AID (CHAID), and a hybrid regression technique.

Evaluating Different Modeling and Segmentation Techniques

The standard techniques for evaluating models and segmentations are generalizations of techniques used to compare the response rates of lists. These generalizations mainly have to do with how the models or segmentations perform for different mailing quantities.

A simple list analysis is based on a comparison of response rates. If list A has a higher response rate than list B, then list A is better than list B. List A will be mailed first, and if additional names are required, they will be selected from list B.

Comparing different modeling or segmentation strategies is as simple as comparing lists when the mailing quantity can be determined beforehand. When the mailing quantity cannot be determined beforehand, there is a simple tool for comparing segmentations or models, called a lift curve.

The main output from modeling or segmentation is a ranking of individuals based on their estimated propensity to respond. If these individuals are ordered according to their rankings, then individuals receiving the highest ranks should be the most responsive. When the individuals from a previous mailing campaign are rank ordered it is possible to compare estimated to actual response rates. Frequently this comparison is accomplished by dividing the universe into 10 equal size groups, or deciles. The top decile contains individuals who were predicted to have the highest chance of responding, and the lowest decile contains those who are least likely to respond. For reference, the response rate for each decile is compared to the overall response rate. For example, if the response rate for the top decile is 2.8% and the overall response rate is 1.9%, then the top decile produces almost 0.5% greater response. This gain in response is often called lift and it is often expressed as an index, called the lift index, which is computed by dividing the response rate for the decile by the overall response rate and multiplying the result by 100, i.e., $100 \times 2.8\%$ / 1.9% = 147. This difference between the lift index and 100 is the percentage boost or drop in the response rate. In our example, the top decile performs 47% better than just mailing to a randomly selected group of prospects.

Typically, a modeling or segmentation effort can identify a decile that performs 30% to 40% better than a random mailing, but it is almost always necessary to mail more than 10% of the available universe. For this reason the cumulative lift index is often calculated. The cumulative lift index measures the boost in response from mailing 10%, 20%, 30%, ..., 100%. In all cases, the cumulative lift index will be greater than 100.

The table on the following page contains the lift information for a typical direct mail campaign.

LIFT TABLE

Decile	Number Mailed	Number Responses	Response Rate	Lift Index	Cumulative Number Mailed	Cumulative Number Responses	Cumulative Response Rate
1-Top	10,000	280	2.80%	147	10,000	280	2.80%
2	10,000	260	2.60	137	20,000	540	2.70
3	10,000	240	2.40	126	30,000	780	2.60
4	10.000	220	2.20	116	40,000	1,000	2.50
5	10,000	200	2.00	105	50,000	1,200	2.40
6	10,000	180	1.80	95	60,000	1,380	2.30
7	10,000	160	1.60	84	70,000	1,540	2.20
8	10,000	140	1.40	74	80,000	1,680	2.10
9	10,000	120	1.20	63	90,000	1,800	2.00
10-Bottom	10,000	100	1.00	53	100,000	1,900	1.90
Overall	100,000	1,900	1.90%	100			

Sometimes the Lift Table is referred to as a "Table of Gains," and frequently the information in the table is illustrated using a line graph, called a Lift Curve or Gains Chart. Information from the preceding Lift Table is graphed below.

GRAPH 1
LIFT CURVE

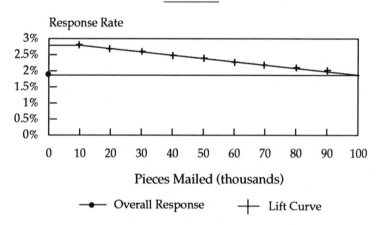

The sloped curve in the graph illustrates the cumulative response rate, while the flat line represents the overall response rate for the mailing. The difference between the heights of the two curves represents the "gains" from modeling. Notice that this difference decreases as larger quantities are mailed. Consequently, if the mailing universe is fixed and a large fraction of the universe will be mailed, the gains from modeling will generally be small.

In the previous example, the lift curve illustrated the gains from developing a single model. This same framework can be used to compare the lifts for two competing models. Here, too, the difference between the heights of the two curves is a measure of the incremental gain from having an alternative model.

One possibility when comparing two alternative models is that one model will perform better for smaller mailing quantities while a competing model does better for larger mailing quantities. The following graph illustrates such a case.

GRAPH 2
LIFT COMPARISON

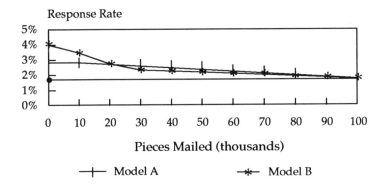

Pieces Mailed (thousands)

──┼── Model A   ──✳── Model B

The two lift curves in Graph 2 illustrate the lift curves for two competing models. Model B performs better for mailings of 20,000 pieces or less, and model A performs better for mailings greater than 20,000 pieces.

Data Sources for Modeling

In the previous section a unifying framework for evaluating different modeling and segmentation techniques was developed. This framework can also be used to evaluate the different types of data that can be used in modeling or segmentation. There are several sources of data that can be used to predict which individuals will respond to a direct mail promotion, including the following:

- Individual Household Level—This is data that is sometimes collected from consumer surveys, but more frequently it is collected by private companies from telephone books, vehicle registrations, credit bureaus, voter registration records, school registration records, and private companies that compile and sell information about their own customers.

- Census Data—This is data collected by the U.S. Government in the Decennial Census, and reported to the public as averages and percentages of Census reporting units, called Block Groups or Enumeration Districts.

- Customer Usage Data—This is customer transactions data, including recency, frequency, and amount of transactions (RFM).

In building a statistical model or segmentation, household level, aggregated household data, and census data work because different household types respond differently to a direct mail promotion. Since household type is best measured by household level data, models built with this type of data almost always produce a higher lift than models built with aggregated household data and carrier route data. Because it has been 10 years since the last census data were released, aggregated household data generally perform better than census data.

Since it would be difficult to obtain household level data for all the households on a database or mailing list, it is frequently possible to combine household level data and aggregate household level data to produce a model that is even better than would be possible with household level data alone. When aggregated household data is substituted into records where actual household level data is missing, the household level is said to be defaulted to area level. Defaulted household level data have been used to develop very powerful predictive models.

Models built on RFM data typically produce a higher lift than models built on other data. A retailer characterized the effectiveness of RFM data by saying that "If you want to know who will shop in the store next week, just take a walk through the store today." This anecdote also illustrates the weaknesses of RFM data; it does not work for acquisition, new customers, and customers who have become inactive. But if reliable RFM data is available, it will produce a significant lift in response.

Segmentation

This section of the chapter deals with segmentation analysis. Segmentation analysis is the process of subdividing the mailing universe so that households in different segments are as different as possible, while households in the same segment are as similar as possible. Several segmentation techniques are available, but AID and CHAID are the two techniques that are most often used in direct marketing.

AID

AID analysis first appeared in academic literature in 1970 as a technique for screening large quantities of survey data. AID is an acronym that stands for Automatic Interaction Detector. Interaction refers to the effect that combinations of characteristics have on response. In marketing, these combinations of characteristics define segments with different response rates.

AID constructs segments by sequentially splitting the mailing universe. First the universe is split into two segments based on either household or usage data. Only one of the household or usage characteristics determines which characteristic makes the "best" split, so each characteristic is tested. The AID algorithm is best defined by comparing the response rate to the overall response rate according to the following formula:

$$\text{ESS} = [n_1(p_1 - p_O)^2] + [n_2(p_2 - p_O)^2]$$

where n_1 and n_2 are the number of pieces mailed to the first and second halves of the split, p_1 and p_2 are the response rates for the first and second halves of the split, and p_O is the overall response rate. The objective of the AID algorithm is to maximize the ESS (Explained Sum of Squares). Intuitively, maximizing the ESS increases the difference in response rates for the resulting segments.

Once the AID algorithm makes the first split, it then resplits each of the resulting segments. Again, the subsequent splitting variables are determined using the ESS formula. Splitting generally stops when the ESS falls below some preselected level, or after the desired number of segments have been derived.

CHAID

In practice, AID sometimes identifies segments whose response rates do not hold up on validation. This inability to always validate is attributed to the sensitivity of the ESS criterion to data anomalies. Several modifications to the ESS criterion have been recommended, and one that has received considerable practical application is CHAID analysis, or Chi-square Automatic Interaction Detector.

One of the main differences between AID and CHAID is that CHAID permits multiway splits. Another difference is that CHAID uses a variation of the ESS criterion based on the approximate chi-square statistic. Many practitioners feel that these two differences make CHAID more stable than AID.

The splitting process for the CHAID algorithm is very similar to that of the AID. Often the splitting process is illustrated using a tree diagram, like the one presented below.

ILLUSTRATION 1
TREE ILLUSTRATION FOR **CHAID** ANALYSIS

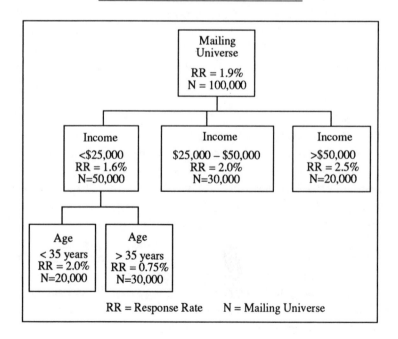

Final Segments

Segment 1	Segment 2	Segment 3	Segment 4
Income more than $50,000	Income $25,000-$50,000	Income less than $25,000 Age less than 35 years	Income less than $25,000 Age more than 35 years
RR = 2.5%	RR = 2.0%	RR = 2.0%	RR = 0.75%
N = 20,000	N = 30,000	N = 20,000	N = 30,000

The CHAID tree illustrates the development of four segments. First, the universe of 100,000 records is split into three segments according to income. High income households were found to be the most responsive. The 20,000 households with incomes greater than $50,000 are found to respond at a rate of 2.5%; 30,000 middle income households respond at 2.0%; and lower income households respond at 1.6%.

In the illustration only the lower income segment was resplit. Possible explanations are that the algorithm was restricted from splitting any segment of 30,000 or less, or that no splitting variable was found. When the lower income segment is resplit, age is the splitting variable. Younger households are found to respond better.

The combinations of characteristics that define the final segments are listed at the top of this page. In general the final segments will be defined by three or four characteristics; 10 to 30 segments are usually manageable.

Selecting a Segmentation

There is some debate about the appropriate segmentation technique and about whether the modeling techniques discussed in the next section are preferred to any segmentation technique. Proponents of CHAID argue that multiway splits are preferred to the two-way restriction imposed by AID. Furthermore, they argue that the approximate chi-square criterion is inherently better than the ESS criterion used in CHAID. These two CHAID features are disputed by AID users. In addition, a new technique called CART (Classification and Regression Trees), which utilizes a two-way splitting methodology, has been developed and appears to be gaining some following.

In practice, none of the theoretical arguments for or against one of the segmentation techniques matters. The lift curve framework makes it possible to make a practical comparison between the techniques. In making such a comparison it is important to use a sample of records that has not been used in developing the segmentation—this process is called split-half testing.

Modeling (Regression)

Modeling, specifically Regression, is the use of statistical analysis to construct a mathematical equation (model) to predict the response rate for *individual prospects*. This compares to the objective of segmentation, which is to divide the prospect universe into *segments*.

There are many different regression techniques, but in direct marketing these different techniques are variations of two different techniques, linear regression and logistic modeling.

Regression Analysis

Regression analysis is sometimes described as curve fitting. The scatter plot below illustrates this notion.

DIAGRAM 1

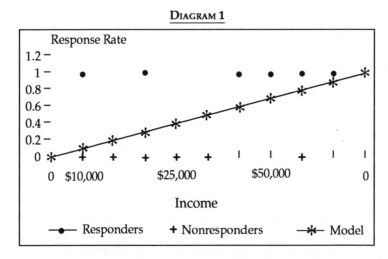

In this diagram "*'s" represent individual prospects, both responders and nonresponders. As drawn, the graph shows that at lower incomes there are many more nonresponders than responders, but at higher incomes there are more responders than nonresponders. The object of regression is to fit a line to the graph that comes as close as possible to the *'s. Often this line is fit using the Ordinary Least Squares (OLS) criterion. OLS is very similar to the ESS criterion described in the segmentation section.

The result of fitting a curve is a regression equation. A simple regression equation has the following form:

$$P = A + B * I$$

where A and B are fixed numbers, and P is the estimated response rate for prospects with income I. P, the estimated response rate, is frequently referred to as a score, and the regression equation is called the scoring equation.

More sophisticated regression equations can be developed using more than one predictor variable. Such regressions are called multiple regression equations.

Logistic Modeling

If you reexamine Diagram 1, you will notice that a better line can be fitted if curved lines are permitted. One class of curved lines has been found to fit these situations particularly well. This class of curves is the "S"-shaped Logistic curves. Diagram 2 illustrates this point.

DIAGRAM 2

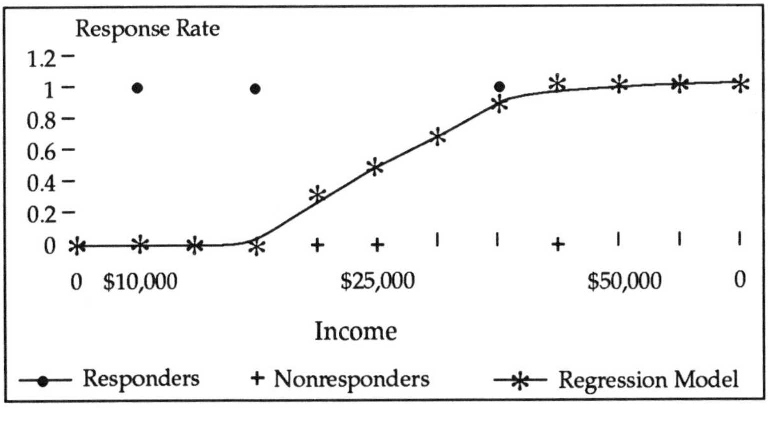

103

The fitting of Logistic Curves is called logistic modeling. As in the case of multiple regression, Logistic models can be built using many explanatory variables, and these models are often called Logistic Scoring equations.

OLS Regression vs. Logistic Modeling

Regression and Logistic scoring models can be compared using the framework developed in the beginning of this chapter. Logistic modeling does perform better than OLS Regression, but sometimes these gains are nominal. Additionally, Logistic modeling requires more statistical training to be used effectively.

Modeling vs. Segmentation

In general, both Regression and Logistic modeling provide better lifts than the segmentation techniques discussed earlier. However, marketing implications, other than the scores, for the modeling techniques are more difficult to understand. Furthermore, the modeling techniques require considerably more training to be used effectively.

9

CREATIVE DEVELOPMENT

Roley D. Altizer
Dominion Bankshares Corporation

Before reading this chapter, you should understand what you will—and will not—gain from it.

This chapter is written for the financial direct marketing *generalist* or the specialist in some particular area of direct marketing who wants to know more about creative development.

I'm very much a financial direct marketing generalist myself, responsible for putting together entire direct marketing programs—from taking part in offer development and list selection to making sure the other 998 scattered pieces of the puzzle actually fit together before the package drops into the mailsack.

I don't consider myself a "creative type," although writing copy and creating direct mail packages have been key responsibilities of my jobs over the past 10+ years. I do consider myself a *communicator* using the written word, hopefully on occasion, creatively.

I make no promise that after reading this chapter you will be a hotshot copywriter. Or that you will be able to turn a so-so direct mail package into a highly profitable one.

But, just maybe my years in the creative and production "trenches" will benefit you. Hopefully, my experiences will shorten the learning curve for you in developing a working knowledge of what's involved in direct marketing creative. Because you'll probably not create the package or produce it yourself, I've spent more time trying to give you guidance in working with others who take care of these challenges for you. If nothing else, you'll have a much better idea of what decisions you need to make—and what questions you need to ask before making a particular decision.

Putting the Importance of Creative into Perspective

Many of us find creative development the most interesting aspect of direct marketing. But let's put its importance into perspective right up front. Creative is the proverbial "tip of the iceberg." It's the most visible aspect but not the most important. As you may have read or heard, creative accounts for about 20% of the success of a direct marketing program. The list and the offer account for a hefty 80%.

Okay, relatively speaking, creative isn't as important. And, while I would never argue that dazzling creative can sell a bad product or that it can sell a weak offer to the wrong list, it *can* make a difference. A great offer to the right list communicated poorly can turn a potential profit into a loss.

How many of us wouldn't welcome a 10% boost in response because of a strong, appealing presentation of the right offer to the right list, or a similar boost to a tried-and-true offer presented to the same audience previously? A 10% difference can push you from a break-even situation into profitability.

The Most Fundamental Fundamental

Let's begin by looking at the building blocks of sound creative execution. I learned early in my professional life, which began in the research department of a broadcast ratings firm, that regardless of how impressive your work (i.e., how great your offer), if you can't communicate with your readers *clearly, precisely, convincingly,* and—often—*quickly,* you're in trouble. Leave off *enthusiasm,* and you're dead!

In direct marketing, there's an even more fundamental point: you're writing *personally* to one individual. Even if your mailing is going to a million people, you must write as if it were going just to *one* person.

While general advertisers have a bit more leeway, it's that *one* individual whom you must constantly keep in mind. You wouldn't write a friend to say "Here's an exciting opportunity for those of you who like to save money." Rather, you'd say "Here's an exciting opportunity for you to save money." See how much stronger the second version is?

Consider these sentences from a recent letter I received: "We're committed to providing our customers with the best service. What our customers think about us really does matter." See if you can make these sentences more *personal*—more one-on-one.

It seems such a basic principle that I'm taken aback by writers who don't realize this critical element of direct response communications. If you learn nothing else from this chapter, I do hope you'll remember this one fundamental: that direct marketing is a *personal* medium.

A Different Kind of Animal in Another Way

While general advertising intends to make you aware of a product or service and build a favorable disposition when you're ready to buy, a direct mail piece asks for the sale, *in addition to* building awareness and a favorable image.

And the direct mail piece contains the method for action: a response piece to fill out and return, an 800 number to call, or, at the very least, a coupon to take to a branch office.

Because it asks for the sale and gives you a method for action, direct response advertising (whether it be a direct mail piece, an ad in a publication, or a broadcast commercial) is *measurable*. General advertisers do before-and-after studies to determine changes in awareness or image over time. Direct marketers measure sales—and profits.

Because direct marketing creativity is measurable, it's *"testable,"* meaning that it can be refined and refined again for even better results.

Maybe that window envelope you use can be replaced by a closed-face envelope and result in greater profits in spite of a higher in-the-mail cost. More about testing later.

The Direct Mail Package

A direct mail package must do many things: build awareness, create interest in a product or service, present benefits in such a way that they establish a desire to own the product or service, *and* motivate the reader to act.

The "classic" direct mail package contains five elements: outside envelope, letter, brochure, response piece, and reply envelope.

The Carrier Envelope

The most-used envelope size still seems to be the #10, the standard letter size envelope used for most business correspondence. But we're seeing a variety of envelope sizes used, from a Monarch size (about 8 by 4") to an invitation size (about 7.5 by 5") to a large 9 by 12" size.

Which one is right for your offer? Good question. Many smart direct marketers have tested and know precisely which envelope size and package format work best for a particular offer. Other envelopes and formats have been chosen at the whims of an art director or, yes, even a direct marketing manager. There are no pat answers, no "truths." The real answer, as I've said, comes from testing.

The safe bet is to begin with the classic package in a #10 window envelope. Then test, test, test. Try third-class postage versus first class; a live stamp versus metered postage; no teaser versus a teaser on the envelope; colored paper versus plain white; an invitation package versus the #10. And so on.

I have my own biases in favor of the classic #10 package without a teaser, particularly if you're mailing to present customers. Let's face it, the classic #10 package without a teaser looks like true business correspondence from a bank. And surely it will be opened. Heaven forbid this is news that I've overdrawn my checking account or that my last loan payment got lost in the mail. You're in an unusual situation in this regard. Wouldn't *Time* magazine love to have such a guarantee that its customers will open its letters?

Going to prospects, particularly for bank card offers, is another matter. These packages today look a lot like magazine offers. Readers are getting wiser. If they see a letter in the mail from a bank of which they're not a customer, they know it's a direct mail piece. So they're predisposed not to open it—unless they happen to be in the market for a particular service. An envelope teaser can be the clincher if the offer is particularly good—a low (really low) interest rate or no annual fee, or both! It gets the reader's attention, and it gambles that the information on the envelope will cause the reader to be more likely to open the envelope than to toss it. My teaser testing is rather inconclusive. So my advice to you is to test for yourself.

The Letter

Once the recipient has opened the envelope—and what a feat it can be to get him or her this far—most of the burden is placed on the direct mail letter. Usually, the first paragraph gets the reader's attention and builds initial interest in the product or service—and the sales message that follows. In other words, it gets the reader started.

The next paragraphs present benefits of the product or service to the reader. And they must be benefits. *Not* attributes. A 7.25% CD earning a 7.41% annual return with compounding is an attribute. The benefit is that you'll be $741 richer in a year if you deposit $10,000 today.

Then you quickly show the reader how easy it is to respond: "You can take advantage of this special offer, reserved for our best customers, just by bringing the enclosed bonus-rate coupon to any convenient branch."

At this point, reinforce the value of the product or service—reinforce the benefits. Then ask for the sale:

> Remember, as our preferred customer, you can earn an additional $223 on a $10,000 investment with your enclosed bonus-rate coupon. Take advantage of this profitable opportunity today at any of our branches. Please don't wait. Your coupon expires February 15.

A P.S.?

Yes. To summarize the offer quickly (some say the P.S. is the first thing a reader goes to after opening the letter) or to present one more sales-clenching benefit.

A Brochure?

Not necessarily. But often, yes. Brochures are to direct response what pictures are to advertisements. They graphically illustrate the benefits. They also reinforce and/or expand upon messages made in your sales letter. They do *not* bring up new benefits unless they aren't critical to decision-making. They work best when your offer is a complicated one or when you have many sales points.

If you feel a brochure is necessary to sell your product or service, it should be written by the same person who writes your sales letter. It should have the same tone or feeling as the letter. Unless you can't avoid it, don't use rack brochures for your direct mail pieces. They're usually written by general advertising copywriters who frequently don't include a call for action. A reasonably happy medium is to use a rack brochure with copy adjustments to turn it into a direct response brochure.

If in doubt, *test*. It will cost more initially to produce the brochure simply to test. But it could be a big money-saver. If you use a brochure now with a particular piece, test to see what happens to results if you don't use it. Or try a less-costly factsheet or buckslip. The gross response might not be quite as good, but take a look at your acquisition cost. Chances are it will be lower, so next time out you can mail more pieces and possibly get more customers at a lower cost each.

The Response Piece

Pick up a direct mail piece you receive over the next few days. Before looking at anything else, pull out the response piece. Read it. Do you have a *complete* understanding of the offer—what you have to do and what you're going to get? If not, someone has failed.

Use this simple test for your own response piece. Look at the response form first. If your offer isn't clear to *you*, then how can it be to someone else? For an even better test, ask several people around your home and office to take the response form test. If it's clear, then move to the other pieces.

The Reply Envelope

This piece deserves a few words. A reply envelope is typically a #9 envelope that fits neatly inside the slightly larger #10 carrier envelope. Who pays the postage? In 99 of 100 cases, the bank should pay it—a small extra cost for getting the order. A small extra cost, by the way, that can make the difference between a person's responding and not responding to your offer. I'm serious.

Other Creative Elements

Please don't assume you're a direct mail expert after having gotten this far. For every generality I made in the previous section, there are probably 20 ands, ifs, or buts. There are, obviously, hundreds of other details you need to think about. Let's get into just a few others.

The General Look of the Package

I hold that a direct mail package should be a reflection of your corporate image. If an upscale image is important to you, then in spite of cost ramifications, carry that image in your direct response packages. Maybe response wouldn't be affected if you used a less expensive package, but is it in your best corporate interest to do so? Is your institution really still seen in the same light? This is a qualitative decision you may need to make in spite of a volume of quantitative data leading you in a different direction.

Package image is important also when it comes to the product or service you're selling. Deposit products should be promoted with more dignity. After all, you're asking people to bring you their money. Credit products can be treated more creatively and with more "hard sell" tactics. Competition for dollars, not to mention attention, is so much greater, particularly for bank card products.

Personalization

Your results will be better if you send a personalized letter to customers or prospects rather than a printed "Dear Friend" letter mailed with a label on an envelope. But merely laser printing the person's name and address on the letter isn't enough. I'm not advocating the mindless capability to stick in the customer's name or city in every paragraph ("Now, Mr. Jones, because you're a valuable customer living in Washington . . .").

The first element to try for is a title in the salutation. Why address the person individually at the top of the letter, then say "Dear Customer" or "Dear John Jones" in the salutation? Why not "Dear Mr. Jones"? If your files aren't genderized, your direct mail vendor can genderize them for you. His software will usually deal with a questionable gender (for example, Pat or Chris) simply by not attempting to genderize it. That's safer for you, too, from a customer relations point of view. But where possible, genderize and use a title in the salutation.

From there, personalize where it's *important*. If you're sending an offer to a good bank card customer to upgrade him to a gold card, show him with laser personalization that he's not just another number:

> Because of your excellent record as a Classic Visa customer since 1971, we want to offer you our Visa Gold card with a $5,000 credit line—an increase of $700 over your present line.

If you're sending a letter to both Visa and MasterCard customers, don't say "because you're a valuable Visa/MasterCard customer . . ." Use direct mail computer power to identify the one card the customer has.

Show account numbers, too, where needed. They're important to customers having more than one account of a particular type. They're invaluable on response pieces, too, for internal processing, even if they're disguised.

Type Fonts

Use a *typewriter* font for your letter. Why go to the trouble to personalize a letter when you turn around and use a laser font that looks typeset? Remember, you're sending a personal letter from one individual to another. I even go so far as to avoid typewriter fonts that have proportional spacing. The old-fashioned typewriter fonts where the "i" takes up as much space as the "w" will give you a more personally typed look. Be sure your laser type is plenty dark. Some fonts look very weak, and your letter will look like a bad photocopy.

Signatures

Speaking of writing from one individual to another—who should sign the letter? Ideally, the person to whom the customer or prospect would go to respond to the direct mail piece. Typically, this would be the branch manager rather than a senior vice president at corporate headquarters, but this can present production nightmares.

If you have relatively few branches, the task isn't so bad. You can collect signatures from each manager and have them digitized (your agency or production company can explain) for use with any letter. Your computer files would have a branch code for each customer, and signatures would be individualized based on this code. (The same applies to phone numbers, which are often helpful on a letter or response piece.) When a manager is transferred or otherwise moves on, you simply have the new manager's signature digitized and go from there.

The task is *much* more complex when you have many branches. To avoid errors and embarrassing oversights, you might need one person working practically full-time to keep up with the changes. Many financial direct marketers have decided to forgo the desired option of localizing signatures in favor of a regional or corporate level signature. Results may not be quite as good, but you avoid errors. Which would you rather have—slightly better results or customer relations problems?

Customer Files

This subject has been covered in much more detail in other chapters, but it bears touching upon here. Bank customer files are notoriously "dirty." So, unless your list is coming from a carefully developed Marketing Customer Information File, have your vendor take extra care to "clean" your files. Imagine how embarrassing it would be to send a piece addressed to "Name Unknown" (Dear Mr. Unknown!) at a clearly good address. Legitimately, for some reason you may not know a customer's name, but you're opening yourself wide for problems if you don't handle the tricky situations up front.

Direct Response Copywriting and Art Direction

Books have been written on both subjects. (See the last section of this chapter.) So how can I possibly cover this subject adequately in a page or two? I can't; so I won't try. I won't tell you my philosophies either. What you or I might think is a great direct mail package or ad might be a bomb, and the one we think looks horrible might be a winner. That's where testing plays its important role. Never play by the seat of your pants in this business. It's too easy and inexpensive to know the truth.

You learn over time what copy style and art direction work best with your audience. Read books. Go to seminars. Read every piece of direct mail you receive. Have others pass along their direct mail to you. Pay attention to what packages you keep seeing over and over. They're the winners!

Okay, if it isn't as easy as listing the "10 points of successful direct mail creative work," where do you get good creative work?

Who Should Do Your Creative Work? Most Likely, Not You.

I strongly advise that unless you've been around the direct marketing business for awhile, you shouldn't try to write your own copy or have your staff artist design your package. Not that it requires decades of experience, but there are just so many professionals out there who can probably do a much better job than you. Pay them to do the job for you; it will save you time and, hopefully, headaches.

Yes, I said *hopefully*. Beware when you choose a direct marketing agency. For too long the orientation of many direct marketing agencies has been (and still is) one of getting short-term profits over thinking about the long-term relationship. You see few long-term relationships in this business; it's very different from general advertising agency-client relationships.

Not that they're impossible to develop. I just want to make you aware of the reality as I've seen it over the years. There are many good direct marketing agencies around that do excellent work and are interested in building a solid relationship with you. There are others with good ideas and good sales presentations, but little else.

When talking with an agency, be sure it has financial marketing experience. Wouldn't you agree that financial direct marketing is a different ballgame from selling magazine subscriptions? Don't be too inflexible, though. Direct marketing principles tend to be very transportable from industry to industry. I moved rather easily from selling shoes by mail to financial direct marketing, for example.

Don't go to a general advertising agency. Most have tried to build some expertise in direct marketing. But often it's just a matter of adding "direct marketing" to their list of capabilities. Your best bet, if your general agency has a *true* experienced direct response arm, just may be to stick with it. After all, it knows your bank.

Given the choice, I'd take a direct marketing agency with financial direct marketing credentials over a general agency. Regardless of your choice, be sure—absolutely sure—to talk with other clients of the agency. How long have they been clients? How does the agency deal with the mistakes that will inevitably happen? How's the client service? Do you really feel this agency is a partner in developing your direct marketing programs? What happens once the sale is made? Do you really get the service you expected? Do you ever see the principals of the agency again?

Check the agency's pricing. Make comparisons. Remember, the world of financial direct marketing is still a relatively young one. Innocent financial institutions are still unnecessarily paying a premium for some direct marketing work. If someone comes to you with a great idea to sell, be careful. Even if it worked for a bank on the other end of the state that doesn't mean it will work for you. Look for solid *planning* experience. Look for an agency that thinks long range, not one interested in making its money and running.

Just one more point. I'm off the soap box now. Be tolerant of your agency. Remember, great offers, list selection, and creativity usually don't happen overnight. You have the burden of knowing when to identify if a program could have been better with a few refinements or if it was purely and simply a bomb. Remember, in direct marketing, *testing* is the real key to success. It's another way to tell if you've found a good agency. Ask about its testing philosophy and experience. If it's clear that the agency doesn't appreciate the importance of testing, head for the door—quickly!

Direct Mail Production

This is a related subject that flows from choosing someone for your creative development.

Assume you have your package designed and your copy written. Where do you go? To a direct mail production house? Back to your agency? Most likely, again unless you have the experience, you ask your agency to handle production for you.

Over the years, direct mail production has caused me more headaches, more sleepless nights, than any other aspect of direct marketing. Why? Several reasons. I'll be fair from the outset. Until you get deeply involved in having a direct mail package produced, you can never understand or appreciate what a complex job it is. For each direct mail project I'm in charge of, I write a fairly detailed set of project specs. While they're somewhat incomplete (I can't do the person's job for him or her), they usually run four or five pages in length. And still mistakes happen.

Fortunately, with experience, you can catch mistakes before your package goes out the door. But, if you don't have that experience, you may pay dearly to get it. Therefore, my advice is to leave production to your agency.

Direct mail production is, indeed, extremely complex. You need people who are extremely detail-oriented to meet the challenge. (If you're not, stay away!)

If you choose to handle production yourself, you'll find that dealing with direct mail production companies can be one of the most exasperating experiences you'll ever have. I'm not bad-mouthing them. It's a job I wouldn't have—trying to keep up with the 900 details of a project while dealing with a customer who really doesn't understand direct mail and doesn't know what he or she wants or needs.

I generally do know what I want and need; I'm very detail oriented, diligent, and usually stay a step or two ahead of my vendors. But I still have problems. Direct mail production companies have small margins. They work on a project-by-project basis, constantly having to find new business. The great majority hire relatively inexperienced people as account representatives who work with clients once the sale has been made to be sure the package is produced properly. They can't afford to pay them well. And it's a thankless job. Clients who don't really know what they want still expect the project to be pulled off flawlessly.

I also believe very strongly that direct mail production houses don't realize that they're in a different arena when they have financial direct marketing projects to complete. The level of accuracy required is so much more critical. If you're selling magazine subscriptions and make a mistake, that's one thing. If you're dealing with a person's money, it's *very* different. Just mail your long-time customer, Mr. Jones, a letter offering him a credit card and put Mr. Smith's response form in his package. Do you think you'll hear from Mr. Jones? And Mr. Smith? And anyone else affected by the slip-up? You bet you will!

I'm convinced that the direct mail production company that hires very experienced account representatives, pays them well, gives them the resources they need, and emphasizes 100% error-free quality will have its investment returned many times in repeat business. Just think how this one step alone would lower the cost of sales. One of my missions in life is to find such a company, where my production representative is at least one step ahead of me.

I've said enough, I hope, to convince you that you really don't need (much less want) day-to-day direct mail production responsibilities.

Pay your agency to handle production for you. Hopefully, you will get your money's worth.

Once more, though, be careful. Agency production people aren't always as conscientious as you would expect given the price you're paying. My first experience with a direct marketing agency production person was a nightmare worse than any I'd had with production companies themselves. Don't assume anything. Be sure they know absolutely what they're doing. The more orderly the agency seems to be—particularly in having detailed production plans and worksheets—the better your chances.

How You Can Help Yourself

Too often I hear from my vendor friends that banks are their worst clients—generally because bankers are unfamiliar with a business built around deadlines. Also, too many bankers don't take the time to learn the direct marketing business.

My advice to you is to find a solid direct marketing vendor, whether it be an agency or a production company. Listen to that vendor. Realize it's a two-way street. Data processing work, for example, takes time. So don't expect your vendor to complete three days of data processing work in one if you've been late getting tapes to him in the first place.

Develop a detailed plan and schedule with your vendor up front. Pay attention to your deadlines. Realize that if you don't meet them something will probably have to slip. Know your options. Be involved with your vendor. Don't get caught finding out after the fact that if you had used paper A instead of paper B the vendor could have met the deadline.

Make your vendor your partner, not just someone to create or produce something for you. Not just someone to kick around and blame for your own ineptness. Be sure you're your vendor's partner, too. Help him. Teach him your business. Make sure he comes to you with problems. Make sure he's straightforward with you. You'll both profit.

120

Additional Reading

This section just may be the most important to you. I've given you many things to think about, many of which aren't printed elsewhere. Usually, you're forced to learn them by doing.

To learn more about copywriting, read any of the books or articles written by Herschell Gordon Lewis. *Direct Mail Copy That Sells* is my favorite. His newer book, *Herschell Gordon Lewis on the Art of Copywriting*, is a winner, too. He also writes a monthly column for *Direct Marketing* magazine.

The classic book by John Caples, *Tested Advertising Methods*, and *Successful Direct Marketing Methods*, by Bob Stone, are both invaluable references. So are any number of other direct marketing publications available from the HCI Library. Write Hoke Communications, Inc., 224 Seventh Street, Garden City, NY 11530, for a catalog.

10

THE BASICS OF PRODUCING WINNING DIRECT MAIL

Thomas J. Collins
Marketing Profiles, Inc.

You've got less than 7 seconds ... In that brief period of time your direct mail readers will:

1. Glance at the envelope.

2. Make a snap decision about the content.

3. Open the letter.

4. Read the first sentence.

At any point during this process, however, they make one of three decisions: throw it away, put it on top of the refrigerator for later consideration, or respond immediately. All in 7 seconds.

Think about all the time you spent to create the product offer, write the copy, and mail the letter . . . just for 7 seconds. Ah, but you say to yourself, 7 seconds of undivided attention is not all bad! Unfortunately, the process does not often end in the positive. You had better sit down for this—out of 1,000 prospecting letters:

- Only 20% decide to open it (200).

- 6% read the letter (60).

- 2% respond to the offer (20).

So regardless of the brilliance of your direct mail copywriting skills, the beauty of your design, or the degree to which you think your customer loves you . . . accept one simple truth. People don't care and they don't want to read your letter.

Your job is clear then; you have got to get your "hook" into them fast. Lead with your benefit statement. Let them know "what's in it for them" before you discuss the strength of your organization, how much you love them as a customer, etc.

Writing Copy That Gets Attention

Writing good direct mail copy is easy . . . if you relax and let it come naturally. Before you set pen to paper (or fingertips to keyboard), consider the following three points:

1. Who are you writing to? Whether you're writing a play or a direct mail promotion, the first thing you must consider is your audience. Create in your mind an idea of the person you're trying to reach: their age, education, likes and dislikes, maybe the type of house they own or car they drive.

2. What's in it for them? In other words, what is your benefit statement? What can you say that will make them stop what they are doing and respond to your offer?

3. What do you want them to do? Send in a response coupon? Call you on the phone? Learn something new about your products? Maybe just give them a "warm and fuzzy" feeling about your organization?

Now, just to clear your mind, list all the other things you are compelled to write about—how strong your institution is, the variety and features of your products, or maybe how much you value their business. Now set these aside . . . someplace where it will be difficult to find them again. Because, unfortunately, this is the type of information that makes your copy boring—and the stuff most people don't read.

A few words about style: Make it simple, and make it fun! Write your copy to an eighth-grade level (just slightly below that of the average newspaper). As much as possible, keep the number of syllables per word down to two or three, and don't use fancy words, long sentences, or banking jargon. Strive for short, snappy paragraphs, and write the copy like you would say it. Ignore the image of your college English professor for a brief moment and go ahead—start a sentence with "and" or dangle an occasional participle. Heck, most participles were made to be dangled.

Remember, you're not writing to impress, but to make your reader feel comfortable, relaxed, interested, and informed. Good copy should take away fear and aversion. Most people have a fear of making the wrong decision or being denied a loan. Nearly all have an aversion to salespeople or anything that might cost them time or money. Your job is to create a positive feeling.

Tell them if the offer is free or if they're prequalified. Then explain how you'll assist them when they respond. ("In three days you will receive a complete package of material that fully explains all the advantages of our IRAs.") Cover the "four W's"—who, what, when, and where—so your prospect knows precisely what to expect. Give your readers options that make their decisions easier. You might say, for example, that their account can be opened by mail or they may call you directly for a personal appointment.

The most important part of your copy is the call to action. Sound the bugle and write a paragraph that specifically tells your reader to respond. Create a sense of urgency by placing time restrictions on the response. (For example, "This offer is only available until July 31.") Consider adding special offers or coupons that provide a tangible feel to the offer. Don't write your copy like you are selling Ginzu knives, but don't be afraid to lead your customer to the sale, either. Finally, don't snatch the carrot from under the horse's nose by forgetting the response mechanism. This includes coupons, phone numbers, and applications; they are essential. Make it easy for your customers to drop their responses back in the mail—without even needing a pen— by preprinting their names on the response device. Remember to put your address and indicia on the mailing response as well.

Salutations

Dear Valued Customer,
You are important to us at 1st Financial, in fact, one of our most valued customers. However, not important enough for us to take a few moments to personalize your letter . . .

You're not kidding anyone but yourself when you try to create a personal flavor in a nonpersonalized letter. Either you make it personal or you don't: Don't try to fake it!

You can solve some of your salutation problems by gendercoding your files. However, the process is not 100% accurate. (In fact, it's not even 90% accurate.) So take the extra precaution of having your branch managers scan the customer files to correct any errors. This should be a priority for your top deposit or income-producing households. Another option is to use the name lines as they are printed in your address fields, i.e., Dear John J. Jones. Make sure you standardize your files to eliminate banking jargon such as ITF, IRA, or other terms. If the gender or salutation is in doubt, have the system default to a bold benefit statement as the introduction.

Likewise, be very careful when using personalization in the body copy. If you include account numbers, balances, rates, or any type of specific information, it must be accurate and current. If it is inaccurate, prepare for some unhappy calls from customers. Ask yourself if the information you wish to include has a significant impact on the objective of the mailing piece. If yes, proceed with caution. Remember, you build a relationship with your customers by establishing trust. Don't damage your image by sending them a letter that shows you don't even know the correct balance of their accounts.

A few years back, every teller at our financial institution hated the marketing department. Every month we did an upscale customer mailing that required personal salutations and signatures—and guess who got to complete the signatures? Today this is no longer necessary. Technology has advanced to allow images of signatures to be digitized and printed right on a laser printer. There is no reason anymore not to personalize at least the branch manager's, department head's, or president's signature. For an extra-special touch, have your new account thank you letter come complete with the signature of the originating service representative.

Stationery

People are more inclined to open direct mail from their financial institution than from any other company. You need to capitalize on that. Make your letter look like the president's secretary just typed it. Use top quality paper—the difference in cost is insignificant compared to the image you're sending. (Keep the rag content low, however, to avoid clogging your laser printer.)

For upscale mailings, use special executive stationery (monarch sized) printed and embossed with the president's name in the upper left corner. (Your boss also will love it for his or her personal use.) If your production house prints the stationery, it also can make sure the embossing, foil stamping, and paper style works on its equipment. Have it store the stationery in a place that limits humidity to prevent the paper from curling and creating a production nightmare.

The envelope is almost as important as the letter itself. It creates the initial impression and gives clues to the customers as to the content of the letter. If your direct mail does not have the "we typed this directly for you" appearance, then consider a message on the envelope that encourages them to open the envelope. The more personalized the appearance, i.e., standard envelope, typed address, stamps rather than indicia, the less you need to "tease" customers with outside printing of benefit statements.

Window envelopes are obviously less personalized than typewritten envelopes. But they are much cheaper to process because they eliminate the nightmare of hand-matching personalized letters to personalized envelopes.

Format

Design your format around who will receive the piece. Self-mailers work well with businesses and in situations where the message needs to be told quickly (no envelope to open). Also, they should be used when you want the piece handed down to others or when it doesn't really require an elite feel or personalization (loans, checking, seminars, etc.).

Letters work better in personal situations and are often easier to produce. But, depending on the quantity and the number of inserts, they may not be cheaper. In general, letter packages pull better than self-mailers . . . but it does depend on your target audience and your message.

Match the Season . . .

When I've got the after-Christmas blues . . . stacks of bills, no cash . . . make your product offer solve my problem. Send me a home equity loan that consolidates my credit cards, makes the interest tax deductible, and gives me a lower monthly payment. Likewise, pursue home improvement loans in the spring, car purchases in the fall, and cash needs for Christmas.

Seasons bring changing needs. Not only should your product mailings tie into the seasons but also your serialized mailings. Change serialized mailings as each season approaches. Send Christmas cards with certificate bonus messages; checking account messages in the summer (when people move); credit card offers before the holidays, vacation periods, school openings, etc.

Think through *when* you are making the offer. The key to good direct mail is the right offer to the right person at the *right time.*

Lists

Boring . . . no doubt about it. Unless you keep a pocket full of pens in a plastic holder in your shirt pocket, this is a boring topic. However, it's the first *and most important* step toward a successful promotion. If you're not reaching the right people, you're not reaching anyone at all.

Fortunately, with a Marketing Customer Information File (MCIF), you can make the process a little more scientific. First, take a crowbar to your marketing department's budget and free up a couple of thousand dollars to get your customers' records appended with demographic information. Consider items such as age, occupation, income, length of residency, value of home, value of car, zip + 4, gendercoding, and geocoding. These can be added to your files for only about $50 per thousand households. Pretty cheap—considering the value of the information.

Finding "Look-Alikes"

Let's look at the relationships that exist between what you would define as your "best" customer for a particular product and what he or she looks like demographically. For example, on a home equity loan, you may define your best customer as having "an approved loan limit of $40,000, an activation balance of $20,000, strong collateral with remaining equity of $10,000, no derogatory credit, and a $1,000 checking account with your financial institution."

Now scan your files based on those parameters to determine what current customers meet that criteria. Next, take that group and have your MCIF determine their demographic profile. You'll find they fit into a pretty tight demographic group related to age, income, value of home, length of residency, value of car, etc.

Here's the payoff: Reverse the process and scan your remaining customers and find those who match the same demographic profile but do not have a home equity loan. This group will most likely not only end up being your most profitable target list but will also contain prospects with the highest propensity toward home equity products.

Using Demographic *and* Customer Information

When appended data is applied in conjunction with existing balance, relationship, and product usage information, you can greatly enhance the quality of your segmentation techniques.

Using the home equity loan example again, scan your file and find all existing mortgage loan customers with a loan-to-value ratio less than 70%, less than $5,000 in total household deposit balances, good credit, who are not members of a fifty-plus club, who are not receiving direct deposit of social security, etc. If you have some demographic fields appended, look for age less than 60, home value greater than $50,000, loan less than 15 years old, income greater than $40,000, live in your selected zip codes, and drive a middle- to up-scale car.

By adding home ownership information to your files, you can also find existing deposit customers who have their mortgages elsewhere. Want to find noncustomers? Piece of cake. Set up the same set of variables and contact a list broker. What you will get back is a list of your competition's "best" customers . . . so go get 'em. **Note:** Be sure to run the tape past your existing customer file to take out duplicates.

It's Easier Than It Sounds

This may all seem confusing, but it is really a fairly simple process. In fact, lists can actually be much more refined, depending on how precise you want to be. The key is to think about what the product is used for, then match it to the various needs of the consumer. For example, on a home equity loan the money can be used for:

Debt Consolidation.	Look for credit users and seasonal cash needs.
Home Improvement.	Look for new residents (they need appliances, drapes, etc.), new child (additions to home), pool season, older homes (new roof, remodeling).
Auto Purchase.	Luxury, classic, or antique car fanatics; cars over 4 years old.
Education.	Look for children ages 17 to 18.

Using Only MCIF Data

Although not as accurate, target segments of existing customers can be developed without demographic data by using an analysis of their current products. The approach is similar to building a demographic profile in reverse. For example, we know the age range of certificate customers to be typically above age 35 and in the middle- to upper-income range. Likewise, you can generate demographic "profiles" of all of your customers by the other products and services they use. Although not as accurate as using appended demographics, this still allows you to:

1. Find prospects who are likely to meet the demographic profile of the typical buyer.

2. Find "qualified" prospects who do not currently have the product.

3. Reduce your segment due to the customers' current financial position (i.e., customers with large deposit balances do not need personal loans).

Advanced Techniques

There are some additional steps that you can take during the segmentation process:

- Prequalify or preapprove the list. Having your credit bureau prescreen the files for credit analysis narrows your file size and improves your approval rate significantly. Don't be afraid to try the procedure. Simply meet with your credit bureau and request a listing of the most popular prescreening techniques. Then take those options and meet with your loan department to match them to its underwriting criteria. One benefit of this is that you are developing a good working relationship with your loan department. The obvious second benefit is that only prospects that will be pre-approved receive the mailing. **Note:** If you use credit bureau information, you must make the prospect a firm offer and cannot turn them down unless their credit has materially changed since your original prescreening.

  You may prequalify credit offers by using data within your MCIF or appended data to identify prospects that will have better credit and likely be approved. Using data such as income, length of residence and payment history from your own loans will increase the approval rate.

- Geodemographic coding of your files can also produce considerable success. This clustering process assumes that people who live in the same neighborhoods have similar life-styles. Whether you believe in the concept or not, it does provide some insight into the segmentation process.

- Become your own database manager to really "turbocharge" your list. You can start by collecting lists of doctors, dentists, churches, organizations, new home owners, or businesses. One good way to use a list of businesses, for example, is to start an officer call program. Use your list to solicit checking, loans, and investment products. The calling officers of your institution can then follow up on the responses received. They like it because they are not making "cold" calls. Management likes it because the costs per acquisition, close ratio, and market penetration are significantly improved. You may gather some lists yourself; purchase others for unlimited use from Dun & Bradstreet or list brokers. However you obtain your list, remember it's important to clean it up twice a year to eliminate stale information.

Production Options

There are two capacity concerns to address when considering producing the direct mail piece internally. Certainly, the capacity of your equipment, staff, logistics of supplies, time and coordination of the folding, stuffing, inserting, sealing, metering, etc., is the first concern. However, the second concern is the lost opportunity costs associated with internal production. The time spent in coordinating, printing, lettershopping, and mailing is time you could have spent in other areas more important to the institution. Shop around before you decide. Not only are costs very competitive, but by using zip sorting and batch processing, the job may actually cost less if done outside.

Internal

Most internal-use laser printers will print 5 to 25 letters per minute. So on small projects, once you select the list, it is merely a task of loading paper. Mailings greater than 2,000 to 3,000 start to get a little unruly. One option is to print the letter internally and job out folding, inserting, etc., to a lettershop. That way, your costs and time are significantly reduced, and the quality of the letter is assured. The first couple of times you use the lettershop, go over and watch it complete the project. It's a good learning experience and you can make sure the job is done right.

External

A thousand things can go wrong in direct mail production. Unfortunately, they will all affect your customer. Lettershop production is a combination of twentieth-century technology and what looks like nineteenth-century equipment. Advanced software packages can merge/purge, standardize addresses, append data, and zip sort, but then it's all handed over for production on equipment that would scare the Marquis de Sade. Here are some things to look for to protect yourself:

1. Tape layout. Give the production house your tape layout well in advance. On your first mailing, require a test run to make sure it

can interpret the data. Use a fixed-length format, if possible, and include a printout of the first few pages of the data. Make sure that the segment you intended to mail is the segment it is printing. For example, when merging two files together, there are two lists developed—matches and nonmatches. Which list is loaded for production is obviously critical.

2. Laser proofs. Don't limit your approval process to just the brochures, coupons, etc. You also should receive a proof of the actual laser-printed letter. Check for layout, general appearance, etc. Use your gut instincts . . . does it look good to you? Have two or three people you can trust proofread the copy. If possible, find employees that are equal to or higher than you in rank. They may be more honest with you if they think the package needs more work.

3. Print quality. High-speed mainframe laser printers have a couple of problems. First, the faster the print speed, the more the quality of the print suffers. Many lasers also have limited image areas that may require additional offset printing. Have your production house review samples throughout the run to guarantee that someone is inspecting what is being printed, not just turning on the equipment and leaving.

4. Mailhouse. This is critical . . . Go visit your mailhouse (the company that actually folds, stuffs, meters, and mails the piece). These steps require a great deal of care—and attention to detail. In a "matched-piece" mailing, it only takes one mistake to mess up the entire run. Unfortunately, the person whom you originally talked to at the mailhouse is typically not the person handling your project. Those that operate the equipment and handle the mailing are not rocket scientists. So watch the results closely until you feel comfortable. Likewise, it would be smart to have a double-check system in place that ensures that names are matched correctly, pieces are inserted properly, and maintains constant quality checks.

Checklists

Do you currently use a complete checklist system to make sure the project is accurate? If not, consider working on your resume . . . because the other shoe is waiting to drop. There are just too many things that can go wrong to not take the time to use a checklist. Here are a few ideas for checklists:

____ 1. Legal approval

____ 2. Is the variable information correct?

     ____ a. Branch names

     ____ b. Phone numbers

     ____ c. Branch managers, CSR names

     ____ d. Addresses

     ____ e. Titles

     ____ f. Digitized signatures

____ 3. Communication Package:

Have you sent a package of material and explanation letter to:

     ____ a. All branches?

     ____ b. Operational/loan departments?

     ____ c. Telephone operators?

     ____ d. Data processing department?

     ____ e. Receptionists?

     ____ f. Board of Directors?

     ____ g. Accounting/bookkeeping?

     ____ h. Training department?

     ____ i. Senior officers?

____ 4. Is the promotion reflected in your:

     ____ a. Rate boards?

     ____ b. Outdoor displays?

     ____ c. Sales brochures?

     ____ d. Phone recorder/hot line?

     ____ e. Rack literature?

     ____ f. Statement stuffers?

____ g. ATM messages?

____ h. Statement messages?

____ i. Staff meetings?

Precautions

Review your mailing list. You may want to possibly exclude:

____ 1. Board of Directors

____ 2. Officers

____ 3. Zip codes outside your market area

____ 4. Business/commercial accounts

____ 5. Organizations

____ 6. Churches

____ 7. Accounts "flagged" no mail

____ 8. Customers with dual addresses in off-season

____ 9. Delinquent accounts

____ 10. NSF/overdraft accounts

____ 11. Dormant accounts

____ 12. Special product accounts (IRAs, trust, annuities)

____ 13. Special groups (upscale, senior citizens, affinity)

____ 14. Names addressed to your branches

____ 15. P.O. boxes

Response Fulfillment

____ 1. How would you handle response processing at the following levels?

•1%

•3%

•5%

•10%

If your response rate is high, make sure that you have the staff and alternatives to process applications quickly.

____ 2. Do you have a central response focal point?

____ 3. How will you handle the distribution of responses?

____ 4. What is your follow-up package?

Sales Tracking System

____ 1. Where are sales recorded?

____ 2. Where are they routed to?

____ 3. "Tickled" or response required by 3 days?

____ 4. Is there a summarized tracking report?

Telemarketing Support to Follow Up Direct Mail

____ 1. Who will make the calls?

____ 2. Who will generate lists?

____ 3. Lists sent by what date?

____ 4. Scripts

____ 5. Incentive system

Regulatory Concerns

____ 1. Rate/yield requirements for deposit and loan products

____ 2. Home-equity disclosure

____ 3. Holding company regulations

____ 4. SEC

____ 5. FDIC/CULIC

____ 6. Reg D

____ 7. Reg E

____ 8. Reg B

_____ 9. Reg Z

_____ 10. CRA compliance

Postal Concerns

_____ 1. Zip sort

_____ 2. Address verification

_____ 3. Bulk/1st-class permit

_____ 4. Number of mailing pieces vs. permit

_____ 5. Piece dimensions and format vs. postal requirements

_____ 6. Are the days necessary for delivery okay?

    _____ a. 1st class

    _____ b. Bulk

_____ 7. Adequate total postage?

_____ 8. Return address requested?

_____ 9. Meter, indicia, stamp, precanceled stamps

_____ 10. Is the date the piece arrives correct (not a holiday season, Friday, or Monday)?

Copy

_____ 1. Punctuation

_____ 2. Tense

_____ 3. Person

_____ 4. Readability (8th grade)

_____ 5. Ease of reading

_____ 6. Believability

_____ 7. Benefit statement

_____ 8. Call to action

_____ 9. Response mechanism (coupon, phone number, etc.)

_____ 10. Professional layout

Mailhouse

____ 1. Do your envelopes and inserts fit with the mailhouse equipment to be used?

____ 2. Do your inserts fit the envelope?

____ 3. Do the folds occur in suitable places on the letter?

____ 4. Does the design allow the name and address to show through the window?

Profit and Politics in Marketing

Ever wonder why most marketing departments are not held in the same high regard as loan departments? Many times it's because marketing people tend to look at numbers and not profits. You need to check constantly the motivation behind any project.

Anyone can sell checking accounts if they are free ... but what do you get? Low-balance accounts that clog up your teller lines, overload your DP and bookkeeping departments, and eat up your profits. And with Reg CC restrictions, the potential losses due to returned checks are scary. Likewise, anyone can get you a 3% response on certificate mailings if you pay a fifty-basis-point bonus and give away a toaster. However, there may be times when these types of promotions make sense. Marketing's job is to know when these programs are necessary, why they are necessary, and the financial and operational impact of the decision.

Look at the incremental profits and costs associated with your promotions before you begin. Get management to agree to the goals, costs, projected response rates, and tactics necessary to complete the task. Know what your margins are prior to making the decision. If the program costs are high or will result in lower margins, know what they are and why—and what you are going to do to increase profits. Track your programs; not just to improve response rates but to give you the data you need at management meetings. If you decide to give away a bonus rate or free account, develop a cross-sell program that eventually forces the customers to purchase multiple products. If they do not buy after a significant time don't be afraid to force them to a fee-based account or lower yielding product. Keep in mind that they are costing you money. Your job is to generate profitable accounts.

Good politicians grease the skids before the bad news hits. You will have complaints . . . Mrs. McGillicuty got two letters. Mr. Schwartz is upset because his neighbor got a bonus rate letter and he didn't. The loan department got a credit application from a deadbeat. The war stories are almost endless. Prepare your staff and management for the bad news. There is no way to prevent it completely. Tell them about potential problems that will arise, but emphasize the benefits and bottom-line results that the program will generate.

Finally, summarize your results for management. Determine your return on investment. Track your respondents over time as you cross-sell them more products. Keep in mind, you are not just selling products, you are selling yourself and your programs to management. Be a little self-serving; it will pay off in more support, appreciation, and responsibility.

11

TRACKING METHODS AND PRACTICES

Ron Bukowski
Security Bank, SSB

One of the attributes of direct marketing is that it is measurable. The process of tracking is the tool that provides the measurability. This article covers how the process of tracking is applied and how databases are used to enable good tracking.

There are three different methods used to track direct marketing campaigns. Each method is based on the type of campaign and the marketing objective for the campaign. The simplest measurement method is *Response Rate* tracking, in which the marketer is concerned only with maximizing the number of responses to a direct marketing solicitation per dollar spent for the campaign. Although this is the method most commonly used as the sole measurement of success, it really should be used exclusively only in cases where the offer is for an isolated product and the total profit to be gained will be the result of the immediate response to the offer. Response rate tracking does not really measure return on investment in those cases where the campaign will produce multiple relationships from the respondents. Since financial institutions depend on customer loyalty for profitability, response tracking alone will not provide adequate analysis.

The second tracking method, *Long Term Value* tracking, measures the progress of a customer household over a period of time and determines the profitability of the campaign over that period. In addition to providing data for return on investment, long-term value tracking provides data about customer retention for the types of campaigns that give customers an incentive to accept the offer. For instance, if the financial institution pays a rate premium on CDs or waives the first year fee on credit cards, some percentage of the respondents will be strictly rate shoppers and will drop the service when the terms return to normal. Other respondents will continue to do business with the institution that provided the incentive. With long-term value tracking, the institution can measure the effectiveness of the incentive offered. Another side benefit of this method is that the discipline required to perform such tracking will also allow the offering institution to conduct follow-up campaigns targeted at one or more of the response outcomes.

The above methods work fine for campaigns with a single offer. However, because of the increasing popularity of marketing databases, financial institutions are using the databases to conduct "serial mail" (sometimes called "matrix mail") campaigns in which customer households with given financial services profiles receive a series of mail and/or telephone solicitations over a long period of time. (The period of time could vary from three months to an infinite repetition of a series of offers.) Tracking of such campaigns must also be on a long-term basis and the method of measuring results differs from the first two tracking methods described. This third type of tracking is known as *Incremental* tracking. This tracking technique requires knowledge of which households received which communications over a long period of time and the ongoing logging of the progress of those households over the same (or longer) periods of time. This is the most complex of the tracking methods and it is most subject to constraints.

Incremental tracking has one major benefit that no other tracking method provides. It is the only credible method of answering the challenge of "How many of these customers would have used this financial service even if we didn't conduct this campaign?" In order to do this, the marketer separates the eligible recipients into two groups — a mail group and a control group. Results for each of the two groups are compared and the campaign is given credit for the incremental difference between the mail group and the control group.

Database

The most fundamental consideration for good tracking is that the tracking database contains adequate information to allow for successful tracking. Database considerations have to be implemented before the campaign is conducted. The first premise here is that the marketer must be able to identify, after the fact, households that received the solicitation and households that accepted the offer. If there are degrees of acceptance, the database must also be capable of distinguishing among the degrees.

Here are some examples of degrees of difference in response. In a credit card offering, there is a need to distinguish between respondents who activate the line of credit and those who don't. Of course, among the active cardholder there is a difference between those who pay off their monthly balances and those who maintain an interest-bearing balance. A marketer who offers a bonus for opening a certain type of checking account may want to separately track customers who converted other types of checking accounts, existing customers who opened their first checking accounts, and customers who are new to the institution. If a marketer offers an incentive for a CD or an IRA, there is usually a computable threshold at which the institution is assured (or more assured) of a profit. The database should be able to separate the so-called winners from the losers. In addition, the database should be able to provide analysis that detects any demographic or financial profile differences between the winners and the losers. The possibilities are endless. However, the marketer must know in advance what he or she is going to look for when it is time to perform the measurements.

Identification of recipients is fairly simple. If a marketing central information file has been used to select the candidates for a campaign, the marketer only needs to uniquely mark the household records that were chosen or to extract those records into a separate tracking file. Marking records within the database is the preferred method. If a household becomes a candidate for more than one solicitation, the marketer may not want to confuse the customer with offers that were not designed to work serially or the marketer may have a hierarchy of customer segments that are eligible for different series of offers. If the database is marked, problems can be avoided. Some databases are completely refreshed every month. In these cases, the markings placed on the records are lost when the file is refreshed. Therefore, an alternative method for knowing who received a solicitation is needed.

One alternative is to create an extract file at the time of the offer and then to load that file back into the database at the time it is refreshed. Another alternative is to create a tracking file that transcends updates but can be matched to the database. This can be done by making a "thumbprint" record of each household that has been solicited. The thumbprint contains the social security numbers of all members of the household at the time that the solicitation is made. A maximum of four social security numbers is adequate since 99.7% of all households have no more than four. If a household gains or loses a person (social security number) in a future update, the tracking record can still be linked to the household record with the remaining social security numbers. When this happens, the thumbprint should be refreshed.

If the marketer uses a rented list for the solicitation, the list should be added to the marketing database as prospects for the service being solicited. If the database does not allow for prospect files, the marketer can use either of two alternatives to match respondents to the mailing list file. The least desirable alternative is to gather coupons or other paperwork from the persons accepting the offer and to post these to the mailing list file. A simpler method is to extract the names and addresses of people in the marketing database who have opened target accounts and match them to the mailing list file. The matching key from both files should be some portion of the last name plus some portion of the street address plus the five-digit zip code. Usually, the first seven characters of the last name will work well. The first seven characters of the address may produce undermatching because of probable inconsistencies in the way that the words North, South, East, and West are abbreviated. The person doing the tracking should first experiment with various lengths of the street address in the matching key since different parts of the country have differing characteristics of address structures. If this is a major problem, it would be wise to purchase microcomputer software that performs address standardization. Both the mail file and the response file can be processed through this software before matching the two files.

Another advantage of incorporating the prospect file into the marketing database is that the prospect names can be enhanced with demographic data along with the rest of the marketing database. These enhancements provide for a much more finite analysis of the respondents (and nonrespondents) to any given offer. Future campaigns for the same product can then be more narrowly targeted with regard to demographics or the financial profiles of prospects. If multiple mailing lists are used and the marketer knows that he or she will be repeating the campaign in the future, codes should be appended to the file that indicate which lists were the sources for each person's name. When results are analyzed, a respondent should be credited to all of the lists that sourced the name. For a narrowly targeted product, there will be very great differences in response rates among various lists. Taking advantage of these differences will result in large improvements in cost-effectiveness.

Tracking Windows

This is another subject that varies in complexity depending on the type of campaign being conducted. If the offer has a time limit for acceptance, the tracking window begins when the mail is dropped and ends when the offer expires. If the offer is open ended with regard to time, a normal tracking window is 2 months from the date of the solicitation. This size window works fine for such services as credit cards, checking accounts, or lines of credit. However, if the marketer is seeking CD money or homeowner's insurance, he or she may have to study how long it takes a given set of prospects to convert their time-specific, unmatured products to the service being offered. As a strategic note, the marketer may find that responses to a homeowner's insurance offer pour in at an acceptable rate for 6 weeks and then fall off dramatically. In this case the marketer would remail the entire prospect base every 6 weeks for a year.

Serial mail and repetitive offers have their own considerations when it comes to tracking windows. Since serial mail has no end and since it quite often involves soft-sell offers, the tracking window needs to be continuous in order to know whether the consumer is being affected by the campaign. Ideally, measurements for serial mail should be taken every time that approximately 100,000 pieces of mail have gone out to a particular prospect group. Then, if the response rate is as low as 0.1%, the tracking cells should include at least one hundred responses, which gives them more statistical credibility. Of course, in smaller institutions, it is not practical to wait for 100,000 pieces of mail to be dropped. In this case, a measurement each 6 months is a practical alternative. Since the tracking cells are liable to be small, the analyst needs to use more than one such measurement as a confirmation of the statistics that result from the tracking analysis. For repetitive offers that overlap the ideal 60-day tracking window, the analyst must first look for names that appear in the prospect file of both offers. If such a person responds after the second mailing, the response must be credited to the second mailing, even though 60 days may not have elapsed since the first mailing.

Control Groups

If incremental tracking is to be performed, a control group, consisting of people who did not receive the solicitation, is essential. The fundamental rule about control groups is that members of the group must not be influenced by the campaign being measured. Without a database that tracks who has received which solicitations, it is impossible to maintain control groups properly, which, in turn, invalidates the incremental tracking analysis. The size of a control group is stated in terms of a percentage of those people eligible to receive the solicitation. The exact percentage to be used depends on the size of the entire target group and the amount of mail (or other solicitations) to be made to the group. Ideally, the control group should have been able to make 100 or more responses to the solicitation during the tracking period. As a practical matter, control groups larger than 10% removes too many candidates from the solicitation, thereby causing the tracking process to reduce the amount of sales to be generated from the solicitation.

At the outset of a campaign (usually serial mail or matrix mail), members of the control group should be identified in the database, and they should be systematically omitted from any campaign conducted during the period of time that the serial mail is produced. If the serial mailing is successful, the members of the control group will be permanently excluded from receiving any solicitations. The reason for ostracizing these people from all mailings is that any campaign will heighten the awareness or affinity of a consumer for the institution, and strong campaigns for one product or service will generate business for other services not even mentioned in the campaign literature.

If a person is in a control group for serial mail concerning deposits and the marketer allows that person to receive a general solicitation for a credit card from another campaign, there is a higher probability that the recipient of a credit mailing rather than a nonrecipient will open a deposit account. The reason is that if the person were properly targeted for the deposit-oriented serial mail in the first place, he or she would be more likely to open or increase a deposit account as a result of any form of communication.

During the life of a serial mail campaign, the financial institution will gain and lose customers in the mailed-to group and the control group. Also, if the target segments of a serial mail campaign are arranged hierarchically, a customer may move from one segment to another by virtue of a change in his or her account structure or by the simple passage of time. Therefore, one of the database processes must include the computation of the size of the mail group and the control group each time the database is refreshed. If both groups grow or shrink proportionately, there is no problem. Of course, this never happens. If the control group grows in proportion to the mailing group, nothing should be done. This should be a temporary phenomenon. (Otherwise, the campaign isn't working!) If the mailed group grows in proportion to the control group, the marketer must select enough eligible new customers (who have never received any solicitations) to rebalance the proportion of control group to mailed group.

One last point about control groups: A customer who is in the control group is eligible to be measured as the control for multiple campaigns. If a serial campaign is aimed at CD holders with over $50,000 in total deposits and another campaign is aimed at customers without checking accounts, any person in the control group who satisfies both conditions can be used as a control for both campaigns. The control group member's status as a direct marketing leper validates him or her for any incremental tracking analysis.

Measurement Methods

If all of the above preparation is done properly and the marketer's central information system database supports selection, prospect identification, and control groups, the measurement process is relatively simple. If the tracking process is limited to response analysis, the measurement technique is a simple count of the number of responses during the tracking window. Long-term value tracking and incremental tracking are a little more involved.

Long-term value tracking requires that the analyst capture the status of the prospect-turned-customer at the time the offer is accepted. At a minimum, the monetary value of the account that was the target of the solicitation should be recorded as of the date opened. If the respondent's household was already a customer, the analyst might want to capture the status of every account in the household at the time the offer is accepted. This is quite often impractical. An adequate substitute is a picture of the total of each major deposit and loan category. If this is not possible, the analyst should at least try for total deposits and total loans. Whenever long-term tracking involves measuring the amount of disintermediation (and subsequent recovery therefrom) caused by the loss of deposits to investment or annuity products, the base month for these customers should be a month before the sale of the investment product. If the on-line marketing database does not contain previous iterations, the analyst may need to reload the previous month's database in order to capture the status of such customers.

The data captured in the base month can be used to analyze the immediate value of the sales campaign and compare results to goals. After this analysis, the analyst should capture the household status of the respondents every 3 months for a period of time that equals the planning horizon of the institution. If current period profitability can be attached to this quarterly status, the final version of the analysis can be used to perform a discounted cash flow (long-term value) of the project. Obviously, management doesn't want to wait several years (length of planning horizon) to determine whether to conduct another such promotion. Therefore, the initial analysis and the quarterly reports are very important. If the interim values and final values of all direct marketing projects are entered into a database of their own, the marketer has an ongoing analysis that can be used for determining what type of campaigns will have the greatest impact in accomplishing management's current objectives.

The ability to capture the current status of a customer or prospect group is the key to incremental tracking. For each mailed group and each control group, the analyst needs to perform this capture at the end of each measurement window. The end of one window becomes the beginning of the next window. Success is measured by comparing the percentage change in total balances of the target product for the mailed group and the control group. If the target product is total deposits, and if the mailed group increased total deposits by 5% during the measurement window and the control group increased total deposits by 3% during the same time, the campaign can be credited with 2% (5% – 3%) of the total deposits of all customers in the mailed group. The statistical supposition is that these customers would have increased their deposits by 3% without any stimulation. This analysis is valid even if both categories of customers decrease their deposits during the measurement period.

Unlike long-term value tracking, the incremental amounts (deposits, loans, fees, etc.) are not accumulated. They are credited to the discrete measurement window in which they were gathered. The reason for this is that the campaign itself is continuous and the withdrawal of serial or matrix mail will result in the cessation of incremental account growth. What may or may not be true is that the results of one measurement window are the cause of mail dropped during the same time window. There is surely some lag time between the inception of a serial mail program and the development of incremental accounts, fees, or balances. The analyst will need to use common sense and some experimentation to determine the amount of lag time. Since serial mail usually involves multiple campaigns conducted simultaneously at a variety of target groups within the database, each of these campaigns may require a different amount of lag time.

Reports

The following are sample reports which can be developed from database analysis of results of various campaigns. Quantities, dollar amounts, and percentages are represented by "#," "$," and "%," respectively, in order to avoid inference of the relative success of any given product or offer.

The above analysis shows only a few of the ways in which a mailing database can be segmented in order to determine the best candidates

Response Analysis							
Campaign: Pre-Approved Credit Card							
Date: December 1, 1989							
Window: December 10, 1989, to January 31, 1990							
Cost/Item: $.$$$							
Audience	Total Mailed	Appli- cations	# of Lines	Resp. Rate	$ of Lines	Cost/ $1,000	In- dex
Total Mailing	##,###	###,###	#,###	%.%%	$$,$$$	$$$.$$	100
Mailing Lists							
New Movers	##,###	###,###	#,###	%.%%	$$,$$$	$$$.$$	###
Active Cr. Card	##,###	###,###	#,###	%.%%	$$,$$$	$$$.$$	###
Mtge. Customers	##,###	###,###	#,###	%.%%	$$,$$$	$$$.$$	###
Total W/Dupl.	##,###						
Total by County							
Marin	##,###	###,###	#,###	%.%%	$$,$$$	$$$.$$	###
Palm Beach	##,###	###,###	#,###	%.%%	$$,$$$	$$$.$$	###
Winnebago	##,###	###,###	#,###	%.%%	$$,$$$	$$$.$$	###
Total Mailing	##,###	###,###	#,###	%.%%	$$,$$$	$$$.$$	100
Total by Age Group							
Under 35	##,###	###,###	#,###	%.%%	$$,$$$	$$$.$$	###
35 - 49	##,###	###,###	#,###	%.%%	$$,$$$	$$$.$$	###
50 and Over	##,###	###,###	#,###	%.%%	$$,$$$	$$$.$$	###
Total Mailing	##,###	###,###	#,###	%.%%	$$,$$$	$$$.$$	100
Total by Household Income							
Under $50M	##,###	###,###	#,###	%.%%	$$,$$$	$$$.$$	###
$50M to $74M	##,###	###,###	#,###	%.%%	$$,$$$	$$$.$$	###
Over $75M	##,###	###,###	#,###	%.%%	$$,$$$	$$$.$$	###
Total Mailing	##,###	###,###	#,###	%.%%	$$,$$$	$$$.$$	###

for a given product or offer. The analyst should seek as many subjects as possible within the database for segmentation. Of course, in order for the analysis to be valid, there should be at least 100 responses in one of the segments of a subject to be analyzed. Possible geographic subjects might include cities, counties, states, metropolitan statistical areas, areas of dominant influence (particularly if the direct marketing campaign was supplemented by media coverage), the first three digits of zip codes, the first five digits of zip codes, telephone exchanges, and census methodology (rural vs. urban). Demographic subjects might include age, income, home ownership, length of residence, value of residence, automobile ownership, customer/noncustomer status, existence of children in the home, and occupation of head of household. In addition, if the marketer subscribes to one of the geodemographic clustering systems, such as Micro-Vision, Prizm, or Acorn, this is the place to analyze the differences among the cluster codes. Of course, the marketing database must contain the geographic, demographic, and cluster codes desired for the analysis. By definition, this is the major reason for having a marketing central file.

The cost per item is calculated by dividing the number of items mailed by the total direct cost of the campaign. Direct costs include all fees to outside vendors plus cost of material and postage. Internal overhead cost should not be included because they are, at best, arbitrary, and inconsistent application of overhead will distort the comparison of one campaign with another. The Response Rate is simply the number of accounts opened stated as a percentage of the number of pieces mailed to a particular segment. This column will provide the greatest degree of analysis for determining how to improve the results of future mailings.

The number of applications were included in this analysis because a credit solicitation can generate a lot of interest from unqualified applicants, and this form of analysis will help determine if there is a segmented source for unqualified applicants. If there is, the segment can be omitted in future campaigns, or the marketer can convince his or her competitors of the unique opportunities available by soliciting this segment. In order to compute the number of applicants, application data must be manually logged into the mailing database. This may be more costly than valuable and the analyst may want to first measure the overall rejection rate and perform the manual entry only if there appears to be a major problem.

A cost index is used as a simple method of determining the degree to which a mailing segment performed better or worse than average. The index is calculated by dividing the average cost of a single segment by the average cost of the entire mailing and multiplying the answer by 100. Indexes above 100 are more costly than average and indexes below 100 are less costly than average. If the solicitation is a "saturation" mailing, that is, if the marketer mails to every household within a measurable piece of geography, a set of demographic indexes (not shown on the sample report) can also be computed.

For example, if the mailing was sent to everyone in a particular county and the analyst knows that 75% of the households in that county own their own homes, the response could be segregated between homeowners and nonhomeowners. If there is no difference between the two groups, then 75% of the responses should be from homeowners. However, if half the responses come from each group, the analyst knows that 25% of the prospects (nonhomeowners) provided 50% of the responses. Therefore, nonhomeowners responded at twice the rate of their existence in the county. Meanwhile, homeowners proved

LONG-TERM VALUE TRACKING ANALYSIS						
Campaign:	Lovable Stuffed Sheep for New Customers					
Date:	July 1988					
Measurement Window:	July 1, 1988, to June 30, 1991					
Campaign Cost:	$$$,$$$					
Original Customers:	##,###					
Date of Report:	December 31, 1989					
Remaining Customers:	##,###					
	Accts.	Balances/ Vol.	Avg. Mos.	Avg. Bal.	Avg. Rate	Cum. Profit
Checking Accounts	#,###	$$$,$$$	###	$,$$$	%%.%	$$,$$$
Savings/Money Market	#,###	$$$,$$$	###	$,$$$	%%.%	$$,$$$
Certificates	#,###	$$$,$$$	###	$,$$$	%%.%	$$,$$$
Retirement Accts.	#,###	$$$,$$$	###	$,$$$	%%.%	$$,$$$
Mortgages	#,###	$$$,$$$	###	$,$$$	%%.%	$$,$$$
Installment Loans	#,###	$$$,$$$	###	$,$$$	%%.%	$$,$$$
Lines of Credit	#,###	$$$,$$$	###	$,$$$	%%.%	$$,$$$
Annuities	#,###	$$$,$$$			%%.%	$$,$$$
Securities	#,###	$$$,$$$			%%.%	$$,$$$
Insurance	#,###	$$$,$$$			%%.%	$$,$$$
Cumulative Profit						$$,$$$

only two-thirds as likely to respond when compared with their share of the population of the county. The index for nonhomeowners is 200 and for homeowners is 67. The indexes can be calculated by dividing the percentage responses by the percentage of this segment in the population and multiplying the result by 100.

This preceding report was designed for a campaign that had a goal of acquiring new customers for the financial institution. Therefore, profit was computed for every service category. If the campaign's objective were to acquire a certain type of account, only the line containing that account category would be extended to the profit column. In either case, all of the account types would be listed and tracked. The "Balance/Volume" column represents current total balance for asset and liability products and cumulative sales volume for fee based products. "Average Months" is computed by summing the number of months that each customer used each product line during the tracking period and dividing the sum by the number of original customers. Likewise, the "Average Balance" is the sum of monthly balances divided by the total number of months. The "Average Rate" is the dollar-weighted monthly average rate paid or collected on each monthly balance. Even though this report may be prepared quarterly or only at the end of the tracking horizon, the tracking and accumulation of statistics must be done on a monthly basis. Otherwise, the time-weighted averages cannot be computed.

"Cumulative Profit" for asset and liability accounts is the combination of spread income on the average balance for the average number of months less operational cost of maintaining the accounts for the same number of months. The profit for fee accounts is the volume multiplied by the rate less the operational cost of managing the account. Each institution has its own method of computing profit on an individual service and there is much debate about application of overhead. The term "Profit" in this case is computed for the sake of determining whether a campaign met its goals and whether a similar campaign in the future is a worthwhile risk. Therefore, "Profit" really stands for contribution to overhead and it should be computed using direct costs only.

This report is the simplest to prepare and understand. It shows a lag period of two months between the time of the mailing and the measurement window. The lag period can be an instinctive number or it can be developed by testing a rolling 3-month period of results compared to mail volume.

Matrix Mail Incremental Deposit Tracking Analysis		
Customer Segment: Household Balances $25M to $49M		
Mailing Period: July 1 to September 30, 1989		
Tracking Period: September 1 to November 30, 1989		
Campaign Cost for Period: $$$,$$$		
Product Objective: Increase Total Deposits		
	Mailed Group	**Control Group**
Group Size	###,###	##,###
Total Deposits September 1	$$,$$$,$$$	$,$$$,$$$
Total Deposits November 30	$$,$$$,$$$	$,$$$,$$$
Net Change	$,$$$,$$$	$$$,$$$
Percent Change	%.%%	%.%%
Net Percent Due to Matrix Mail	%.%%	
Deposit Incr. Due to Matrix Mail	$,$$$,$$$	
Cost of New Money	%.%%%	

The difficult part of the process is the maintenance of the mailed and control groups. The marketer who wishes to use a database as a source of new business from existing customers via matrix mail must investigate the tracking methodology of the MCIF vendor very thoroughly before buying a database system. If the product objective for this customer segment were "Cross Sell New Customers," the analysis would include a second section for total loans and possibly a third section for fee business generated. If the product objective were "Checking Accounts to Credit Card Holders," the analysis would include only the checking account balances of the target segment.

The "Net Percent Due to Matrix Mail" is computed by subtracting the percent change in the control group from the percent change in the mailed group. This is an algebraic sum. The answer could be a negative number. The "Deposit Increment Due to Matrix Mail" is computed by applying the net percent computed above to the beginning deposit balances of the mailed group. The "Cost of New Money," then, is simply the campaign cost for the mailing period divided by the incremental deposit balances.

Campaign Taxonomy

The results of any one direct marketing campaign could be a statistical aberration or the consequence of a one-time economic or social event (e.g., All Savers certificates). Therefore, the analyst needs to compare the results at hand with the results of other campaigns for the same product, but with variances in message, offer, media, timing, or packaging. In order to do this the analyst needs a simple database, or taxonomy, that defines the who, what, when, where, and how of all campaigns. The database should be hierarchical with a base record that can be sorted and that uses the same words or codes to describe like elements. The contents of the base records are as follows:

     Unique Campaign Code

     Campaign Name

     Objective

*   Campaign Dates

*   Medium (Mail, Phone, etc.)

     Target Segment

*   Target Age

*   Target Income

*   Target Balance Range

*   Target Geography

*   Target Product

*   Planned Quantity

*   Planned Cost

*   Account Goal

*   Balance/Volume Goal

*   Actual Quantity

*   Actual Cost

*   Response Window

*   Gross Responses

*   Actual Accounts

*   Actual Balances/Volume

*   Cost Per Account

*   Cost Per $1,000 Balances/Volume

    Long Term Tracking Period

    Beginning Deposits

    Beginning Loans

    Ending Deposits

    Ending Loans

The items in the above base record list that are preceded by asterisks are the ones for which standard names and standard codes should be developed. The taxonomy can then be sorted or queried on the basis of these elements. Lower levels of the hierarchy could contain names of vendors; rates paid per 1,000 names rented; results by geographic, demographic, or cluster code segments; and interim tracking reports or studies of statistical peculiarities.

A favorite inquiry is to request all of the campaigns for a given product and have the records rank ordered according to cost per $1,000 of balances generated. All other data elements can then be plotted against the cost element to uncover visible trends. Statistically, the elements can be converted to quantitative values (or Yes/No binary values for qualitative data) and regression analysis can be applied to the database.

Because the database entries for any one product might be small, the analyst would tend to use a more intuitive method of reaching a conclusion from the data. This is why the subsidiary levels of the taxonomy are important. The analyst might find no regular trends in the base records of solicitations for a given product. However, when looking at the subsidiary records, he or she might discover that all mailings that used new movers lists resulted in higher response rates. Again, the possibilities are endless. However, the probability of finding the most profitable path is zero unless some form of structured analysis is applied. Using a marketing database for tracking and a tracking database for analysis is clearly a way to increase profits from direct marketing.

12

THE IMPORTANCE OF CROSS-SELLING

Mike Newes
OKRA Marketing

I would like to share a few facts that could have a dramatic impact on your future marketing plans.

According to financial industry research:

- 70% to 80% of any growth in your loans and deposits will need to come from existing customers.

- 60% or more of your existing customers may have more than one account, but they probably utilize just one service.

- At least 50% of your current customer relationships are unprofitable.

- Customers are five times less likely to leave a financial institution if they are utilizing two services than if they are utilizing just one.

- On average, both the individual deposit balances in each service and the overall profitability of the customer relationship increase as the number of services utilized increases.

What that says is that cross-selling is critical to the future of your institution. It may even be critical to your survival as an independent institution.

So what's new? You've heard that before in trade journal articles, association conferences, and consultant presentations. In fact, you're going to hear it as well in the next few articles that follow this one.

What's new is that now, with the advent of PC-based customer information database marketing systems, you have a way of accomplishing the cross-selling task far more efficiently and economically than ever before.

Traditional Marketing Tools Don't Help Cross-Selling

Traditional advertising media have never been a cost-effective way to handle cross-selling. They are too limited in reach and impact and too expensive to use with any frequency in addressing existing customers. Statement stuffers have become so commonplace that they are easily ignored.

Platform systems are too general. They may prompt a customer service representative to cross-sell the "product du jour," but that product is probably not appropriate to every customer or prospect who walks in. In addition, platform systems have limited ability to "personalize" to the needs of a particular customer.

Conventional Customer Information File (CIF) systems are also too limited to be an effective cross-selling tool. They are a powerful tool for customer service, but they were never designed for marketing applications. Conventional CIF systems have a tremendous amount of information available about individual account holders, even complete individual account relationships. However, they do not have the capability to associate and combine those customers into complete households, so you can understand and measure the value of the total relationship of each individual household.

While typical CIF systems will show current balances, they cannot make a determination of the profitability or value of either individual accounts or the total customer household relationships. Although the CIF will give you a snapshot of the immediate individual customer relationship, it cannot give you any measure of what impact cross-selling success has on the profitability of a customer household, an individual branch, an entire product line.

Early Marketing CIF (MCIF) systems offered some assistance, but realistically, they were too expensive to own and too difficult to use to be valuable to all financial institutions. However, the advent of simple but powerful PC-based MCIF technology now provides financial institutions of any size with the tool that has been missing, a tool that will allow any institution, large or small, to do a more effective job of cross-selling and do it with lower marketing costs. The result—and the real benefit to your institution—will be more business and more profits.

Several of the chapters in this book outline ways of targeting specific customer segments for specific types of products. If you already understand how an MCIF system can contribute to the basic cross-selling process, you may want to refer directly to the chapters that address the specific applications that interest you the most. If you'd like a more fundamental overview before embarking into specific product areas, read on.

MCIF Puts Cross-Selling Information at Your Fingertips

As you probably know from reading earlier articles, an MCIF system will capture and organize all your customer information from all of your product and service areas. It will associate accounts with customers, then assemble the customers into an economic marketing unit called a customer household. (Householding techniques—and the resulting householding accuracy—will vary from vendor to vendor, and should be investigated carefully before you make any investment.) Many of the better systems also perform name and address standardization, geocoding, zip + 4 appending, life-style coding, and other services.

The reason why MCIF systems are an important tool for cross-selling is that the MCIF puts this comprehensive customer information database in-house, at your fingertips, and makes the information easily available, anytime, through an on-site PC.

The cross-selling implications of collecting all your customer information into a single database are tremendous. Basically, the MCIF will give you a complete and comprehensive understanding of three critical information components necessary for effective cross-selling.

- Because you know all of the accounts owned by all of the customers in each household, the MCIF allows you to measure the scope and profitability of individual account and complete customer household relationships. You will be able to separate single-service households from those with multiple services; see balances associated with the various types of services; and see how profitability increases as the number of services increases.

- By definition, by knowing what products and services a customer household has with your institution, you know what they don't have. That means they have the potential to purchase them from you. That's the beginning of cross-selling.

- The most critical cross-selling information component that an MCIF provides is a measure of demonstrated propensity, or the inclination of any given customer household to purchase additional products or services in various combinations from your specific institution or branches.

It is this ability to determine the propensity of specific customer segments to purchase various products and services in particular combinations that allows an MCIF to play such a critical role in making your cross-selling efforts more effective. The MCIF allows you to identify and target specific customer segments for cross-selling programs, and determine the exact products or services to offer them that will both motivate response and increase the profitability of the overall relationship.

Equally important, MCIF systems allow you to track and measure the results of such efforts.

Reports Let You Measure Propensity

MCIF systems typically offer comprehensive reporting, but the better systems all offer three types of reports that can help you plan and execute a propensity-based cross-selling strategy. They may be called by slightly different names in different systems from competitive vendors, but they commonly cover three areas:

1. Current cross-sell ratios and penetration

2. Combination of services, ranked by popularity

3. Combination of services, ranked by profitability

The cross-sell reports are typically in a matrix format that allows you to identify how many customers that hold one type of service have been cross-sold another. This type of report has two uses. First and most obvious, it allows you to measure overall cross-sell ratios and the cross-sell ratio of specific product combinations. For example, it might show that among all money market customers, 69% have been cross-sold a savings account, 50% have been sold a short-term CD, 18% have been sold a retirement account, etc.

More important, it shows you cross-selling opportunities. For example, the high cross-sell ratio (69%) of the savings service to money market households says that in your particular institution, your customers have a propensity to combine a money market account with a savings account. They also have a high propensity (50%) to combine a money market with a short-term CD (50%).

What that tells you is that, if you could only do one or two direct mail programs directed toward money market account holders, you could try to sell them a home equity line of credit or installment loan, and you might generate some business, but your response would most likely be low. However, if you identified those money market holders who do not have a savings account—and that's 31% of your account base in this example—and mailed them a savings service offer, you could expect a much higher response rate because money market customers in your particular institution have demonstrated a propensity to combine money market accounts with savings accounts.

The same is true if you identified those money market holders who do not have a short-term CD—and that's 50% of your base—and mailed them a CD offer with a rate incentive. You could expect a high rate of return because your customers have also demonstrated a propensity to combine those two services.

The Combination of Services Report identifies the number of house-holds in your institution that have every possible individual service or combination of services. The combinations are listed in rank order so you can see which are your most popular single services and which are your most popular combinations of services.

For example, in reviewing such a report, you might find that the three most popular combinations of services are not combinations at all, but rather are single-service checking, single-service savings and single-service money market households. In continuing to review the report, however, you might see that the next most popular combination might be a combination of checking with savings, and that such combinations as money market with checking and money market with short-term CD might also rank high.

That says your customers have a propensity to combine these prod-ucts. More important, it says that within your particular customer base, the next logical purchase that single-service checking account customers typically make is a savings service; the next logical pur-chase of single-service money market customers is either a checking account or a short-term CD.

Now you can cross-sell to "propensity." Using the MCIF system, you can identify single-service checking customers and send them a savings service offer. You can find single-service money market customers and first send them a checking solicitation, then send a short-term CD mailer. You are likely to get a higher than normal rate of response because you are making these customers an offer to which your data indicates they are likely to respond positively.

The Combination of Services ranked by profitability gives you similar capabilities with one important difference. Now you can target your cross-selling efforts, not only against those combinations that are most popular but, among those combinations, you can also choose to promote those that will deliver the most improvement in profitability.

In the example above, I said that you might find that money market customers have a propensity to combine either a checking service or a short-term CD. If you wanted to choose which combination to promote first, you could review which combination has the higher average profitability and choose that one.

Making Cross-Selling a Strategy, Not Just a Wish

For many years, banking leaders have been discussing the advantages of cross-selling, and most institutions have listed cross-selling as one of their strategic objectives. Unfortunately, because institutions did not have an effective way to implement cross-selling programs, cross-selling was more of a wish than a true strategy.

Today, with the advent of powerful MCIF systems, marketers have a single tool that allows them to set the strategy, execute the tactics necessary to support the strategy, and then measure the resultant impact on profitability.

13

TARGETING HIGH DEPOSITORS

Marianne A. Diericks
First Banks System

 $\mathbf{W}$ hen attempting to build their business, financial institutions often focus on capturing customers from competitors and neglect growing relationships with current customers. Yet it is much easier to ask for more money from customers who already trust you than it is to convince a person to change banks. By using your Marketing Customer Information File (MCIF), you can develop precise lists of prospects to cross-sell services that will far outperform purchased lists of noncustomers.

What do you need to know about your customers in order to find prospects for new deposits? You begin with an analysis of your MCIF, which tells you where your customer product penetration is strong, where it's weak, and where windows of opportunity exist. The key benefit of the database analysis is that it defines the extent to which you can expect to reach each of your marketing goals through sales to existing customers versus new customers.

You can tell your MCIF what you want to sell and it will unerringly target the best prospects for that product in your customer base. But you have to learn how to tell it what you want. You do that through segmentation strategies, which are derived from your database analysis, coupled with an understanding of the factors that motivate the need or desire for a specific financial service. Experience at other financial institutions shows that prior product usage and balance levels are the most powerful predictors of future product usage.

That's precisely the information you have on your MCIF, and you can use that information to define segments within your customer base that offer the greatest potential to bring you additional business. These segments can be identified and quantified using a set of principles commonly called AFRA:

AFFINITY: prior product usage is the best predictor of future product needs. High deposit customers are poor prospects for credit services.

FREQUENCY: the more business a household has with you, the more it is likely to give you. It's easier to sell the sixth product to a customer than the second.

RECENCY: likelihood to purchase declines as length of time since previous purchase increases.

AMOUNT: the more dollars a household has with you, the more it is likely to give you. It's easier to get an extra $25,000 from a high deposit household than $2,500 from an average deposit household.

Let's look at an example of a typical database analysis of deposit customers, which combines checking, savings, certificates of deposits, and retirement account dollars for all household members. Table 1-A shows a breakout of deposit households into eight deposit segments, with the top segment including households having >$100,000 in total deposits (left), to the bottom segment, containing households with <$2,500 in total deposits. The solid bars represent deposit dollars controlled by the particular segment, and the striped bar shows number of households in the segment.

The key message is this: a very small number of households control the majority of deposit dollars. On the flip side, there are many house

TABLE 1A

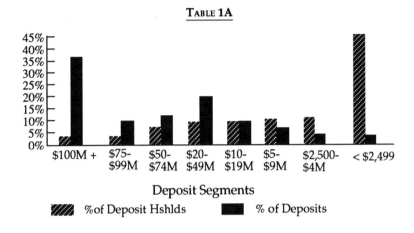

Deposit Segments

▨ %of Deposit Hshlds   ■ % of Deposits

holds with low deposit balances. Typically, the 80-20 rule holds true for deposit dollars: 80% or more of your deposit dollars are controlled by 20% of your total households.

A traditional direct marketer looking at this table might conclude that mailings be conducted to segments containing the largest number of households, thinking that a modest amount of additional deposits from each of these customers would generate a high total dollar volume. In contrast, a database direct marketer targets the opposite end of the table: the small number of households who already have high deposit levels at your institution. The reason: people who have high deposits with you also have money in other financial institutions. If you give them appropriate incentives, they will give you more of their total deposit dollars. On the other hand, the numerous low-deposit households probably do not have money scattered around town, and even the best incentive cannot bring you dollars that do not exist.

While traditional direct marketing is based on mailing large volumes, a database marketing strategy is based on mailing as few pieces as possible to reach marketing objectives. Therefore, you focus effort and promotion dollars on your top 20% of customers. This approach provides clear advantages to the marketer: mailing costs are lower, offers can be more aggressive because of the selective audience, bankers obtain more qualified leads, customers receive offers with genuine appeal, and new business acquisition costs are less. With very few exceptions, and regardless of your product offer, you should never mail deeper than 30% into your customer base. And the top 20% is the place to start.

If that seems too simplistic, you are right. This top 20% does not hold similar deposit potential from one institution to another, and the top 20% is not a homogeneous customer segment. For some institutions, the top 20% may have a deposit level of $6,500, while $22,000 may be the cutoff level at another institution. Deposit level is, by far, a much better indicator of deposit potential than a simplistic segmentation strategy.

A further breakout of your top 20% by centile segments, as shown in table 1-B, demonstrates the value of using absolute deposit level to predict cost effective deposit potential. The top 2 centiles have an average balance of well over $100,000, while the average balance of the "lower" deciles within the top 20% is under $20,550 — a difference of $80,000. This difference is a strong measurement of relative deposit potential, which can be used to establish high deposit mailing subsegments that you can test, measure, and refine.

If your database has been enhanced with appended demographics, you have additional segmentation options open to you. Household specific demographic enhancement is particularly useful in identifying those customers who are not currently in your top 20% to 30%, but have the potential to be. Product usage segmentation falls short in this application because these customers probably are doing the bulk of their business with your competition, so they won't show up in your key segments.

It's important to recognize that you have a finite number of good prospects in your customer base for additional deposit sales. A database marketing plan emphasizes regularly scheduled promotions to these prospects to maximize the effectiveness of your marketing budget. The segmentation strategies, which lie at the heart of your database plan, result from the MCIF analysis combined with your marketing/sales objectives. Since the list is the single most critical element of any direct marketing plan, these strategies require careful attention. It makes sense to test these segment definitions and continually refine them, based on your tracking results.

	Households	Average Deposit	Total Deposits ($000's)	% of Total	Cumulative % of Total	Deposit to Qualify
			TABLE 1B			
		Top 20% Deposit Households Centile Segmentation				
1%	4,631	$322,090	$1,491,600	28.0	28.0	$145,050
2	4,631	122,112	565,500	10.6	38.6	106,090
3	4,630	97,084	449,500	8.4	47.0	88,450
4	4,631	80,954	374,900	7.0	54.1	74,360
5	4,630	68,487	317,000	5.9	60.0	63,360
6	4,631	63,334	293,300	5.5	65.5	55,010
7	4,631	51,652	239,200	4.5	70.0	48,610
8	4,630	45,080	211,500	4.0	74.0	42,960
9	4,631	40,596	188,000	3.5	77.5	38,381
10	4,630	36,328	168,200	3.2	80.6	34,417
11	4,631	32,628	151,100	2.8	83.5	30,961
12	4,631	29,562	136,900	2.6	86.0	28,159
13	4,630	26,825	124,200	2.3	88.4	25,563
14	4,631	24,466	113,300	2.1	90.5	23,373
15	4,631	22,349	103,500	1.9	92.4	21,340
16	4,630	20,475	94,800	1.8	94.2	19,749
17	4,631	18,894	87,500	1.6	95.9	18,068
18	4,630	17,322	80,200	1.5	97.4	16,637
19	4,631	15,958	73,900	1.4	98.7	15,317
20	4,630	14,795	68,500	1.3	100.0	14,237
	92,612		$5,332,600			

Although it's difficult to create a need for a financial service, you can motivate customers with latent needs to act now. Your segmentation strategies should include varying offers, and the strength of those offers, to different segments, based on the profitability of the business they are likely to bring you. For example, you should be willing to pay more for a checking account with a $10,000 average balance than one with a $750 average balance.

Noncustomer Deposit Prospects

While most direct mail dollars should be targeted to existing customers, financial institutions cannot overlook the importance of bringing new customers into the database. Database marketing can be used to bring in selected new households that are then more likely to buy additional products after they become customers. Investing in new customers should be viewed as investing in long-term customers rather than single product sales. Most new customer direct mail solicitations in the past have been product driven. Generally, this strategy limits the objective of the promotion to product goals rather than multiple sales and relationship building goals. This strategy also fails to realize the full potential of the market. The targeted prospect may not respond to an offer because they did not have the need for the product or the capacity to purchase at the time they received the solicitation. For the most part, consumers buy financial services on their own timetables. Therefore, timeliness of the offer has a significant impact on response rates, particularly for product-specific, one-time mailings.

Noncustomers are also less likely than customers to read direct mail from a financial institution. Therefore, one mailing may not cut through the clutter and get opened. A series of mailings may be more effective in establishing the prospect as someone with whom the financial institution would like to do business. Then, when that person needs a particular product, they may think of your institution first.

Another way to identify noncustomer prospects is by constructing a profile model of existing customers and conducting primary research, which together help formulate a noncustomer mailing list and product offers. It is helpful to realize that prospects usually will not buy a financial service they do not already have. This is almost universally true for high deposit prospects.

Classic Deposit Offers to Get You Started

Let's suppose your marketing plan calls for increasing deposits, and you want to try database marketing to see if it can help achieve your goals. You can begin with a modest budget and two classic mailings that can give you early success. If you can select your top deposit households (with third-class deliverable addresses) off your database, segment them by deposit levels, and set up tracking to measure sales results for each segment during the promotion period, you can proceed with these mailings:

- A checking-with-bonus offer to high deposit households who do not have a DDA with you

- A bonus-rate Certificate of Deposit offer to high deposit households who do not have a CD maturing during the promotion period (to generate new money)

Establish several segments for each offer, for which you track results, so you can measure relative cost- effectiveness.

Segment quantities should be large enough to provide statistically valid and projectable results, include customers from various branches, and be fairly equal in size. If you are choosing households from a large base, select names randomly.

Once you've determined your development and mailing costs, expected response rate, and desired acquisition cost, you can define your offers. Since these are your best customers, you can afford to be more aggressive with offers than if you were advertising in the newspaper. A strong offer that competes well in your marketplace is critical.

Your tracking results will usually vary by segment, with top deposit segments responding more favorably. It is not unusual for checking response to range from 1% to 6% among segments, and for CD response to vary from 2% to 10%.

Database mailings are quite simple in their message, since high deposit customers don't need to be sold on the value of free checking or bonus-rate CDs — they simply need to understand the offer, the deadline, and how to take advantage of the offer. In most cases, the letter sent to your high deposit households should be signed by the manager of the branch at which they do business. The desired response is a branch visit, returning a coupon, or calling the branch for more information.

Important Direct Mail Basics

Database marketing is a sophisticated approach to direct mail, and knowing direct mail principles will help you achieve greater success with your cross-sell mailings.

Financial institutions are accustomed to general advertising, having run newspaper or radio promotions for particular products. But developing an effective direct mail campaign requires a significantly different focus from developing product advertising.

In direct marketing, **your list is 60% of your success.** It is more important to be sending the right offer to the right prospect than it is to have an attractive mailing package. Your mailing list requires careful selection and attention to production details in order to assure that your mailing gets delivered to the right persons.

Your offer accounts for 25% of direct mail success. If you have a great mailing list for a CD promotion but your offer pales in comparison to the competition, your response rate will drop. High deposit customers may be loyal to you, but they also shop rates.

The creative materials account for 15% of a mailing's success. While creating the direct mail letter or brochure may be the most "fun" part of developing a promotion, it has less impact on response than the list and offer. Once you've perfected your lists and developed unbeatable offers, then creative approach becomes your point of leverage. Be sure your mailing package is understandable, emphasizes benefits to the customer, and makes it easy to respond.

Direct marketing is a testing medium, through which lists, offers, and creative approaches are continually tested, analyzed, and refined. Tracking reports are critical in demonstrating the value of database marketing, and a mailing that is not tracked is not direct mail, but is simply advertising in an envelope.

Still another important key to direct marketing success is **persistency**: find your best prospects and keep going back to them. If they didn't respond to your offer the first time, don't assume they won't buy from you. Perhaps they didn't need your product at the time they received the mailing, and if you contact them three and six months later, your offer may arrive just when they're ready to buy.

Myths About Direct Mail

If direct marketing is relatively new to your institution, you may encounter resistance to using it, especially for affluent audiences.

Some managers simply think of it as "junk mail," and believe it conflicts with the institution's image. This shouldn't be the case when mailings are appropriate for the audience. In fact, direct mail is the most personal of promotional media, and database mailings are designed to acknowledge customers for their current business and generate new business.

But myths exist, and these are a few you may encounter:

Myth	Fact
Affluent customers don't like direct mail.	Research shows that most upscale consumers welcome the convenience of direct mail, because they are often too busy to notice other forms of advertising.
A mailing to affluent customers must not look or sound like direct mail (no tear-offs, window envelopes, or third-class postage); message is "soft-sell."	It's important to follow direct mail principles when preparing a mailing, regardless of the audience. You must get the person's attention, clearly state the benefits of your offer, ask for a response, and make it easy to respond. If you are too "soft-sell," your offer may be overlooked. If you don't directly ask for a response, you won't get one.
You don't need a mailing program because branch officers are already in touch with best prospects.	Although branches are in contact with customers, they can't reach large numbers. They may know their most frequent customers better than their most affluent.
It takes a large incentive for affluent customers to respond to an offer, so direct mail becomes too costly.	It's smart to test incentive levels, but a modest bonus of $20 is often enough to convince a person to open new account—even customers with high deposit levels.

Necessary Resources

Initiating a database marketing program involves changing the way your institution approaches cross-selling, and you'll need some critical resources to help launch the program.

- **Financial resources:** Your budget amount will depend greatly on whether you need to develop an MCIF. Beyond that, you can begin a mailing program with a small budget by approaching the first six months as a test phase. Then, armed with tracking results, you can justify additional dollars. If you've already been doing "mass mailings," you'll find you need less money to achieve better results through database marketing.

- **Senior management sponsorship:** When you begin database marketing, a high-level sponsor is invaluable in paving the way for implementation. Without this support, obstacles can derail you.

- **Focused, central coordination:** Central management of the database program is essential because planning and implementation must be driven with a broad view of the customer base, rather than by specific product goals. It is the manager's job to keep the institution focused on pockets of opportunity within the customer base, and to avoid spending dollars where little potential exists.

- **Competent, creative systems support:** Ideally, you need a person who knows the intricacies of your customer files and internal systems, and who can translate data into marketing information. This support is critical in developing an MCIF, and selecting lists, tracking, and updating customer files.

- **Excellent production coordinator:** This person watches every detail of your mailings: corporate graphic standards; postal requirements; managing vendors; quality control; deadlines; and more. Once a database program is underway, several offers may be sent to various customer segments during a given month, and the potential for error is great. An experienced direct mail production coordinator works magic.

- **Database marketing expertise:** This resource can help you "hit the ground running," and create early success with database marketing. If consultants have worked with other financial institutions, they know which offers work with specific customer segments.

This can save much testing, and help to generate more dollars the first year. If you hire external consultants, be sure to request a current database client list, details about their campaigns, and references.

Preparing Your Branches

Customers receiving database mailings will usually be asked to contact their branch to "redeem" the offer or to obtain more information. Branch personnel must therefore be familiar with your program in order to support it, feel confident about fulfilling offers, and answer customer questions.

Inform branch managers about the program early in its development in order to address their concerns and gain their endorsement. Preferably, they will share information with bankers, to prepare them for a new way of generating sales.

Several weeks prior to the first mail drop, your bankers should receive samples of the letter text, a description of the mailing package, target audience, codes used on response coupons, and any required tracking. Then, as the mailing drops, each bank should receive a listing of customers mailed, by offer. Since third-class postage is used, there will usually be a 1-week to 10-day delay before customers receive the mailing. Encourage bankers to follow up the mailing with telephone calls to their customers to improve response.

Do yourself a favor: let bankers know that mailing lists are imperfect. They will receive telephone calls from families to say you mailed to a deceased person or to persons who closed their accounts. They may also hear complaints from people who do not want to receive promotional mailings. If bankers are unprepared for such calls, they will blame marketing for using "bad lists," and have doubts about the database program. When they know in advance that telephone calls are a normal part of any mailing program, they can be prepared. As a guideline, up to 10% of a list may contain errors.

Related to this, you'll want to establish procedures for correcting customer information received from banks as a result of mailings. Equally important, provide the opportunity for disgruntled customers to be placed on a "do not mail" list, which is run against every mailing list you use.

Database Mailings Work

Financial institutions across the country, large and small, have begun to reap the benefits of database marketing. There is no more efficient and effective way to reach selected customers for cross-selling, and the more you delay beginning your program, the more you risk losing your customers to the competition.

Affluent deposit customers aren't easy to find. Most of them are not in Private Banking or the Trust department, as some would assume, and they don't necessarily "look wealthy" when they walk into your branches. On the contrary, they may be large savers because they have lived frugal lives. That's why it's so important to look carefully into your database to identify your best deposit prospects, then to develop ongoing communications with them. They will appreciate the attention, respond to offers that provide genuine value, and do more and more business with you as their preferred financial institution.

14

DEVELOPING AN INTEGRATED COMMERCIAL DATABASE

Jane Gedicks
Banc One Corporation

To manage a business well is to manage its future; and to manage it's future is to manage information.   Marion Harper, Jr.

I skate to where I think the puck will be.   Wayne Gretzky

For aggressive users of household databases to analyze retail banking customers, it is only a modest leap to imagine the value of such information for commercial relationships. The array of benefits from an integrated commercial database is compelling, including:

- Better design of products/services

- Identification and targeting of profitable segments and opportunities

- Greater productivity of sales forces

- Enhanced customer service through knowledge of total business needs

- Heightened leverage of corporate strengths and coordination of resources

The number of businesses in a market is usually small, relative to the number of retail households. However, the number of services used and the related balances are likely to be substantially higher than those of the average retail household. Unfortunately, the smaller quantity does not simplify the task of linking together the array of commercial applications. It is common practice to project geodemographic, lifestyle, and financial product usage for the retail market. There is substantially less linkage and projectability of business demographics (e.g., sales size, number of employees, SIC code, age of firm, historic and cyclical patterns of growth or decline, business and industry risk) that are readily available regarding commercial relationships.

There are several major obstacles to an integrated commercial database. First, the tools available are limited. Most of the software available today was designed for retail applications, and it is being retrofitted to commercial needs. Second, marketing analysis for commercial banking traditionally has been low tech; the emphasis has been on the operating systems that support the pricing and product needs of cash management or lending officers, not on market penetration analysis.

There are three levels of development in the evolution of both the tools and the analysis needs for an integrated commercial database. First, the *classification* scheme of commercial relationships, accounts, and activities must be developed. Vocabulary and nomenclature need to be standardized if internal classifications are to be matched against external benchmarks of product usage, service preference, and market size and opportunities. Second, *segmentation* of customer and market characteristics can be used to classify current position in the market as well as to quantify additional opportunities. Finally, the total *business relationship can be maximized* across profit centers, business units and operational systems through diagnosis and alleviation of impediments that arise from organizational politics.

Classification of Commercial Relationships, Accounts, and Activities in Customer and Market Databases

---

Nothing in this world is so powerful as an idea whose time has come.
Victor Hugo

. . . A rose by any other name . . .
Shakespeare

The complexity of the commercial relationship is amplified by the multiple hierarchies of commercial relationships. On the retail side we view accounts, individuals, and households in a simple vertical structure. On the commercial side there are multidirectional interrelationships among parent companies, subsidiaries, franchises, branches, affiliates, partnerships, business units, etc., which pose an enormous challenge both to our technology and to our analytic capabilities. (See Diagram 1.)

DIAGRAM 1

Commercial Relationship

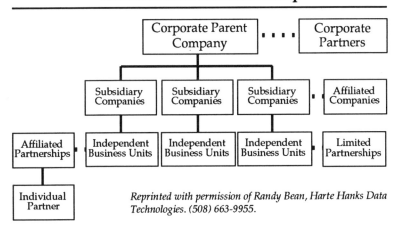

Reprinted with permission of Randy Bean, Harte Hanks Data Technologies. (508) 663-9955.

Building a commercial database involves bringing together the various financial relationships of a business. This is done through "enterprising,"[1] the commercial counterpart of "householding," i.e., the bringing together of the financial services of a business, to create a comprehensive look at the quality and quantity of the relationship across a broad array of applications, operating systems, and name and address structures. (See Diagram 2.)

To do business name matching, more effective parameters for business name and address matching must be developed. File standardization, account numbers, tax identifiers, and customer keys are some of the parameters that help establish interrelationships of accounts. Traditionally, the term *forced householding* was used at this stage. Unfortunately this was a euphemism for the process of alienating the

[1] Terminology suggested by Tom Swithenbank, CEO of Harte Hanks Data Technologies.

181

DIAGRAM 2

Commercial Relationship

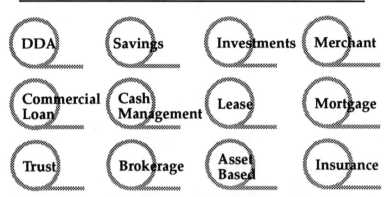

commercial lending officer by demanding that he or she manually identify all the accounts and industry classifications of his or her customers and prospects, so they could be appended to the database. Needless to say, this process did not create a reliable, updatable source of information for use in prospecting and supporting business applications. Worse yet, if one was successful in getting commercial bankers to use it, it was very labor intensive to maintain because the technology did not readily support ongoing linkages and updates.

The task is certainly not simple. The interrelationships among business units of a commercial relationship are relevant for some applications while superfluous to others. For example, a subsidiary of General Motors based in Akron, Ohio, may get its checking and payroll services from a local financial institution, whereas its lockbox services come from a multistate holding company selected by the corporate parent in Detroit. The Akron banker is probably only interested in the subsidiary's accounts when he sets pricing and evaluates his market opportunities, but the multi-state holding company may wish to match its market coverage to that of the corporate parent and its subsidiaries.

The final element of commercial product and service classifications relates to the need for a common vocabulary. Businesses use a broad array of products, relationship packages, and account management and reconciliation systems. It is important that the classification

DIAGRAM 3

"Matchmaker"

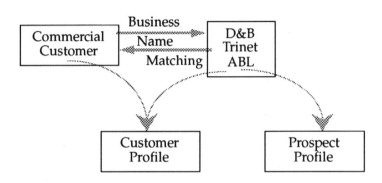

scheme be developed with an eye toward both internal communication and external benchmarks of primary, syndicated, and secondary research. (See Diagram 3.)

The ability to match the business customer to the external market is critical to ensure the integrity of the market size, share, and segmentation analysis that it drives.

Market Size, Share, and Segmentation

"Cheshire Puss," she [Alice] began..."would you please tell me which way I ought to go from here?" "That depends on where you want to get to" said the cat.   Lewis Carroll

Give me a lever long enough...and single-handed I can move the world.
                                                                     Archimedes

When the classification tools are in place, the segmentation opportunities are quite intuitive. If the business application is defined, the customers can be matched to the market, so estimates of penetration and share, as well as product usage and profitability, can be projected.

In defining the business market, it is important to consider the business application when selecting from various sources. For example, if the target market is core DDA accounts from small service

183

DIAGRAM 4

Defining the Market

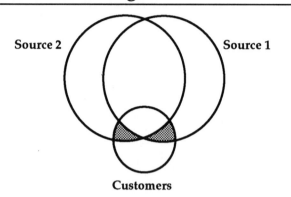

Source 2   Source 1

Customers

businesses, then a market source driven largely by credit history may not accurately reflect the true prospect base.

Through experimentation and tracking, we can identify both the overlap of our market sources and the unique strengths of a particular source for a business application, as shown in Diagram 4. The quality of information also plays a key role here; recency of update, level of detail, accuracy, and delivery media all play a role in the viability of information.

The customer profile now begins to emerge, as in Diagram 5. At the core are internal measures of accounts, dollar volumes, activity levels and history. These measures are reformulated to calculate profitability, growth, risk and cyclicality.

This data is further enhanced by appending additional "demographics," such as sales size, number of employees, industry, age of firm, etc., as in Diagram 6. This information is used to model the market opportunity by projecting product usage, cross-selling, servicing preferences, and incremental profitability.

This integration of primary or secondary research and syndicated studies with proprietary customer and profitability information is the

DIAGRAM 5

Customer Profile

INTERNAL DATA:

- Profitability
- Growth
- Risk
- Cycles
- Accounts
- $ Volume
- Activities
- Account
  History

DIAGRAM 6

Customer Profile

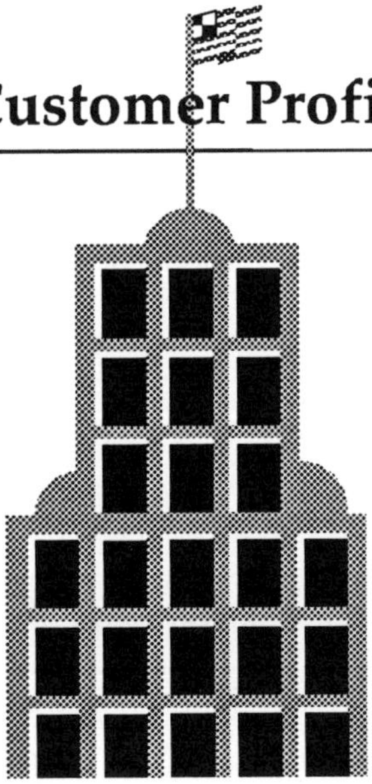

INTERNAL DATA:

- Profitability
- Growth
- Risk
- Cycles
- Accounts
- $ Volume
- Activities
- Account
  History

APPEND DATA:

- Product Usage
  Projections
- Cross Selling
  Opportunities
- Servicing
  Preferences
- Incremental
  Profits
- Sales Size
- No. of Employees
- Industry
- Age of Firm

185

DIAGRAM 7

Customer Opportunities

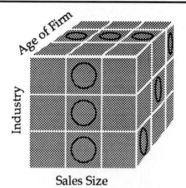

Sales Size

key to a treasure chest of opportunities. (See Diagram 7.) The parameters can be as simple or as complex as you can reliably model, preferably with reality checks against experience in known markets!

Maximizing the Business Relationship

There are three types of companies, those who make things happen, those who watch things happen, those who wonder what happened.   Anonymous

Having lost sight of our objective, we redoubled our efforts.   Old Adage

At this point we have successfully classified business entities by their accounts and activities; we have identified their relationship within their parent company, when appropriate; and we have sized and segmented our key marketing opportunities and applied analysis to prioritize them.

The remaining task is to execute programs against these strategies. Within a bank there are a variety of customer ownership, referral, and tracking issues that are critical to successful implementation. The internal politics of cross-selling and referrals across profit centers and business units has the potential to nurture or poison any program. There are tough tradeoffs involved in many day-to-day decisions that should be managed strategically. Policies on upselling, referrals to other business units, private banking, etc., may channel through areas that do not share a common reporting or accountability structure.

Needless to say, what is best for one business unit may not coincide with what is best for the corporation or the business customer. The tools and analytic framework that have seen maturation on the retail database (Diagram 8) are still latent and disjointed for the commercial database. The component pieces that could be integrated are already quite powerful and have often been used to manage the business intuitively, with great success.

Yet the economics of managing the business relationship are compelling, particularly in a large organization based on estimated costs of $240 for the average business-to-business sales call: Fifty calling officers with four unproductive calls per week would cost $2.5 million per year! Compounding this waste is the risk that the competition *is* doing a better job targeting your customers and prospects and leveraging its corporate strengths to address the total business needs of its targets. Fostering the integration of information systems to support better decisions through portfolio mix, risk management, and resource allocation will be a critical investment for banks that wish to survive in the '90s.

DIAGRAM 8

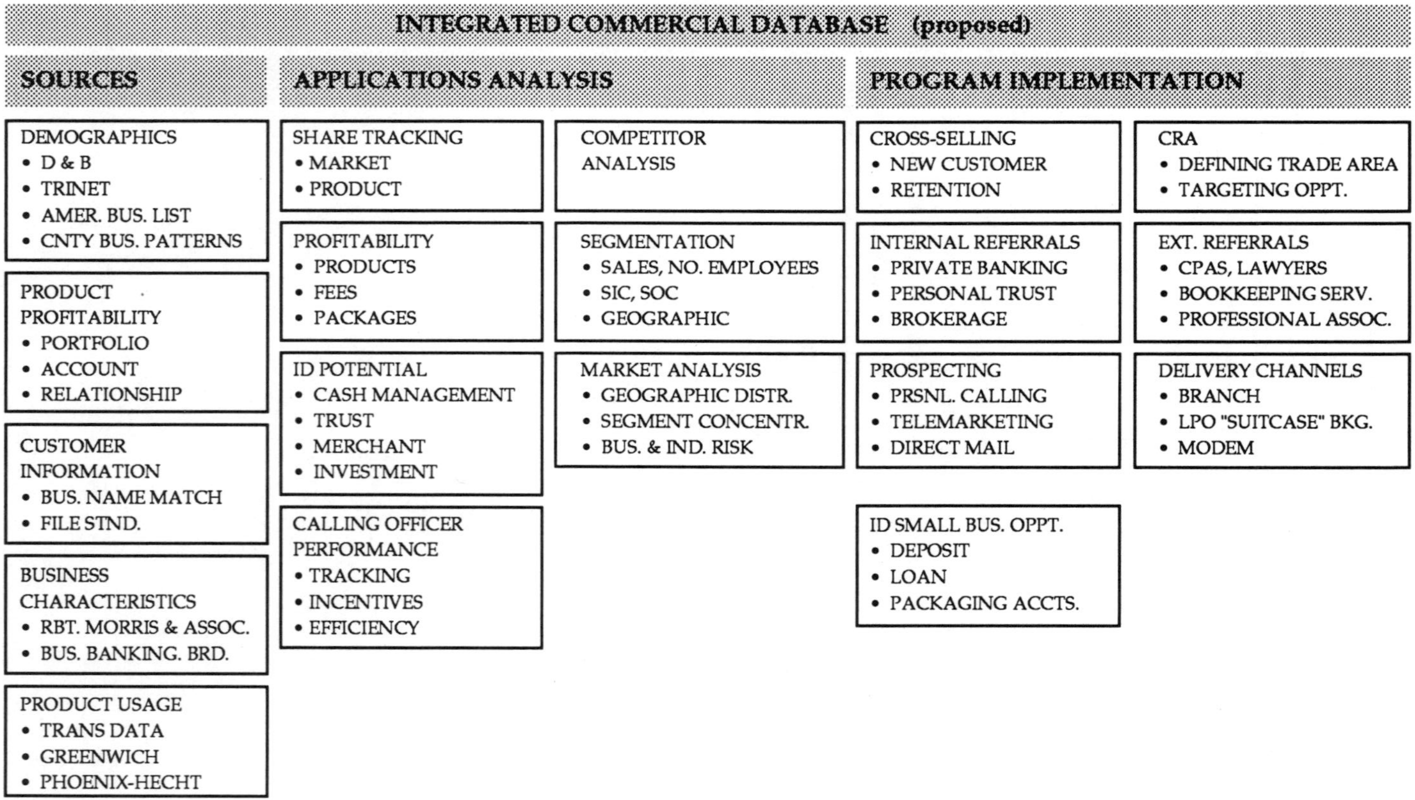

INTEGRATED COMMERCIAL DATABASE (proposed)

SOURCES

DEMOGRAPHICS
- D & B
- TRINET
- AMER. BUS. LIST
- CNTY BUS. PATTERNS

PRODUCT PROFITABILITY
- PORTFOLIO
- ACCOUNT
- RELATIONSHIP

CUSTOMER INFORMATION
- BUS. NAME MATCH
- FILE STND.

BUSINESS CHARACTERISTICS
- RBT. MORRIS & ASSOC.
- BUS. BANKING. BRD.

PRODUCT USAGE
- TRANS DATA
- GREENWICH
- PHOENIX-HECHT

APPLICATIONS ANALYSIS

SHARE TRACKING
- MARKET
- PRODUCT

PROFITABILITY
- PRODUCTS
- FEES
- PACKAGES

ID POTENTIAL
- CASH MANAGEMENT
- TRUST
- MERCHANT
- INVESTMENT

CALLING OFFICER PERFORMANCE
- TRACKING
- INCENTIVES
- EFFICIENCY

COMPETITOR ANALYSIS

SEGMENTATION
- SALES, NO. EMPLOYEES
- SIC, SOC
- GEOGRAPHIC

MARKET ANALYSIS
- GEOGRAPHIC DISTR.
- SEGMENT CONCENTR.
- BUS. & IND. RISK

PROGRAM IMPLEMENTATION

CROSS-SELLING
- NEW CUSTOMER
- RETENTION

INTERNAL REFERRALS
- PRIVATE BANKING
- PERSONAL TRUST
- BROKERAGE

PROSPECTING
- PRSNL. CALLING
- TELEMARKETING
- DIRECT MAIL

ID SMALL BUS. OPPT.
- DEPOSIT
- LOAN
- PACKAGING ACCTS.

CRA
- DEFINING TRADE AREA
- TARGETING OPPT.

EXT. REFERRALS
- CPAS, LAWYERS
- BOOKKEEPING SERV.
- PROFESSIONAL ASSOC.

DELIVERY CHANNELS
- BRANCH
- LPO "SUITCASE" BKG.
- MODEM

PART 5 | SELLING TRANSACTION PRODUCTS

15

USING YOUR MCIF TO INCREASE THE MARKETING EFFECTIVENESS OF CHECKING ACCOUNTS

Brad Champlin
Leader Federal Bank for Savings

The marketing importance of the "Checking Account" has been recognized by financial services marketers for many years. It has generally been agreed that the Checking Account enabled the financial institution to become the customer's "primary institution." Financial services marketing theory taught us that the Checking Account was the core account that would make cross-selling other services much more effective.

The competition for the customer's checking account through cross-selling has been long and hard. In the late '60s, Wells Fargo Bank took the market by storm by introducing the Gold Account—a group of services that were packaged together around the checking account. As with virtually every financial services product innovation, this concept was quickly adopted by major banks across the country and the playing field was again level.

Considering that the checking account is a basic product, there have been significant changes and product enhancements developed through the years, all aimed at increasing checking account growth and customer satisfaction. To name a few checking account enhancements, in addition to the "package" account:

- Overdraft Protection

- Automatic Teller Machines

- Telephone Transfer

- Telephone Bill Paying

- Debit Card

As with most product-driven strategies, competitors quickly followed with "me too" products. Shifts in checking account market share were more dependent upon media and promotional clout than marketing expertise.

Perhaps the change that had the greatest impact on checking and the financial services industry took place on January 1, 1981, with the authorization for savings and loans and savings banks to offer Negotiable Order of Withdrawal (NOW) accounts. While not officially a checking account because it paid interest (5.25%), it nevertheless looked like a checking account, tasted like a checking account, and smelled like a checking account.

Even with the minor marketing problem of not being able to call this account a checking account, there was an intense marketing war as savings institutions were given an opportunity to capture significant checking account market share because a regulatory change created a unique situation. And the banks had to protect their turf. Now (no pun intended), the battle was on to capture the primary relationship of a customer through aggressive checking account promotion. Marketing strategies varied from giving the account away free to anyone who could walk through the door and write their name to requiring high deposit balances to qualify for the account. And the market responded positively to this new product.

Determining the Value of the Checking Account

The development of more sophisticated Marketing Customer Information Files (MCIFs) has tremendously increased the opportunity for an institution to shift checking account market share and, particularly, attract "quality" checking accounts (as measured by high average balance). The MCIF enables the institution to analyze the impact of the checking account on a customer relationship and to more accurately measure the profitability of the account or relationship. (Do we really want to be the primary financial institution of this customer?) And the astute marketer can take advantage of this data and access to the customer base to more effectively market the checking account through database marketing.

How important is the checking account? First, let us address the issue of the value of the checking account to a customer's relationship. The theoretical benefits of being the customer's primary financial institution are to solidify that relationship and to more effectively sell other services. The MCIF has the ability to verify these theories that usually were seriously questioned by the Chief Financial Officer.

Analysis of an important market segment—High Deposit Households—can help quantify the impact of checking on this group of customers. Chart I shows the comparative product usage between customers (households) that have more than $10,000 in total deposits with Institution A segmented by those who have a Checking Account and those that do not.

This basic product usage comparison clearly demonstrates the positive impact of checking on product usage among this all-important customer segment. High Deposit Households with a Checking Account relationship had:

- About 50% greater usage of Savings Account

- Over 75% greater usage of Money Market Account

- Over one third greater usage of Retirement Account

- Twice the usage of nontraditional products (Brokerage and Annuity)

- Almost 300% greater usage of Credit Card

This actual data strongly supports the premise that a Checking Account customer, at least from a selected market segment, offers

CHART I

INSTITUTION A

COMPARATIVE IMPACT ON PRODUCT USAGE OF

HIGH DEPOSIT HOUSEHOLDS

	With Checking		Without Checking	
	% Using	Avg. Balance	% Using	Avg. Balance
Checking	100	$ 5,100	-	-
Savings	34	5,762	22	$ 8,585
Money Market	38	25,655	21	29,185
Long-Term CD	30	35,475	31	37,568
Short-Term CD	59	36,530	58	41,138
Retirement	31	18,217	23	21,413
Brokerage	5	-	2	-
Annuity	8	-	4	-
Credit Card	22	443	8	454
Equity Loan	5	14,458	2	14,102
Installment Loan	1	6,259	<1	9,267
Mortgage	10	41,528	5	48,484
Average Total Deposits		54,520		48,649
Number of Services per Hshld.		3.1		1.8
Number of Accts. per Hshld.		6.2		3.0

increased product cross-sell potential. For this institution, the number of services increases almost 75% (from 1.8 to 3.1) and the number of accounts increases over 50% (from 3.0 to 6.2). However, the Chief Financial Officer may not understand the impact.

Perhaps the most important difference between these High Deposit Customer segments was that Total Cost of Funds for High Deposit Households that *did* have a Checking Account was approximately 75 *Basis Points lower* compared to High Deposit Households that *did not* have a Checking Account. This is a measurable value of the elusive benefit of the checking account relationship on a specific customer segment that even the Chief Financial Officer will take notice of.

Another important figure that should be noted is the average checking account balance of over $5,000 of these High Deposit Households. While account profitability is recognized as a better measurement of checking account value, we are assuming that most institutions do not have cost accounting systems in place or agreed-upon cost accounting assumptions to accurately measure the checking account value with this methodology. While somewhat simplistic, average checking account balance at least does give a relative measurement of checking account value. In other words, a higher checking balance is probably more profitable than a lower checking balance.

These findings support the prioritized strategic recommendation to increase checking account penetration among High Deposit Households and even give the marketer some preliminary data to project an acceptable acquisition cost for the promotion. A similar analysis can be conducted to determine the value of any customer segment an institution has identified as a potential target market.

Product-Driven vs. Market-Driven Strategies

The way in which an institution analyzes and establishes this acceptable acquisition cost will depend upon the marketing focus of the institution. Specifically, an institution that is Product-focused will establish the acquisition cost based on the value of the specific checking account and related costs, while an institution that is Customer focused will review the "profitability" (however that can be defined) of the household's total account relationship.

A Product-focused strategy may select checking account balance as the driving factor in determining profitability depending upon the capabilities of the profitability module of their MCIF and, *more importantly*, the validity of product cost allocations. A Customer-focused strategy identifies the target customer segment for checking account growth and then develops products and offers for each segment. Whatever the strategy, the MCIF is a necessity for identifying and targeting the most potentially profitable new checking account customer profile.

Offer Development

Using checking account balance as the primary criteria for determining the value or potential profitability of a checking account enables an institution to use the MCIF to prioritize customers that do not have checking accounts based on their projected checking account balance. Offers can then be specifically designed for each of these customer segments identified by the MCIF. The strength of the offer is all important in getting customers to switch their checking account relationship. With this exercise, we are attempting to project the average checking account balances of prospective checking customers and then developing a strategy based on this value to attract their checking accounts.

This can be accomplished by ranking checking account customers by balance range and analyzing these groups of customers on a variety of product usage characteristics that are maintained on the database to identify common characteristics for clustering segmentation (based on *household specific* data). Using appended data for this segmentation of customers based on product usage can increase the effectiveness of this segmentation. Some examples are given below.

Checking Account Balance	Household Definition
$10,000+	- Total Deposits >$35,000, Regular Savings >$5,000 - Total Deposits >$35,000, Multiple Service User
$7,500–$9,999	- Total Deposits >$20,000, Multiple Service User+ 4 Services - Total Deposits >$20,000, Nontraditional Product Usage
$5,000–$4,999	- Home Equity Credit Line >$7,500 - Mortgage Loan >$150,000

While Total Household Deposit Balance is virtually always a key indicator of a high checking balance, other product usage can be used to identify nuggets of opportunity for high balance checking accounts such as high loan balances or non-traditional product usage (in combination with deposit usage) as indicated above.

While I have focused on using the MCIF to identify and rank checking account potential based on projected checking balances, this same methodology can be used to identify the target market for whatever type of checking account the institution has identified as "profitable" and decided to market.

This type of analysis can identify customers whose checking account relationship a financial institution would like to have. However, the likelihood of these prioritized customer segments actually opening a checking account will vary. For example, a customer with greater than $50,000 in total deposits and 5 or more accounts, who is also a member of the institution's Seniors Club, may be 10 times more likely to open a checking account than a single service mortgage loan customer with a $150,000+ balance. My point is that while the value of the checking account of each segment (measured by average balance) may be similar, the relative acquisition cost will vary significantly by segment.

How can we be sure that the nonchecking customers we have identified for checking promotion will maintain the projected checking balances when they do open an account? Chart II and III show a comparison of checking account usage among high balance customer segments and the average checking balance of high deposit segments over a one-year period that included aggressive checking account promotion for two institutions. Chart II presents comparative checking account penetration and Chart III presents comparative average checking balances.

As you can see, both institutions had a significant increase in checking account penetration among their targeted segments during this measurement period, which was the result of aggressive target offers. Most importantly with this increase in checking penetration, the average checking account balance remained about the same. This confirms our basic assumption that high deposit customers that open new checking accounts will increase their checking account balances to the average balances of the group.

Clearly the estimated value of a new checking account dictates the acceptable acquisition cost of that account. In determining this acceptable acquisition cost you should include all hard, incremental costs associated with the checking promotion. Optimally, the long-term value of the relationship should be taken into consideration in estab-

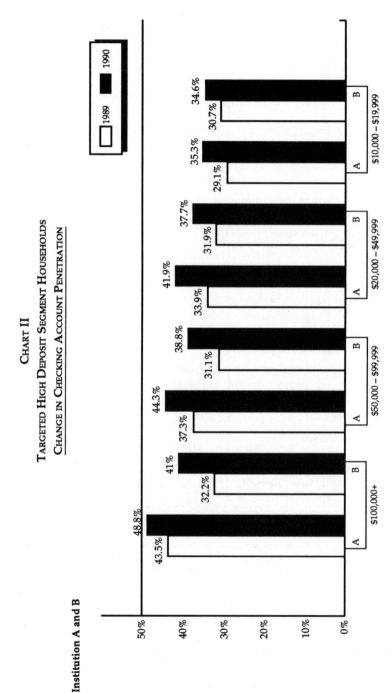

CHART II
TARGETED HIGH DEPOSIT SEGMENT HOUSEHOLDS
CHANGE IN CHECKING ACCOUNT PENETRATION

Institution A and B

1989 1990

$100,000+

A 43.5% 48.8%
B 32.2% 41%

$50,000 – $99,999

A 37.3% 44.3%
B 31.1% 38.8%

$20,000 – $49,999

A 33.9% 41.9%
B 31.9% 37.7%

$10,000 – $19,999

A 29.1% 35.3%
B 30.7% 34.6%

Source: FUSION Marketing Group

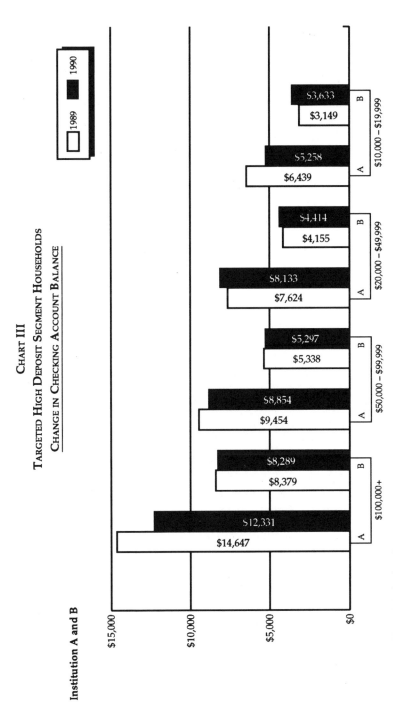

Chart III
Targeted High Deposit Segment Households
Change in Checking Account Balance

Source: FUSION Marketing Group

lishing this value. However, at least checking balance and potential impact on cost of funds are starting points.

This predetermined value has a direct impact on the strength offer that will be targeted to each identified customer segment. The MCIF's segmentation and select capabilities also enable an institution to vary the checking account offer based on the value it has determined for each targeted segment. Financial institutions do not have to make the same checking offer to all customers.

In a targeted direct mail promotion execution, there are a number of variables that are interrelated in tailoring the checking account offer to the targeted customer segment:

- Product
- Offer
- Copy Tone

On the following page is an offer grid for five hypothetical customer segments that illustrate some possible variations.

The segmentation capabilities of the MCIF and offer variables like those above give an institution the ability to design a checking account solicitation plan for virtually every customer *based on the value of checking account or household relationship*. This is what Rapp and Collins in their book *The Great Marketing Turnaround* described as **Individualized Marketing**—which is the essence of Database Marketing. The ability to segment and analyze the "profitability" (based on whatever measurement an institution uses) of the checking account of homogeneous groupings of customers enables the fine tuning of both the product *and* the strength of offer, as detailed above.

The key element in offer development is the ability to *predict* the value of the checking account relationship from identified customer segments. Instead of forcing the relationship for the customer to qualify for the offer, we can predict the relationship and individualize the offer. If an institution determines that a household with $50,000 in total deposits maintains an Average Checking Account Balance of greater than $6,500 compared to Credit Card Households with Credit Line of $1,000 who maintain an average Checking Account balance of less than $750, then offer development is relatively easy. (**Note:** Again, this is a very simplistic example of measuring the value of the

Checking Account based on balance level. This same methodology can be used if an institution can establish profitability measures by account or customer segment.)

Segment	Product	Offer	Copy
• $100,000+ Deposit Hshld	- Money Market checking	- Guaranteed Free Checking For Life (regardless of balance) - Unlimited Free Checks. - $100 Cash Bonus.	"As one of our best customers, we want to extend an offer you cannot refuse. We will even come to your home to open your account."
• $50,000+ Deposit Hshld, Age 55+	- Seniors Checking Package	- Free Checking. - Free Checks. - $25 Cash Bonus.	"In reviewing your account relationship we noticed that you do not have a checking account and want to make a personal, special offer for you to open one."
• <$10,000 Deposit Hshld, Age 55+	- Seniors Checking Package	- Free Checking. - First Order of Checks Free.	"You may qualify for our Senior Checking Package."
• Mortgage or Installment Loan (identified as Homeowner), Age 25-45	- Homeowner Checking Package	- Free Checking. - Free Checks. - Free ATM Card. - No Annual Fee Credit Card. - Discount on Loans.	"We want to do more business with customers like you, and have a group of services that fit your financial needs."
• Low Deposit Households, Age <55, Unknown	- Thrifty Checking	- $250 Minimum Balance - First Order of Checks Free. - Free ATM Card.	"You can get the best checking account in town from 1st National."

Timing/Event Triggers

Timing is all important to maximize the effectiveness of Database Marketing. Database Marketing Plans attempt to take advantage of predicting future buying behavior. For example, IRA and Home Equity Lending promotions were traditionally scheduled during the March-April period because of the increased associated new account activity during this period. Institutions can use their MCIF to analyze new account activity in order to identify the best schedule for Checking Account solicitations.

The basic buying pattern of "normal" activity for new checking accounts can be identified by an institution simply by looking its own new checking account activity by month for the past 12 to 18 months (of course, taking into consideration the timing of any checking account promotions). This data should reflect the new checking account activity of the market.

Our experience indicates that there is little seasonality in new checking account response if the prime target market can be identified and solicited with an appealing offer.

This is not to say that an optimum promotion window for new checking accounts cannot be identified by account activity within the customer base (i.e., Event Triggers). This can be done and *is very effective*. There are certain database Account Activity/Event Triggers that *can be easily identified* that increase the likelihood of a customer opening a new checking account. For example, a New Household or Approaching Maturing CD are Event Triggers that can be identified as increasing the response to checking account offers.

Effective database marketing is based on simply picking up previous buying behavior and taking advantage of these patterns through selective, targeted promotion. Virtually everyone wants to cross-sell, but relatively few cross-selling promotions are effective. Checking account cross-sell can be very effective if the customer segment is "right," the offer is "right," and the timing is "right."

Cross-Selling Existing Checking Account Customers

While we have focused on cross-selling Checking Accounts to existing customers, an institution must also look at the cross-sell potential that exists within its checking account customers. After all, haven't we

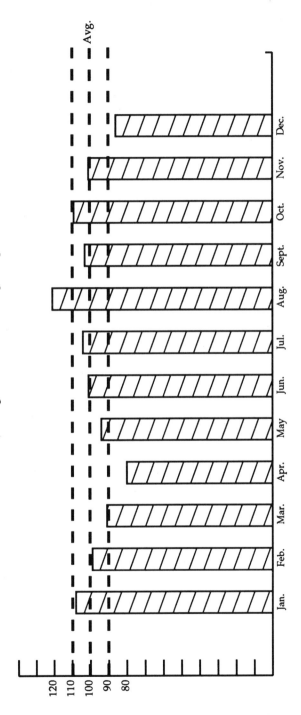

CHART IV

MONTHLY NEW CHECKING ACCOUNT ACTIVITY INDEX

100 Index Base = Average Number Accounts Opened per Month

Source: FUSION Marketing Group

been assuming that checking account usage increases the cross-sell opportunities and effectiveness?

Most financial institutions rely on statement stuffers, point of sale and media advertising to cross-sell their checking account customers (and other customers). Significant resources have been put behind statement stuffers and point of sale advertising with little consideration for the target market. While checking account customers are prime prospects for cross-selling other products, statement stuffers are terrifically wasteful when compared to the targeting efficiencies of an MCIF. Consider these examples of product promotions through checking account statement stuffers (all actual!) that are probably ineffective because they cannot be targeted to the most potentially responsive customers:

- Home Equity Loan/Line—How many receiving statements are Homeowners (typically less than 50%) and how many of those have enough equity to qualify for a 80% loan-to-value loan?

- IRAs —The target market of this product is shrinking. The IRA is an example of a product that absolutely *requires* comprehensive targeting methodologies to ensure success.

- High Deposit Package Account—this product requires a $10,000 aggregate deposit balance. Less than 20% of present checking account customers will qualify.

To increase the effectiveness of statement stuffers for a financial institution, you can use database marketing techniques of analyzing the target market product usage, previous buying behavior, and demographics to determine what products should be included in a statement stuffer program. For example, if 65% of Checking Account households have an average balance of less than $750, they likely hold little potential for certificates of deposits or annuities. Conversely, if 40% of the Money Market Account households have balances greater than $20,000, they likely do hold cost effective deposit potential through statement stuffer communication.

We have seen that Checking Account usage increases the cross-sell potential of that customer. However, to be most effective the products and offers must be tailored to the subsegments that can be identified within the overall customer base. Again, an institution can use its MCIF to identify checking account customer subsegments, and by analyzing their previous buying behavior (based on product usage and balance levels) determine the products that they (as a group) are most likely to buy. This identifies their financial service needs and their capacity to buy.

Using Affinity and Amount segmentation strategies of database marketing can significantly increase cross-selling efficiencies. Following are some specific, basic examples of checking customer subsegments identified through the MCIF and developing specific product/offers for each.

$100,000+ Mortgage Loan/Open Date Less Than 5 Years

These checking customers offer excellent cross-sell potential because they are heavy financial service users. These customers are most likely heavy credit users with limited deposit potential *at the present time*. Their greatest product cross-sell product potential: Credit Cards, Line Of Credit/Installment Loan, Money Market Account/Regular Savings/Low Balance Withdrawable CD (they do want to start saving), and possibly home equity loans/lines (additional analysis from the MCIF enables an institution to determine their equity and to selectively offer equity lending products). These customers have virtually no capacity for significant deposit generation from traditional certificates.

High Deposit/Money Market/Multiple Certificates

These identified checking customers are very loyal customers. They hold *excellent* additional deposit potential. Their primary product potential is additional Certificates of Deposit (since most are multiple CD households). Because of the loyalty factor they also likely hold potential for nontraditional investment products because they will listen and believe advice from their primary financial institution. These high deposit households hold very little credit potential, although they will be responsive to credit card offers (particularly if age can be used as a deselect). Once they have the credit card they will maintain relatively low balances.

205

Single Service/Checking Balance Less Than $500

These checking customers make up a large majority of the checking account base of most financial institutions but they hold limited cross-sell potential. The primary cross-sell opportunities are credit products, particularly Credit Cards, Overdraft Protection and Debit Cards. However, be aware that the turn-down rate of this customer group will be *very high*. They (as a group) hold *no potential for additional deposits* (at this time or in the near future). If they do open a Savings Account, their average balance will be $250–$300.

Concluding

The MCIF is a powerful tool to develop specific products and special offers, and to communicate one-on-one to meet the needs of the customer on an individualized basis. This special recognition gives a financial institution the opportunity to increase sales/product usage through customer satisfaction.

In *Megatrends 2000,* John Naisbitt and Patricia Aburdene conclude with this statement: "Recognition of the individual is the thread connecting every trend described in this book." They talk of the "Age of the Individual" and comment that "when the focus was on the institution, individuals got what suited the institution; everybody got the same thing. No more. With the focus on the individual has come the primacy of the consumer."

Hopefully, this has given readers some insights as to how to use their MCIFs to cost effectively increase checking account penetration within their customer base and to increase product usage among existing checking account customers. More importantly, it is hoped that it will stimulate ideas for more creative uses of the MCIF for more effective marketing.

16

LINE OF CREDIT— A CASE HISTORY

Tom Bourdage
U.S. Bank of Oregon

I n 1982, U.S. Bank developed a line of credit product that would enhance our consumer product mix and attract new customers to the bank. This product has evolved into one of our most profitable. This chapter describes our bank and discusses our current marketing environment, our current marketing tactics, short- and long-term objectives, strategy and tactics, and monitoring measurement related to the direct response marketing of our line of credit product. The basis for this chapter is a paper I submitted to the Bank Marketing School in December 1989, titled "1-3 Year Direct Response Marketing Plan, Line of Credit Product." That paper, which details the development of our program, is available from the BMA Information Center.

Present Marketing Environment

The Northwest Market

The historical market for U. S. Bank has been the state of Oregon. With recent expansions in Northern California and potential responsibility for Idaho, our market responsibilities are expanding. Economically, the marketing environment is dominated by the timber, tourism, and service industries. During the late seventies and the early eighties our market's economy was severely affected by the high interest rates and national decline in the demand for wood products.

A large portion of our market is dependent on farming and agricultural products. Population concentrations are located west of the Cascade Mountains and along the interstate highway. The people are conservative and responsible in their use of credit. They are slow to change and have generally used fixed-rate, fixed-term borrowing for consumer debt. Only recently has our customer base begun using revolving, variable-rate line of credit for major purchase transactions. This change may have occurred because of increased awareness resulting from the marketing efforts of lenders. Recently, a favorable interest rate environment has also made lines of credit a less expensive way to borrow. Until the last couple of years, bank cards were the predominant source of revolving credit.

Economic Factors

Our market is very dependent on the economy of the rest of the country. If interest rates rise and the demand for wood products slows, our economy will suffer. Historically, in an economic slowdown, we are one of the first economies to feel the effects.

Presently, Oregon ranks as one of the fastest growing states measured by wage and salary employment in 1989. We have current wage and salary growth rates of 4.1%, an increase of 45,700 over 1988. Personal income growth is at a rate that keeps us in the top ten in the nation. [1]

Oregon is also experiencing a strong growth in new business development. Recently a number of foreign companies have located here. New people are coming here in support of the high-tech business growth. Over the past few years Oregon, like much of the country, has experienced an economic boom.

Changes in the Market

A number of changes have occurred in the banking industry in our market in the past 5 years.

---

[1] John W. Mitchell, Ph.D.; *N.W. Business Barometer*, U.S. Bancorp Publication, Volume 28, No. 2, May 1990.

1. Banking deregulation has heated competition for the retail customers.

2. State banking regulations have allowed the entrance of new banks.

3. Consumers have become more sophisticated in shopping for banking products.

4. Technology has provided the ability to deliver consumer loan products faster and more economically.

5. Banks have become more dependent on fee income as interest margins shrink.

6. New financial products have been introduced.

7. Customers demand quality service.

U.S. Bank of Oregon

U.S. Bank of Oregon is the largest subsidiary of the parent holding company U.S. Bancorp. Some statistics as of the end of June 1990 for U.S. Bancorp:

Financial Results (June 1990)	U.S. Bancorp
Total Assets	$17.7 Billion
Total Deposits	$13.7 Billion
Total Bank Branches	370
Total Employees	9,900
1990 YTD Net Income	$89.4 Million
Return on Assets	1.10%
Return on Equity	17.20%

Over the years, U.S. Bank of Oregon has maintained the corporate image as a local hometown bank. After the consolidation of consumer loan processing and approval, our perceived image changed. Our overall corporate goal is to deliver competitive retail loan products with the best possible level of customer service. We have positioned our products and delivery to be competitive, customer driven, and efficient.

Share of Retail Bank Products

In the Oregon market more than 50% of the total households have checking accounts and/or savings accounts. Approximately 35%-

40% of the households have a mortgage loan, auto loan, or VISA card. From our research, only 20% had a line of credit product. We estimate we have 15% of the line of credit market in Oregon.

On average, each of our customers has 1.5 account relationships with our bank. This presents a real marketing opportunity since we have about a 37% market share of all Oregon households maintaining a retail banking relationship. The demographics of our customers show them to be older and more upscale than the general population. We have the largest share of the market in the Portland area. [2]

Product profitability is foremost in our delivery of consumer loan products. We now understand that we do not have to be the lowest-cost provider to maintain market share.

Our Line of Credit Product

Our product was first introduced to the Oregon market eight years ago. Our original product was accessible through branch advances, overdrafts, and telephone transfers. About three years ago we added direct check access. This enhancement was necessary to develop a longer-range strategy for soliciting new markets.

An analysis of our line of credit product was necessary in developing a long-term marketing plan. The process included asking such questions as: [3]

1. How many customers are currently using this product?

2. How are these customers segmented (i.e., what are the similarities among customers using this product)?

3. What is the current volume?

4. What is the projected volume for next year?

5. What are the costs and revenues?

6. How price sensitive is this service?

---

[2] Source: *1990 Oregon Funds Probe Presentation*, U.S. Bank of Oregon, April 1990, Presentation by Marketing Research.

[3] Diane M. Marien, Robert P. Ford, Robert J. Losh; *The Product Managers Handbook—A Practical Guide for Bank Product Managers*, 1983.

7. What are the present and projected gross profit and profit margins?

8. What are the product's major strengths and weaknesses?

9. What enhancements could be developed to increase volume?

The need to know your customers is the foundation for the development of any product enhancements. Even after you fully understand the factors related to the product enhancements, continued analysis is necessary to ensure continued profitability.

Competitors' Marketing Efforts

Competition for the line of credit products in our market started with the introduction of the product by a local savings and loan about 8 years ago. At the time the new product hit the market, our only revolving product was a bank credit card. The savings and loan that first introduced the product was attempting to develop a niche in the revolving consumer market without the cost of bank card franchising. We developed our version of the product about 6 months later.

As the market matured there was additional competition for the same customers. A number of out-of-state lending institutions began to offer line of credit products. In many cases, limits offered were more aggressive. In order to compete, it was necessary to differentiate our product.

With an analysis of the current users in our customer base, we determined the product was a relationship product. More than 70% of the customers that have a line of credit product also had a demand deposit relationship. As an attempt to maintain the relationship, we introduced a relationship-pricing benefit when the customer chooses automatic payment from a U.S. Bank checking account. We continue to enjoy a marketing advantage over our competition with this relationship-priced product.

Where will we be in the next five years?

1. Increased reliance on fee income as interest margins continue to shrink.

2. Changes in technology to deliver services more profitably.

3. Banks being forced to eliminate nonprofitable, traditional retail products.

4. Expanded hours.

5. Fewer banks (as more banks are acquired).

6. More reliance on other distribution channels to market products (direct response marketing).

7. More dependence on new markets.

8. More dependence on multiple-product relationships.

The next five years will require the banking industry to deliver the products that best fit the needs of the customer and return a profit to the bank. This means the products that have been marginally profitable to the bank must be evaluated for their benefit. Banks will be required to know the profitability and potential of each product, relationship, customer, and market.

Current Marketing Strategies

Two years ago we developed a direct response marketing proposal for our line of credit product to be marketed to our current customer base. The marketing effort focused on the "mass market" appeal of a line of credit as a secondary consumer loan. The offer was targeted to current customers with other consumer relationships. The intent was to offer a line of credit to customers as a retention strategy.

We have also attempted to market the line of credit product using general advertising, such as newspapers and radio. As with any general advertising campaign, the results were difficult to measure. Our last campaigns have not included general media advertising.

Direct Mail Strategy

Our earliest promotional efforts in marketing our personal line of credit products consisted of developing a test for a direct mail strategy to cross-sell our current customer base. Our target market strategy for the personal line of credit of $5,000 is summarized below:

- Retail customer with a current borrowing relationship.
- Lives in Oregon.

- Evidence of a good payment history.
- Offer was "preapproved" or "invitation," depending on Credit Bureau screen.
- Not a current line of credit customer with us.

Source of names for our test solicitation was limited to our customers with the following relationships:

- Direct and indirect consumer borrowing customers with a minimum 6-month credit history.
- Our first-mortgage customers.
- VISA customers with limits under $10,000.

Results from our first efforts with the direct mail solicitation were higher than forecast. Response rates were 4.5% to 5%, twice as high as industry averages. The number of new relationships from this first effort justified the further development of a marketing strategy to our current customer base.

The biannual mail strategy of our current customer base was renamed the "Continuity Mailing." As of the end of 1989, we had mailed to the same target base four times and continued to receive response rates higher than industry averages.

Direct mail efforts have contributed about 40% of our 1989 and 1990 volume for our line of credit products. Our success with the direct response solicitation has resulted in placing a greater emphasis on direct mail marketing in the 1990s.

At the same time general advertising of other retail consumer products resulted in an overall increase in new openings and activation of existing lines. About 20% of the new lines opened were single-service relationships. Short-range plans include a cross-sell offer to those new customers for an additional product.

In summary, our direct mail strategy for soliciting lines of credit products over the past two years has resulted in a substantial increase in new business. The direct response mail has proven to be the most measurable method of marketing. This strategy is the foundation for the marketing plans over the next 3 years for our line of credit product.

Strategy for the Next 1-3 Years

Our line of credit products has been one of the fastest growing direct consumer loan products in our portfolio for the past 2 years. Delinquencies and losses have remained manageable. From a profitability standpoint, the line of credit product is a very profitable product in our retail consumer product mix.

One of the objectives in the delivery and servicing of consumer loans at our bank is streamlining the process. A line of credit product, unlike an installment loan, is a very cost-effective product to acquire. Once the account is established the relationship can be serviced very economically. Historically, the product has complemented the sale of other retail products with the bank.

As competition among lenders for consumer loans heats up, it becomes necessary to adjust our long-term strategy. Early in 1990 we were given approval to test market the direct response mailing concept in a new market. This was our first effort in marketing lines of credit to noncustomers.

Our previous experience in direct response marketing, delivering, and servicing has opened the possibilities of entering new markets. With an overall corporate strategy of expanding into new markets, this product is a natural for market entry. It could also work well as a product to test market before a decision to enter a market is finalized. The test could be accomplished with existing servicing capacities using a proven direct response mailing strategy.

Marketing plans involving the expansion of existing product lines into new markets require that we first determine market potential. Here is how we determined market potential in the targeted markets for our test:

- We surveyed the market
  Market research
    Measures current product offerings.
    Surveys potential users and determines the desirability of product offer.
    Focus groups to test concept.
    National research available.

- Other vendor-provided services
  Credit Bureaus.
  Number of households.
  Income levels.
  Number of trades on file.

- Segmentation Clustering
  Cluster segmentation.
  Demographic/psychographic clustering.

- Evaluate market potential using indirect lending and the mail
  Indirect Business.
  Enter a new market with indirect business.
  Minimize the cost without branch overhead.
  Evaluate the competitive environment.

- Direct Response Mailing
  Cost effective.
  Measurable.
  Targeted.

Research using bureau files for these markets determined a potential market sufficient to test 10,000-15,000 potential customers with a mailing. The mail results were just under 2% overall, which is consistent with industry averages.

Untapped Markets

Up to now, even within our own market, potential customers have not been solicited for our line of credit product. Our plan includes a solicitation of noncustomers who meet the demographic profile of our current line of credit customers.

Existing Customers

We will continue to market the line of credit products to our current market base. The ability to target segments of our current base using cross-sell, household, and cluster grouping allows us to refresh the potential market with additional names each time we mail.

Our longer-term strategy for the line of credit products is ever changing. Continued reliance on the current market to provide the customers necessary to meet the corporate growth goals is shortsighted. We must continue to refine our product offerings and identify new markets where the product will compete.

Supporting the Strategy Using Segmentation

Concept of segmentation:

> Market segmentation is based on the idea that not all consumers seek the same benefits nor do they necessarily desire to pay the same price. A segment is a group of customers who are alike in the specific features they seek from a class of products or services. Market segmentation implies designing products for specific market segments and adopting marketing strategies accordingly. The simplest forms of market segmentation involve clustering customers according to geographic variables, psychographic or lifestyle variables, attitudes, for example, risk aversions and behavior. Once customers are organized into market segments, marketers can capitalize on commonalities within these segments and reach their target audiences more effectively and efficiently. A product can be molded to the peculiarities of the target cluster, and the differentiating traits of the cluster can be exploited for communication purposes. [4]

At U.S. Bank we are using Claritas Corporation's PRIZM program to assist in segmentation. This program is based on census information where neighborhoods are classified into one of forty clusters. Each of the clusters has a descriptive name, such as "Gray Power," "Blue Blood Estates," and is further grouped into twelve broad social groups. The social groups are identified as urban, suburban, town, or rural.

Estimating the market demand for our product involves the process of segmentation. Our past efforts in estimating market potential started by segmenting our customers that are currently using our line of credit products. After we understood our current customer profile, we used that profile in determining our target customers that currently had other relationships with the bank. Our segmentation process

---

[4] Deborah L. Colletti, Melvin R. Crask, Richard J. Fox, D. Mark Jackson, John H. Lindgren, William J. Wichman: *Effective Bank Product Management*, Bank Administration Institute, 1988.

has continued to result in direct mail response rates double the industry averages.

As we enter new markets, or add names to our potential mail solicitations, it first becomes necessary to determine the market potential. The next step is segmenting the new market into likely users of our line of credit products. This preplanning will result in a more targeted, higher-responding customer.

Market segmentation is the basis for our direct response mailing strategy. For the next three years, we are focused on a process to better identify the customers who can be solicited with a line of credit product that minimizes risk and maximizes return. Mass marketing a line of credit product is not only costly but risky when a segmentation strategy is not considered. We are committed to better understanding our customers and their needs.

Measuring and Monitoring Results

One of the most important aspects of this or any marketing plan is the ability to monitor and measure the results. Our strategy in marketing our line of credit product using direct mail anticipated the need to monitor the accounts after they were acquired.

Each of the marketing efforts within our bank is supported by a written proposal to senior management. That proposal outlines the concept, benefit, target, and the expected results. Prior to any marketing campaign, expected results are clearly defined with the production, sales, and operational management to gain their support for the proposal.

Once the campaign is in the market, the same people are informed on the progress of the results on a weekly basis. Since the success of the promotion is dependent on the sales and support staff, communication of the progress is vital to measure progress of the efforts.

Additionally, once the promotion or the focused marketing effort has ended, the evaluation of the results is accomplished with a wrapup session. In that session we evaluate how we did in relation to the goal, what went smoothly, what was lacking, how realistic the goal was, and what opportunities we should exploit.

Our monitoring system provides a management report monthly that identifies the accounts from each mail solicitation. A monthly report tracks the outstanding accounts, the delinquency, and the losses for each mailing group. This gives product management the tools to compare usage patterns of direct mail respondents with the branch-acquired accounts. If it is determined that accounts react differently to the portfolio, adjustments in the product offer can be made to either the mailing or the branch origination.

Another monitoring requirement for understanding the overall marketing strategy is measuring the profitability of separate acquisition strategies. This is a key element in determining and supporting the corporate profitability goals. The goal is to generate quality asset growth while maintaining the necessary return to support the overall corporate goals.

The overall marketing plan must consider the corporate goals in the support of individual product profitability. This enables us to focus the selling efforts on the products that give us the best return. Additionally, if we understand the cost difference in acquiring and boarding line of credit accounts using direct mail vs. the branch, we can better understand the overall profit contribution.

A management report allows us to monitor the profitability over the life of the product. By monitoring and measuring we will have the ability to determine long-term profitability of direct response marketing as a marketing strategy.

Conclusion

The marketing plan for the next 3 years for our line of credit products was developed because of results of our direct response marketing for the past 2 years. Our decision to enter new markets is consistent with the corporate goal of market expansion. The profitability of this product has allowed us to expand the plan into new markets. This line of credit product is our entry level product, to be used as a predictor of product acceptance and market potential in new markets.

This market plan works very well to fulfill the growth goals of U.S. Bank of Oregon as well as U.S. Bancorp.

Reference List

Deborah L. Colletti, Melvin R. Crask, Richard J. Fox, D. Mark Jackson, John H. Lindgren, William J. Wichman. *Effective Bank Product Management*, Bank Administration Institute, Rolling Meadows, Illinois, 1988.

Diane M. Marien, Robert P. Ford, Robert J. Losh. *The Product Managers Handbook—A Practical Guide for Bank Product Managers*, Bank Administration Institute, Rolling Meadows, Illinois, 1983.

John W. Mitchell, Ph.D. *N.W. Business Barometer*, U.S. Bancorp Publication, Volume 28, No. 2, May 1990.

1990 Oregon Funds Probe Presentation, U.S. Bank of Oregon, July 1989, Presentation by Marketing Research.

U.S. Bancorp's 1988 Annual Report to Stockholders.

Marketing Research, *1989 Segmentation Application for Personal Line of Credit Product*, U.S. Bank of Oregon.

17

ACTIVATION OF CREDIT LINES

Jonathan Cohn
FUSION Marketing Group

The cost of acquiring loans (whether credit card, home equity, or line of credit) can be very high. Depending on the variables of the program—type of loan acquired, the method of soliciting (direct mail, branch, telemarketing, multistep application, etc.), mailing quantities of the solicitation, account-opening incentives such as bonuses or fee waivers, customers or prospects—the acquisition cost can range from as little as $5 per credit card accounts for current customers to several hundred dollars for multistep non-customer home equity lines. Besides the initial acquisition cost, there are annual processing expenses for statements, postage, legal reserves for the loan commitments, and much more that make the activation of accounts vital to the long-term success and profitability of these accounts.

In this chapter, activation is defined as the consumer's using an acquired credit line for purchases (credit cards) and/or for revolving credit (credit lines and credit cards). The payment of an annual fee by a consumer with no other transaction or borrowing activity *does not* constitute usage. Most institutions have instituted annual fees as a means of partially recouping the operating costs of credit card accounts or credit lines.

The activation of credit line accounts has received a great deal of attention over the past several years, as institutions have attempted to increase their profit margins on credit cards and lines of credit, especially as deposit interest rates have been deregulated. While companies have used a variety of programs, this chapter will address the most widely used and successful of these programs. The activation programs used by institutions include:

- Convenience checks

- Fee waivers

- Usage programs

- Sweepstakes

- Special program tie-ins

- Rebate programs

The above programs are applicable to all types of credit line accounts. While most of the historical data on account activation is related to credit cards, the increased penetration of home equity lines and unsecured credit lines has generated similar account activation programs. As in other areas of financial services marketing, a number of institutions with mature activation programs are beginning to analyze their customer bases to identify the customers most likely to respond to activation programs. Through the application of segmentation and modeling methodologies, these institutions are moving toward more targeted activation mailings, which result in reduced costs while maintaining, or in some cases exceeding, historical revenue flows.

Convenience Checks

Of all programs developed by financial institutions for the activation of credit lines and the generation of both cash advance fees and revolving, interest-earning balances, convenience checks have proved to be the best program by a wide margin. A recent survey of the most profitable credit card issuers by a credit card trade organization showed that the *issuers ranked convenience checks as the single most successful and profitable program for account activation.*

Convenience checks are basically checks that consumers use to draw funds from the available balances in their credit card or credit line accounts. The checks look just like regular consumer checks and are normally personalized with the customer's name and address. The customer may receive a book of checks when the account is opened or may receive a small supply of checks periodically during the year to coincide with high usage periods.

These items clear through the banking system like any other check. The depositing bank clears the item to the issuing bank as shown in the magnetic ink character recognition (MICR) line. Depending on the issuing institution, the customer's account number may or may not be shown in the MICR line. For some issuers, the check volume does not warrant an automated posting system; the checks clear through a "dead pocket" in the check reader/sorter and are posted to the card account by key entry. The items are posted as a *cash advance* (via check) and begin to accrue interest immediately. At the same time, a cash advance fee, if applicable, is assessed.

Surveys of check usage have shown that the primary uses are:

- Debt consolidation
- Taxes (quarterly estimated, real estate and income taxes)
- Home improvements
- Holiday purchases
- Vacations

To encourage usage of these checks by customers, promotional packages of the checks are mailed by financial institutions to account holders in early spring (to catch income tax and real estate tax payments), early summer (for vacations and home improvements), and mid-fall (for holiday purchases). Bill consolidation takes place at all periods of the year, but the above mailing schedule accommodates the bill consolidation feature. Although most usage of the checks occurs in the 5 weeks immediately after a mailing, checks continue to clear throughout the remainder of the year as consumers require funds.

More advanced programs incorporate monthly activator check mailings to carefully selected subsegments of their files. These mailings are in addition to the standard new account check mailings. Such programs use sophisticated database management techniques to identify and track convenience check usage on the application file level. Specified transactor activity is used as an event trigger to select accounts for the monthly mailings. By targeting high-transaction potential customers, these institutions maximize the revenue potential of their portfolios.

Most institutions promote convenience checks as a debt-consolidation tool with which customers can consolidate many smaller bills into one and make a single, lower monthly payment at a more advantageous rate than that offered on other charge cards. This single monthly payment can be lower because monthly minimums for *all* of the various bills are avoided.

As mentioned above, most issuers view convenience checks as a major profit generator for their credit line accounts. The financial case for using checks is illustrated in the Convenience Check Worksheet. Institutions can use the worksheet to determine if they should proceed with such a program.

CONVENIENCE CHECK WORKSHEET

Total accounts: _____

Total active accounts*: _____

Planned mailing quantity: _____

Estimated Monthly Clearings and Revenues

Month	No. of items	$ cleared	Advance Fees[†]
January			
February			
March			
April			
May			
June			
July			
August			
September			
October			
November			
December			
Total			

* *Accounts with transactions (excluding charges for annual fees) or revolving balances in the past 12 months.*

[†] *Cash advance fees, if applicable, or not waived for promotional reasons.*

<u>CONVENIENCE CHECK PROGRAM PROFITABILITY</u>

1. Total advances: _____
2. Average number of months on books: _____
3. Net interest spread*: _____
Net interest revenue: (#1/#2) × #3 _____
Plus: cash advance fees, if any _____
Less: marketing costs _____
Program net income _____
* Net funding cost of the portfolio.

Example:

A typical card issuer with 500,000 active accounts can expect that 10% to 20% of its customers will use checks during a 12-month period. Average check size varies by season, with peak borrowings around the Christmas holidays and in April. "Average check" size is approximately $550. Assuming a 15% penetration of the file, or 75,000 items annually, the program will generate balances of more than $41 million. Most consumers will carry a cash advance balance between 4 and 6 months before paying off the balance.

Marketing costs vary by the size of the mailings, frequency of issuance, and other services that may provide for automatic replenishment of checks to account holders. A typical institution, mailing to a portion of its customer file twice annually, will have marketing costs that range from 50 to 65 cents per item mailed, including first class postage. Using these assumptions, we can complete the program profitability worksheet:

<u>SAMPLE PROGRAM PROFITABILITY</u>

1. Total advances: $41,000,000
2. Average number of months on books: 4
3. Net interest spread: 5.5%
Net interest revenue: (#1/#2) * #3: $563,750

Plus: cash advance fees, if any   -0-
Less: marketing costs $275,000
(500,000 pieces mailed)
Program net income $288,750

Cash advance fees are zero in the above example. At institutions with cash advance fees, this provides additional revenue. Many institutions have found that having promotional periods during which cash advance fees are waived is very effective in increasing response levels. One issuer showed *a 33% increase in response during the promotional fee-waiver period vs. the same period the year before when fees were not waived.* While sacrificing some fee income, consumers' response levels during the promotional periods and the resulting interest income justify the fee waiver. In the above example, a 2% cash advance fee would have generated more than $800,000 in fee income, ignoring promotional fee waivers.

Convenience Check User Characteristics

Users of convenience checks mirror the normal characteristics of most credit users. Most institutions do not mail to their entire customer base but select the most promising segments for receipt of the checks. In general, the prime prospects for convenience checks (in order of importance) are

- Previous cash advance history in past 12 months

- Maintained revolving balances in past 12 months

- Opened the account in past 18 months

- Has high average monthly transaction volume (more than six transactions per month)

Important Operational Considerations

Offering convenience checks to credit card holders poses some potential operational problems for institutions to consider.

Replacement Checks
- Because convenience checks are not used on a daily or regular basis, the institution will receive calls from customers who have misplaced their checks. Because these customers only call when they foresee an imminent need for using a check, a rapid check-replacement program is essential.

Lost/Stolen Checks
- The institution needs to determine how these items will be handled: Will the accounts be closed; new checks issued; stop payments made; etc.?

Check Minimums
- While convenience checks average approximately $500, most institutions impose a minimum check size, normally $250 or more.

Annual Fee Waivers

For many years, virtually all credit cards were available without an annual fee. Heavy pressures on bank profit margins in the late 1970s and early 1980s forced many issuers to begin imposing modest ($15-$25) annual fees on the cards. Gold cards typically carry a $40-$50 annual fee, which issuers justify because of the additional services provided to these cardholders. Most admit, however, that the additional cost for purchase protection programs, car rental insurance, and other services is nominal, and much of the higher annual fee goes directly to the bank's net profits.

When the charges were instituted, most issuers justified the expense to consumers as an offset to the convenience of carrying the credit card. As the average household had more than two bank credit cards and eight or more department store, gas, and other charge cards, many consumers used the annual fee charges as a reason to select which card to carry.

In the past several years, some card issuers have introduced new marketing programs for credit cards and credit lines with the annual fee (or the lack of one) as a major selling point. Some of these programs, besides offering a promotional first year free of annual charges, have annual fee waiver programs based on the dollar amount of transactions (purchases) during a year. Depending on the amount spent, all or part of the fee is waived. The dollar thresholds vary, but surveys have shown that $2,500 or more in annual card purchases is an average "waiver" amount at most issuers.

Most issuers are reluctant to share specific data on fee waiver programs; however, several points have been made.
- Waivers of first year fees are now virtually mandatory for gold card acquisitions.
- Fee waivers are less important to consumers who are "revolvers"—they are more interested in the amount of credit and interest rates on the lines.

- Initial studies by several large issuers show that gold programs with fee waivers based on dollar transactions actually have a lower account activation rate than accounts without fee waivers!

- The AT&T Universal Card currently offers a fee-free card if a consumer makes at least one transaction per year on the card. While the card has only been offered for 1 year, the company has attracted almost 5 million accounts. Only time will tell whether the marketing strategy of offering the card without a fee in exchange for one transaction will produce "active" accounts above the banking industry average.

Usage Programs

A number of issuers have used usage bonus programs as a means of providing an incentive to customers to use their cards for purchases. The most notable and ongoing program is that offered by Citibank with its CitiDollars program. Other institutions offer similar programs on a seasonal basis as a means of creating spikes in transaction usage.

Although the mechanics of each program vary, the basic program awards points or rewards based on the number of purchases made and/or the dollar amounts of these purchases. Awards usually consist of free or discounted merchandise, travel, and entertainment. Travel awards are very popular because of the high perceived value of the awards by consumers (although the cost to the issuer can be low, due to volume discount arrangements with the travel providers). A recent program included prizes such as weekend stays in the California wine country, free tickets to Broadway shows, and vacations in Europe.

The major question is Do these programs work? Depending on the particular usage program, competing offers, and the complexity of the award structure, the programs have generally proven to be effective in *activating inactive accounts* and *encouraging increased usage from active accounts*. One issuer who regularly offers bonus programs noted that the programs have provided an activation rate of 15% of *inactive* accounts (accounts with no transactions in 6 months) and have increased the transaction level of active accounts by an average of more than 30%.

However, usage bonus programs can create serious operational, marketing and management problems that can outweigh the benefits of the programs. Data processing systems must be able to calculate points monthly and to accumulate totals and disbursements. The programs increase calls to customer service personnel concerning program eligibility, disputes on transactions, and award fulfillment.

The most serious problem usually involves the fulfillment of awards. While many companies with usage programs provide support services to help bank customer service personnel as well as to directly fulfill prize awards, unexpected program successes can strain their facilities. Miscalculating the projected response rates of the programs can create serious customer relations problems when prizes are not awarded quickly.

In one usage bonus program, an institution had a top award of free travel and hotel in Europe for high performers. The institution miscalculated the number of awards that would be claimed and found itself with more winners than the hotels could handle *in several years*. This created a serious customer relations problem that took years to correct, and it upset many of the issuer's most active accounts. The bank's management, gun-shy over its previous experience, has since shied away from other programs that could have been useful in activating accounts.

Other Activation Programs

The above programs represent the major efforts of most institutions for account activation of credit cards and credit lines. There are a number of other programs that have been used as a means of activating accounts, although they have been limited to a smaller number of programs. These programs include rebate programs, travel company affinity cards, and sweepstakes.

The use of rebates as a reward for using a product is a standard tool in every consumer marketer's arsenal. However, credit card issuers have normally not used this tool, with one notable exception—the Discover Card from Sears. The basic reason for most companies not offering a rebate on credit card transactions has been economic. For many

229

issuers, card volume and portfolio size do not support the additional marketing expense of a rebate for transactions.

The Discover Card uses rebates as a major selling point for the card. The account provides customers with up to a 1% rebate on annual card purchases, and recent surveys have shown that this has been a major incentive for consumers to acquire the card and use it instead of other credit or travel and entertainment cards. The company can afford to provide the rebates primarily because it does not have to share interchange fees with other issuers (as required with MasterCard and VISA). These fees, which average approximately 1.5%, more than cover the promotional costs of the rebates.

Another popular usage activator for a limited number of credit card issuers is the affinity card tie-ins with the frequent flyer programs of the airlines and other travel industry providers.

In the early 1980s, the airline industry created customer loyalty with its frequent flyer programs. Most of the major programs (United, American, and Delta) have upwards of 5 million members each, representing travelers who are heavy users of their credit cards for business and personal trips. These programs provide for additional "miles" as a reward for purchases made using the particular credit cards. These programs have much higher account activation rates than other card programs; however, operating expenses for the cards are also higher, due to the cost of awarding the travel rewards.

Finally, in the past several years, the industry has seen the use of sweepstakes as part of account activation marketing programs. In these campaigns, the sponsoring institution (CitiCorp, VISA, and MasterCard) selects a number of transactions every day and either makes them "free" to consumers or provides for another prize, consisting of free travel, merchandise, or other awards.

These companies note that sweepstakes generally increase transaction volumes significantly, although they have been reluctant to share whether, on a long-term basis, these programs have activated inactive accounts or provided a lasting improvement in the transaction levels of active users.

Conclusions

Account activation of credit line and credit card accounts is necessary for program profitability. Each institution needs to assess the impact of the variety of programs that are available, not only from a program profitability perspective but from the perspective of customer relations and operations. Not every activation program will be successful with every institution—some portfolios will be too small, or operational constraints may make provision of specific programs unwieldy. Only a careful analysis by each institution of its particular capabilities will determine which program, if any, to offer.

However, management needs to recognize that account activation, with its resulting increased interest income and transaction fee income, measures the success of every credit line program and warrants ongoing testing and analysis by the institution. Profitability of the program can be significantly enhanced through the application of database marketing strategies such as segmentation, modeling/scoring, and tracking analysis.

PART 6
SUPPORTING BRANCH OPERATIONS

18

BRANCH LOCATION DECISIONS

Robert Nascenzi
National Decision Systems
Dr. David Hornbeck
Area Location Systems, Inc.

Have you ever seen a McDonald's go out of business? How about a bank branch close down? Consider that in 1988, 329 bank branches were closed in California alone—more than the total number of McDonald's that have ever closed their doors to the public. The difference? Effective location decision making.

Within banking, the importance of a well-defined location strategy is paramount to success. Indeed, the choice of branch locations is the most important decision a bank marketeer must make. A branch is a long-term fixed investment, so the disadvantages of a poor site are difficult to overcome. Products, prices, services, and promotions can be easily imitated, but the advantages of a good site may take years for competitors to overcome.

Historical Context

Most financial institutions in nonunitary states engaged in heavy construction of brick and mortar full-service branches from the 1950s through the 1970s. Since federal and state regulations precluded price competition among financial institutions in terms of interest rates on deposits and loans, banks competed with one another in terms of convenience to the consumer. This basically entailed saturating an area with branches in a variation of the "gas-station-on-every-corner" approach.

The increasing deregulation of banking markets in the 1980s has drastically altered the nature of competition in the industry and its expression in delivery outlets. As banks began to compete with one another in terms of interest paid on accounts and charged on loans, the interest spread between the two narrowed. The resulting squeeze on profits compelled financial institutions to search for means of controlling costs and of generating additional revenues.

Two areas of particular concern were labor costs and the construction and maintenance costs of traditional brick and mortar offices. On the one hand, wages and salaries tended to rise. On the other hand, and probably of more immediate concern, were the costs of constructing and maintaining brick and mortar full-service branches. With the advent of technology potentially allowing more customer self-service at a time of competitive pressure on profits, these costs are less and less tolerable for a bank.

Additionally, many banks are seeking to expand their base of operations in anticipation of Federal laws rescinding limitations on interstate banking, to be better situated competitively when interstate banking is finally permitted. Banks are, therefore, reexamining their entire delivery systems. Consequently, location analysis has become focused above the level of single site decisions: the service network is being viewed as a whole, with an eye to optimizing present service provision while simultaneously supporting the extension of service to entirely new areas.

Impact of Technology

A further pressure for such evaluation is the self-service technological revolution underway. Automatic teller machines (ATMs) have become nearly ubiquitous, particularly since the late 1970s. Originally mere cash-dispensing devices, ATMs have increasingly taken on all routine teller transaction functions: cash withdrawals, deposits, balance inquiries, interaccount transfers, and bill-paying. Trying to increase the availability and convenience of ATMs and thus generate transaction volumes exceeding the break-even level, most banks joined their ATMs into interbank networks, such as Star, Plus, and Cirrus.

Network development, however, contributes to the image of convenience and ubiquity a bank needs. It also cuts the costs of installing a huge network of proprietary ATMs and reduces the danger of oversaturating an area with one's own terminals and thus dropping per-machine transaction volumes permanently below the break-even point.

Another important technological development underway is electronic funds transfer at point of sale (POS) machines. This technology permits direct electronic debiting of a customer's account and crediting of a merchant's account at the point of sale. Wider application of this self-service technology is currently hindered by the debates between banks and retailers as to who should bear the costs of installing and running POS terminals.

While several firms have written off home banking, a new approach is underway. In 1989, it is estimated that there were about 100,000 home banking users nationwide, with a large fraction tied into Prodigy (the IBM and Sears videotex service). Home banking's acceptance and growth, to date, has been limited by the fact that a consumer must have a personal computer. To overcome this limitation, Citicorp unveiled the Enhanced Telephone, a hybrid telephone with a small screen, which it hopes will revive the home banking concept.

These technological developments are extremely important from the point of view of a bank struggling to cut its delivery costs. They reduce customer traffic to a branch, or at least through its lobby, while maintaining or increasing deposit levels and transaction volume. The less face-to-face contact needed to carry out business, the less rationale an institution has for maintaining a dense network of full-service brick and mortar branches.

In short, deregulation and intensified price competition among banks, together with the development of self-service banking technologies, are forcing banks to reevaluate and reconceptualize their entire delivery system.

Location Decision Making

All businesses, whether retailing, manufacturing, or services, are located in a manner to take advantage of market, labor, and/or raw materials. Financial institutions are almost always market-oriented. A financial institution must be accessible to people, and it is this fact that governs site selection. A financial institution, therefore, is primarily a place that the consumer must visit, and the site selection problem has to do entirely with making those consumer visits both possible and convenient.

Location decision making involves a three-step process: (1) selecting a region; (2) choosing a location; (3) picking an actual site. The first step includes the evaluation and selection of a county or MSA that appears to offer opportunity for expansion. The decision to investigate certain areas is usually a policy decision based on in-house information, secondary data, or simply a hunch.

The next stage is to analyze locations, or subareas, within the identified region to determine which location within the region offers the most opportunity. This may be a census tract, zipcode, or, for more consistency, a one-mile or half-mile grid square. Much of this analysis relies on the availability of secondary data. In recent years, huge quantities of demographic and financial data at these low levels of geography have been made available on PCs for easy access and evaluation of specific locations.

Suppose a set of n census tracts is to be evaluated. Let P_i represent the profit potential of the ith tract, C_i the cost associated with developing tract i, and D_i the anticipated demand within tract i. The potential of each tract, then, is a function of development costs and demand, i.e.:

$$P_i = f(C_i D_i)$$

The third stage is the selection of an actual site. This is perhaps the most important step in the process, because the identification, evaluation, and selection of sites is crucial to the successful development of a branch network. Site selection, as opposed to the first two stages, should be based upon primary data gathered from site visits, in addition to available secondary data.

Goals and Objectives

In practice, banks and thrifts vary considerably in the methods they use to make locational decisions. However, three goals are shared by both types of institutions:

1. to maximize the utility of their branch network;

2. to avoid the development of a poor performing site; and

3. to reduce their acquisition ratio (sites evaluated to sites developed).

While striving to meet these goals, several common objectives serve as input to the decision-making process:

1. to narrow the scope of information used to develop key variables that affect a branch's success;

2. to develop consistent and systematic application tools and methods for evaluating proposed sites; and

3. to train staff in those tools and methods.

With these goals and objectives in mind, several different approaches to locational research can be explored.

Location Models

The object of a location strategy and the selection of branch sites is to determine the pattern of branches that best meets corporate goals and objectives, and thus create a balance between the requirements of the institution and the needs of the marketplace. Branch site decisions are not merely the act of choosing new sites, but a complex process that involves a number of serious decisions. Within this framework, guidelines are needed for selecting optimal sites and estimating expected deposits and profits of each site.

Given the importance of branch location decisions, a number of analytical procedures have been developed for location analysis and site selection; they constitute a distinct body of knowledge from both theoretical and practical perspectives.

Methods of branch location and deposit forecasting are distinctly different from the techniques normally used in the nonfinancial retail market environment. Financial institutions depend not so much on the quality and price of their products to attract customers but rather lean heavily on physical characteristics, such as location type, accessibility, and visibility. The following identifies six branch location strategies and deposit forecasting methods that are utilized by financial institutions. These procedures can be extremely useful in aiding the site location process. Since the different models have varying strengths and weaknesses and require particular types of data, it is essential that the model utilized for a specific analysis best suit the needs of both the user and the available data.

Floor Space: Space Deposit Ratio Method

Under this approach, it is assumed that a branch's share of deposits in a market area is directly proportional to its share of total bank floor space within the market. First, the size of the branch's trade area is estimated by an area around it, say a one-mile radius, with the radius equal to the distance consumers are willing to travel to the branch. Demographic data from the defined trade area are combined with sales by product to obtain overall market potential. The branch's share of deposits simply equals its share of bank floor space in the area.

The floor space:deposit ratio method is the simplest way to estimate branch potential. However, the assumption that deposits equal a branch's share of floor space is not always applicable, and it assumes that all customers travel the same distance for all products.

Proximal Area Method

This method assumes that depositors will travel to the closest financial institution for each financial product. A branch's trade area is the geographic area that is closer to that branch than the area is to any other branch. That is, consumers within the branch's trade area are closer to that branch than to any other.

Because of the distance traveled assumption, the proximal area method is best suited for forecasting potential for areas in which branches are similar in size and attractiveness and sell undifferentiated products. This makes it a good model for ATMs. However, consumers do not always travel to the closest branch, and the model does not consider traffic patterns that may route consumers away from the branch. In addition, the model fails to reflect differences in consumer segments in terms of banking habits.

Cluster Model

This approach is based on the theory that the proportion of deposits attracted to a location with multiple institutions is directly proportional to the sum of each institution's size and inversely related to the distance from other clustered bank locations.

While applicable to estimating profits in an area with daytime population or in large urban areas with multiple urban centers, it can be very difficult for this model to determine a branch's trade area. In addition, the model assumes that a consumer will bypass the nearest branch if the extra effort is compensated for by a better price, improved image, or differentiated product. Moreover, the clustering of branches of different institutions does not always increase the number of customers.

Analog Method

The analog method assumes that a new branch's potential can be based upon the performance of existing branches. Branch locations similar or analogous to the proposed site are identified. The selected branches should be similar in socioeconomic and demographic characteristics, competition, and shopping patterns. Using internal data, trade areas and market penetration are determined.

This approach is very versatile and can be adopted to a variety of uses. It is the basis for geodemographic screening models, whereby market segments that are concentrated around successful branches are identified and used to "screen" new markets and sites. Nevertheless, the potential of a new site needs to be adjusted to reflect any differences between the analogous branches and the new branch.

Regression Models

A regression model mathematically describes the relationship between demographic and socioeconomic variables and the potential of a given site. For instance, let P_i once again represent the potential of site i, and $x_1, x_2, \ldots, x_n$ represent the significant independent variables that influence potential. A regression model would yield the following equation, where a is the intercept term and $b, c, \ldots, z$ are the regression coefficients corresponding to each independent variable:

$$P_i = a + bx_1i + cx_2i + \ldots + zx_ni$$

The integrity of a regression model depends on the quality and quantity of data used. In addition, it is a static model in that it represents only one point in time. It does, however, isolate key performance variables that have the greatest impact on a site's potential.

Gravity Models

A spatial interaction or gravity model assumes that the share of customers that a branch attracts is inversely proportional to the distance a consumer must travel and directly related to the attraction or characteristics of the branch. If done properly, this model provides valuable insights into consumer preferences and will reasonably predict potential. It is an ideal model for "what if" analysis of alternative sites. However, there is no way to measure the number of consumers within the trade area who purchase financial services outside the trade area, or the number of consumers outside the trade area who purchase products within the trade area.

Data Sources for Estimating Demand

Regardless of the methodology used, locational research is nothing more than a process by which data is generated, organized, and analyzed to support site decisions. This process results in an analytical tool that rates and subsequently ranks the profit potential of various markets.

All locational research applications rely upon the generation of pertinent data. In fact, the major premise of locational research is to identify what factors affect demand and sales performance. This data is market or site related, depending upon the application, and can be drawn from a variety of sources: customer information files, syndicated databases, market audits, proprietary databases, government data, and primary field data collection.

Five major categories of data should be considered.

1. Demographic—population, income, age, education, occupation, persons per household, housing value, etc.

2. Businesses—units and revenues by SIC code, daytime employment.

3. Consumer Demand—syndicated surveys, local market audits.

4. Physical Attributes—unit type (e.g., full service, limited service), visibility, traffic patterns, shopping centers.

5. Competition—number, type, size, deposits.

Each of these broad categories of data varies in impact in explaining variations in sales. In general, the impact of demographic factors increases as the size of the trade area decreases and the frequency of patronage increases. This decay function is depicted by Figure 1. Note that the impact of distance is greatest on suburban locations. In our example, 50% of a suburban branch's customer base falls within a three-mile radius, while in a rural location, less than 20% falls within the same radius. The urban location falls between the two, with bank-at-work consumers offsetting the close proximity of urban dwelling customers. Consumer travel distance also varies by product type. In general, the higher the transaction frequency, the smaller the distance a customer is willing to travel.

Business factors tend to have the greatest impact on performance in urban areas and are usually measured through daytime employment characteristics and data regarding local businesses. Daytime employment data can be broken down by occupation for more detailed analysis, while business data typically includes revenues and number of employees by SIC code.

To effectively associate demographic and daytime employment characteristics with demand potential, it is useful to gather industrywide product usage behavior for the products and services that the proposed site will offer. Sources of industrywide purchasing behavior

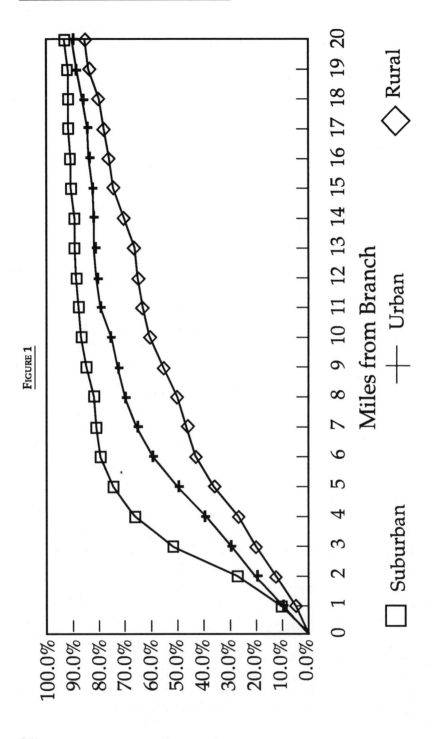

FIGURE 1

include syndicated surveys, data exchanges, local market audits, and an institution's own customer file. Each of these sources has it own strengths and weaknesses. Syndicated surveys are generally consistent and product specific, but may not be accurate in terms of reflecting differences in local markets. Market audits are product specific and reflect local markets, but lack consistency across markets. Data exchanges usually lack product and market detail, but are generally current. Overall, an institution's own customer data within its Marketing Customer Information File (MCIF) may be the best source for estimating demand. It is current, product specific, and consistent.

The remaining two categories of data, competition and physical attributes, have a significant influence on accurately predicting a site's sales potential. In many instances, traffic flow, competitor locations, and activity generators such as shopping centers combine to have more bearing on a site's success than demographic considerations.

Competitive data can be gathered from governmental sources such as the FDIC and FHLBB, as well as from regional data exchanges (e.g., Florida Bankers Association, Financial Institutions Data Exchange). Information required includes number, size, deposits, and location of competitive branches. Physical attributes require individual site evaluations to gather items such as accessibility, visibility, signage, building type, and the like. It is surprising how many branch sites are identified by secondary data and then evaluated and recommended by local real estate salesmen.

Sample Selection

The choice of which branches to use in the modeling process is very important. The sample of branches used should closely represent the types of branches and geographies that the bank is currently operating or plans to expand into. Items to consider in selecting a representative sample are as follows:

- Sales variation—the sample should include branches with an even distribution of performance, rather than evaluating only top performing branches.

- Age of branch—branches with less than one year of operation are normally excluded due to lack of adequate experience.

- Market type—the sample should include branches representing all markets (i.e., suburban, urban, rural) in which the bank operates. This allows for the separation of the sample into subgroups. In most instances, rural markets are excluded from samples used to forecast the potential of an urban or suburban location due to the diverse trade areas normally served in rural markets.

- Branch type—the sample must also include all branch types, that is, full-service, limited service, ATM, etc. However, branches located in shopping malls without outside access are generally excluded. Position in the mall and the large drawing area of shopping malls dictates that these units be analyzed independently.

These sample selection considerations are integral to the development of an effective locational model, particularly when the Analog Method or Regression Model approaches are utilized.

Definition of Trade Area and Product Mix

When analyzing a specific location it is important that the site's trade area and product mix be accurately defined. In this regard, the financial industry might be wise to adopt the concepts of a product's range, threshold, and order. Use of these three concepts can help a bank to define its branch's particular trade area and product mix.

Range essentially is the distance people are willing to travel to get a given product. As mentioned above, it is a function of the frequency with which a product or service must be accessed. It also reflects local competition among the providers of given products and services. Perhaps consumers as a whole are willing to travel ten minutes to do routine banking. If the density of banking competitors in a particular area exceeds one every ten minutes, a customer may not want to travel the full ten minutes to use Bank A's facilities: Banks B and C may provide intervening opportunities to satisfy this need. The concept of range is understood on a site-by-site basis in the banking industry and is expressed in the idea of primary, secondary, and fringe market areas. A full-service branch may have a primary market area with a radius of five minutes in which the majority of customers live or work. The secondary market area may extend another two minutes beyond and provide a significant minority of customers. The fringe or occasional market area may extend another two or three minutes. These are well-established concepts in the literature, but their implications for entire systems of branches do not seem clearly grasped.

A second key spatial concept is that of **threshold**. For a given product or service to be profitable for its provider, there must be sufficient demand for it within its range. There have to be enough people in a product's range who, multiplied by the rate of purchase and the cost of purchase, will generate enough effective demand to cover the cost of providing that product. There is no point in offering a product in so many places that competition within a branch network reduces the range, and thus the threshold, of that product below the break-even point for each branch.

The third important spatial idea is that of **order**. Order is a concept having to do with the price of product and the typical frequency of its purchase. High order describes high-value products and services, infrequently accessed, which people are willing to travel a relatively great distance to purchase. Thus, high order products have large ranges and thresholds. Low order products are those commodities accessed frequently, generally of low value, that people are not at all willing to travel far for. They have small ranges and thresholds and can, therefore, be densely spaced.

A tricky aspect of order is that each product or service has its own order, range and threshold, which usually do not perfectly coincide with those of other products. Their orders, ranges, and thresholds can be grouped together into similar clusters, though, and products of similar order can be offered together in correspondingly high or low order centers or delivery outlets. Low order products can be offered together in densely spaced low order outlets; medium order products can be offered with one another and with products of a lower order in less densely spaced medium order centers; high order products can be provided with one another and with the full gamut of lower order products at widely spaced high order centers. The only time high order products should be subdivided into distinct and separate arrays of similarly ordered products is when their target populations are so very different that it would be useless to offer the full gamut at all high order centers. The highest to the lowest order centers should be arranged in such a way that an entire region is completely covered by the market areas of adjacent centers at each level, barring areas of sparse population and areas of thick intervening opportunities offered by the competition.

These concepts of range, threshold, and order can be easily applied to banking practices. Banks should recognize how far customers are willing to travel to get different types of services. Obviously, customers are less willing to travel far to use an ATM than to procure a home-improvement loan. Range also differs for various types of accounts. Customers may travel some distance to get a high-interest CD but wish to be close to the branch in which their everyday checking account is established. A spatial analysis of consumer banking habits is therefore essential in determining the range of different bank services.

The need to understand ranges is particularly important when contemplating the offering of nontraditional products and services such as discount brokering, insurance services, and investment counseling. These need to be grouped into similar arrays based on range and then situated in some high order branches with a numerically, demographically, and sociologically adequate population base, or threshold, within the offerings' ranges. Pilot experiments in offering such high order products and services can be used to generate range data from actual experience.

Determination of threshold of a given product or service in an area will enable the bank to assess potential profits more accurately. This will also help in establishing the number and types of products and services to be offered in an area, which, in turn, will affect the type and size of branch to be established. A thorough understanding of each product's threshold implies a solid grasp of general consumer trends and the idiosyncrasies of the local market. Knowledge of the local market also includes an evaluation of competitors: where they are located, which types of products and services are offered in each location, and their success. If too many competitors are offering a particular service in a specified area, the profitability of that service is lessened through a reduction in range and threshold. Entry into that market is unlikely to generate business levels exceeding the costs involved.

With more conventional products and services, most institutions have an idea as to how many and what types of people must be found in an outlet's range or market area, depending on the intensity of the competition. Thresholds will definitely be affected by the socio-economic status of local populations. A much smaller population base of wealthier customers can support high-tech, high order products. The smaller the population threshold, of course, the smaller the ranges of the offerings. High order and specialized branches can sometimes be surprisingly close together in wealthier neighborhoods, but the competition of many financial institutions for access to the top 20% of customers may create excessive density in such neighborhoods and correspondingly increase delivery costs relative to branch revenues.

Order needs to be appreciated as integral to the concepts of range and threshold. Once the bank has established the range and threshold of services, they can be ranked and categorized into low, medium, and high order products. Combining knowledge of local market idio-syncrasies, the location of competition, and the order of a bank's services will allow a bank to plan a delivery strategy that takes the various factors into account. For example, financial counseling and brokering services might not have to be included in a high order branch servicing a relatively modest income region. They can be saved for comparable order centers in wealthier districts. Once all factors have been analyzed, then each newly planned branch or ATM can be evaluated in terms of how it fits the bank's network and goals overall.

A particularly strong point of analysis using range, threshold, and order is the overall view their implementation encourages. That is, a bank increasingly takes overall performance as its point of departure rather than just the performance of single outlets. This type of view compels a bank to address the monumental problems involved in assessing branch-level performance problems before deciding to close branches. A narrow site-based performance evaluation may cause a bank to close a branch that plays a key role in raising the profitability of several nearby branches. From this perspective, it is easier to appreciate the very different functions performed by different types of branches and, thus, devise performance criteria appropriate to a particular branch's purpose in the entire network.

Conclusion

Deregulation and intensified price competition, together with the advent of self-service banking technologies, are forcing banks to re-evaluate and reconceptualize their entire delivery systems. Consequently, developing a location strategy requires in-depth analysis and a movement away from simple duplicative brick and mortar systems.

When planning a branch network, the profitability of potential sites must be explored through a systematic approach, several of which we have discussed. Since no one method is applicable in all circumstances, we have focused on the strengths, weaknesses, and application issues associated with each technique, three of which are detailed in the case studies that follow.

Case Study - Analog Method

Introduction

To meet the growing needs of its marketplace, ABC Bank decided to undertake an ambitious network delivery expansion program in the rapidly growing markets surrounding its central metropolitan location. The approach chosen by ABC Bank was to identify the market characteristics that predominated around its top performing units, then screen the markets based upon those characteristics to pinpoint areas for site expansion.

For this project, ABC Bank utilized a geo-demographic segmentation system. The system classified every household in the U.S. into one of forty-eight distinct market segments based upon the demographic, socio-economic, and housing characteristics of the neighborhood in which the household was located.

Selection of Sample

The first step in the model building process was to select a group of branches located throughout the ABC Bank branch network. The sample was constructed to contain a number of branches with high, average, and low performance, as well as to include a variety of locational situations.

Initially, fifty-six sites were chosen. These sites were then examined along the following criteria:

1. Branches open less than twelve months were eliminated for having inadequate history.

2. Branches over five years old were deleted to ensure that sample reflected recent real estate conditions.

3. Branches with extreme conditions (unusually high/low deposits or population) were also removed.

Based upon these three criteria, a final sample of fifty-three branches become the base for developing the analog screening model.

Developing Profiles and the Analog Indices

The geo-demographic market segments surrounding each of the fifty-three branch locations was determined, with a total of twelve considered to be top performing units. The twelve became the basis of the analysis, with the households surrounding these branches aggregated to product a top performing branch profile.

To create branch profiles, a base area was defined to represent the universe from which ABC Bank's top performing branches were drawn. The base area served to compare the top performing branch profile with a larger group of households to determine average conditions so that analog indices could be created. The base area used by ABC Bank consisted of the trade areas of all fifty-three branches.

The profile of the top performing branches not only identified target market segments and the number of households they represented, but also quantified the relative importance of each of the forty-eight market segments by calculating an analog index. The index was derived by relating the percentage of households that surrounded ABC Bank's top performing branches in a given segment to the percentage of all households in the base area within the same segment as follows:

$$(\% \text{ Top}_i / \% \text{ Base}_i) \times 100$$

where i equalled the one to forty-eight segments. An index of 100 was average, while an index of 300 showed that households in that segment were located three times more often than average around top performing branches.

Findings

ABC Bank's households were divided in to three groups: Core, Evaluative, and Non-Key. The Non-Key segments were those that represented a significant portion of total households found around ABC Bank's branches and did not have high analog indices.

Overall, ABC Bank's household base was segmented as follows:

	# Segments	%Top Perf. Unit HHs	% Base Area HHs
Core	7	44.6%	33.7%
Evaluative	34	31.7%	31.3%
High Index	11	25.4%	13.5%
Low Index	23	6.3%	17.8%
Non-Key	7	23.7%	34.9%

Core households were found in seven segments that accounted for 44.6 percent of all top performing unit households. They came from only 33.7 percent of the base area of the seven segments. Segment 33 had the highest analog index at 188, indicating that these households were found almost two times as often around top performing branches. The seven Core segments are shown below:

Segment	% of Top HHs	% of Base HHs	Analog Index
30	9.9%	7.3%	135
15	8.5%	6.1%	138
16	6.3%	4.9%	128
10	5.9%	4.7%	126
33	5.8%	3.1%	188
11	4.6%	4.3%	108
20	3.6%	3.4%	109
	44.6%	33.7%	132

Non-Key households were found in seven segments that accounted for 23.7 percent of all top performing branch households. These seven segments were concentrated around poorer performing units and are shown below.

Segment	% of Top HHs	% of Base HHs	Analog Index
17	6.1%	6.7%	91
14	3.9%	5.1%	75
18	3.8%	5.1%	75
13	3.5%	7.6%	46
12	2.4%	3.6%	67
7	2.4%	3.2%	76
8	1.6%	3.6%	45
	23.7%	34.9%	67

The Evaluative households were divided into two categories. The first group, High Index Evaluative, was made up of segments that had high analog indices but accounted for a relatively smaller proportion of the top performing unit households than the Core households. The High Index Evaluative households, in essence, had high likelihoods of being good for a branch, but were not represented adequately in the market.

The other Evaluative group, Low Index Evaluative, was made up of segments that accounted for small proportions of the top performing branch households and had a low analog index. These Low Index

Evaluative households had low likelihoods of being good for a branch, but were not represented adequately to be sure.

Model Performance

The initial phase in determining the model's performance was to define high volume locations and establish a minimum analog index associated with these branches. For ABC Bank, a deposit level of $ defined high volume locations. An analog index of 120 or higher was associated with the high volume branches. This meant that locations with an analog index of 120 or above should attract deposits of $40MM or more. For the sample, 85 percent of the branches scoring 120 or above had deposits exceeding $40MM.

The next phase was to validate the analog index associated with a hold-out sample. Using the 120 cut-off and the $40MM deposit level, 80 percent of the test sites scoring over 120 had actual deposits greater than $40MM.

The following table illustrates the model's performance. It displays the model's ability to screen new and existing sites, highlighting the model's ability to avoid predicting bad sites as good, and visa-versa.

| | | PERFORMANCE | | | |
		<500,000	>500,000	Total	%Classified Correctly
	>120	out of pocket loss 6	correct 10	16	62
ANALOG INDEX	<120	correct 29	opportunity loss 8	37	78
	Total	35	18	40	74

Given the model's relatively accurate performance, ABC Bank was able to screen new markets around its metropolitan area and dramatically limit site possibilities to a select few that offered the greatest opportunity. Of the thirty-nine census tracts initially screened by ABC Bank with the model, eleven had an analog index above 120. Within the eleven tracts, six new branch sites were chosen.

Case Study - Regression Method

Introduction

To identify new markets which might be suitable for de nova expansion, a metropolitan Atlanta commercial bank developed a model that predicted total deposits at the county level. The model was also used to project deposit growth to measure future trends, and with continued enhancement, could be applied at a more micro level.

Building the Model

The bank decided that the best approach to predict deposits would be to build a regression model based upon FDIC/FHLBB deposit data. All counties within Georgia that had five or more bank or thrift branches were included in their analysis. However, Fulton county, which comprised downtown Atlanta, was excluded due to the large concentration of main office deposits. This left a total sample of ninety-three counties.

Because of the highly skewed nature of data associated with Georgia's counties, it became necessary to transform the data to provide normal distributions. Consequently, the dependent variable in the equation was the log of total FDIC/FHLBB deposits (DEPOSITS) for each county as of June 1988. The independent variables, all in log format as well, were as follows:

1. Number of households in 1988 (HH88)

2. Percent of households in 1988 with income exceeding $75,000 (Y75)

3. The number of jobs in the county less the number of employed persons living in the county (JOBS)

These variables were selected based upon a stepwise multiple regression methodology. While the theoretical impact of the first two variables is obvious, the third variable measures the relative inflow or outflow of deposits from one county to another.

The resulting model was as follows:

DEPOSITS = 3.662 + 0.916 (HH88) + 0.261 (JOBS) + 0.152 (Y75)

255

The adjusted square for the model was just over .92 indicating that the model accounted for roughly 92 percent of the variation in deposits across counties.

Model Performance

Looking at the predicted total deposits for each county versus the actual data, the model was able to estimate total deposits within 25 percent of actual for seventy-two of the ninety-three counties.

Overall, the model tended to over estimate deposits for the rapidly expanding counties in Georgia, while established urban areas were under predicted. This was explained by the fact that deposits were still booked in a former county of residence as families relocate to the newer suburban areas, and by the JOBS variable not being weighted sufficiently for these fast growing counties due to the higher significance of bank-at-work outflows. For the established urban areas, the shortfall in predicated deposits resulted from the influence of corporate monies.

Keeping these considerations in mind and knowing the growth dynamics and urbanicity of a market, the bank was able to explore and evaluate macro-level expansion opportunities, pinpointing those markets offering the greatest deposit potential.

Case Study - Gravity Model

Introduction

A large California commercial bank wished to evaluate the trade areas of four branches located in Northern California as part of a consolidation and relocation project. For the study, the bank compiled demographic and income data for the markets, conducted detailed site evaluations, retrieved customer data from their MCIF, and gathered competitive information from a proprietary database for all bank and thrift branches in California.

Approach

Rather than define trade areas by ZIP codes or census tracts, the bank relied upon their MCIF data for each branch. All customer households for each branch in the MCIF were point geocoded (assigned to a specific latitude and longitude) and mapped to determine actual trade areas. The distance between each household and respective branch was then calculated to determine how far customers were traveling. In addition, distance decay curves were calculated by branch for two key products.

The trade area for each branch was defined as the area around a branch that contained 70 percent of the households assigned to that branch. By this definition, each branch had a different trade area reflecting, to some extent, site characteristics and market penetration.

Results

Of the four branches evaluated, one branch had the largest trade area and greatest market share, yet was unable to achieve the necessary threshold of customers to maintain a viable branch. As a result, the branch was closed.

Another branch had a sufficient threshold of customers, but was performing poorly and had low market penetration even though it had limited competition. Consequently, marketing campaigns were escalated at the branch and were focused on very specific market segments in an effort to increase share.

257

The other two branches were identified as above average performers. Nevertheless, marketing efforts were boosted since it was felt that market share could be improved even further.

Post-Script

While all the data gathered for each site has not yet been presented, this case study highlights the importance of understanding trade areas. Defining trade areas in terms of distance travelled by customers for different products shows that branches have more than one trade area - each varying according to how frequently a product is used, accessed, or purchased.

19

BRANCH EVALUATION THE RIGHT WAY:

NUMBERS, TECHNOLOGY, AND THE HUMAN TOUCH

Jack D. Chamblin
Integrated Database Technologies

Since the early '70s when the financial services industry began recognizing the importance of marketing, marketers have been on a frustrating quest for the "perfect" branch evaluation system.

For the most part, that quest has emphasized the means ("system") and, in the process, lost sight of the end ("branch evaluation"). Too frequently, the consequences are either downright embarrassing or, worse still, misleading and inaccurate.

So often, the entire focus of the effort is on collecting and crunching numbers to produce a "scorecard" in the false belief that the scorecard will identify the winners, the losers, and the also-rans. In effect, simply deriving a score for each branch constitutes a branch evaluation.

What's forgotten in the process is the "why" behind undertaking the process at all. Its purpose is not simply to create a scorecard to rate one branch against another or one branch system against another.

Its purpose is to determine how precious millions of dollars in investment will be committed as branches are opened, closed, or reconfigured.

Even beyond critical resource-allocation decisions are those that impact the people at each branch. Based on the scorecard, and the scorecard alone, management frequently (and often inappropriately) establishes expectations, goals, rewards (positive and negative) for the branch and its personnel, doing so without regard for extenuating circumstances that impact and explain the scorecard itself.

A scorecard is certainly required. However, one must always appreciate these axioms in branch evaluation:

- Numbers do not always reflect the truth.

- Numbers, even when truthful, do not always reflect the whole truth.

- Numbers, even when truthful and complete, often deliver only the "what's happening" portion of the equation.

- Numbers, even when capable of delivering the "what's happening" portion of the equation, can often be of only limited value unless they've been integrated into a true database.

- Numbers, even when integrated into a single useful database, can often be of only limited value without the appropriate technology for unlimited, user-friendly access to and analysis of the database for diagnostic purposes.

- Numbers, even when diagnosed thoroughly, often fail to deliver the "why it's happening" portion of the equation.

- Numbers, even when truthful, complete, integrated into database, and diagnosed thoroughly, cannot replace the human factor in performing a branch evaluation that can serve as a sound foundation for making critical and sensitive decisions.

How Do I Get Started?

Having stated what is obvious (but often neglected) by marketers, what then is required for that ever-elusive "perfect" (or, at least, near-perfect) branch evaluation system?

These are the basic requirements:

- An understanding of the history and present state of each branch being evaluated and the market areas in which the branch is situated.

- An understanding and definition of the distinct and unique market areas within the geography of the branches being evaluated.

- An understanding and definition of the primary trade area of each branch being evaluated.

- Numbers that describe the defined market areas and branch trade areas.

- An understanding of the limitations of those numbers.

- A way to integrate those numbers into a database.

- A way to quickly, efficiently, and flexibly analyze those numbers in a diagnostic process.

In short, the "perfect" branch evaluation system requires a combination of objective data, technology, and human involvement.

What Numbers Are Needed?

There's no argument. For a marketer to do the job the right way, numbers are necessary—and lots of them. Numbers, after all, are the basis of answering the question: "What's going on?"

You'll Need Both Internal (Customer) and External (Market) Data

You'll need numbers that profile both the "internal market" and the external market. (When we speak of the "internal" market, we are referring to data on the customer base.)

Ideally, internal numbers should be:

- "Householded"—i.e., all account information merged, where appropriate, into a household or a business. (Generally, these merged files are referred to as Marketing Customer Information Files—or MCIFs.)

- All merged data must be assigned to a specific branch, and should be related to micromarket geography, ideally at the Census Tract level but no higher than the zip code level.

External (market) data must be related to micromarket geography, ideally at the Census Tract level, but no higher than the zip code level.

You'll Need Both Retail and Commercial Data

The numbers need to profile both the retail and commercial sides of the market and the customer base, even when the focus of the evaluation is exclusively on the retail side.

Why is that?

- The service component of any branch is directly related to and must be defined by the mix between the retail and commercial business and their different and conflicting requirements.

- Peak hours, platform expertise, product knowledge, special services, branch configuration all vary according to that retail-commercial mix.

- The retail potential of a branch no longer relates exclusively to where consumers live. ATMs and ATM networks are widespread, giving consumers almost total flexibility in deciding where to bank. Most heads of household, whether male or female, work outside the home. The combination of numbers and flexibility makes it imperative that the workplace be factored into a branch evaluation.

- Without understanding the commercial composition of a market area or primary branch trade area, one can neither accurately size a branch's potential retail market nor fully explain its performance and recommendation.

What the Numbers Need to Tell You

Think of the numbers as falling into four different "buckets":

Retail Segment . . . . Internal (Customer) Data
Retail Segment . . . . External (Market) Data
Commercial Segment . . . . Internal (Customer) Data
Commercial Segment . . . . External (Market) Data

Within each bucket, here's what you want to know. (It's a given that you can't always get what you want when it comes to the numbers. If you get more than this, so much the better; if you get less, you'll need to find a way to overcome the gaps, perhaps through the human factor.)

	Customers	Market
Retail Segment	Service types used How many accounts Dollars by service type Branch uses in cycle ATM uses in cycle When became customer Assigned to what branch Household head age Household life cycle Household income Household head occupation Home ownership	Projected service usage Projected service dollars Number of households Number of people Age distribution Life cycle distribution Income distribution Occupation distribution Home owning distribution Number branches by type Number ATMs
Commercial Segment	Service types used How many accounts Dollars by service type When became customer Assigned to what branch SIC Number employees Sales at location Type location Type ownership	Projected services usage Projected service dollars Number businesses by SIC Number employees by SIC Sales by SIC Type locations Type ownership Number branches by type

Where the Numbers Come From

These are the key sources of data by general category.

	Customers	Market
Retail Segment	MCIF with demographic data appended or attributed where needed In absence of MCIF data, internal account data	Updated Census demographics FDIC branch data Syndicated and proprietary market research data modeled for micromarket projections Competitive branch and ATM "census" of all providers in marketplace (shopping studies)
Commercial Segment	MCIF with demographic data appended or attributed where needed In absence of MCIF data, internal account data	Business "census" data FDIC branch data Syndicated and proprietary market research data modeled for micromarket projections Competitive branch and ATM "census" of all providers in marketplace (shopping studies)

Now What?

Assuming you've accumulated as many numbers as time, budget, and patience permit, now what?

Harness the numbers!

More often than not, a marketer expends his or her energy and resources on accumulating the data only to then face a severe case of the "shorts"—short of time, short of budget, short of patience, short of discipline, short of commitment, and, worst of all, short of goal. This is when the best intentions come face to face with reality.

Here's a tip: When you plan the branch evaluation effort, put as much emphasis on how you'll make the data useful as you do on what data you'll assemble. It's not enough to simply have the numbers; you've got to have a means of working with them and a structure for your analysis.

Enter Technology

You'll need the power of the computer.

When we speak of "power," though, we're not speaking of the computer's power as measured in MIPS, RAM, and megahertz; we're speaking of *your* power as measured by what you have at your fingertips, including:

- A true database in which all those numbers you've accumulated are integrated and can be related to one another regardless of their source, format, and content.

- A system that will allow you unlimited access to that database.

- A system that will allow you to query, analyze, report on, and map that database in an infinite variety of ways to support your diagnostic process.

- A system that doesn't require you to have an advanced degree in computer sciences—one that frees you up to spend your time using the database, not writing programs.

- A system that produces output, whether statistical or graphic, in a form that can be immediately used in your finished product.

- A system that allows you to operate independently of your main-frame and MIS department. (If you're like most marketers, you know what it's like to be a "computer power orphan" in your own organization.)

(For the skeptics among us, yes, such technology exists!)

Define a Structure

In so many cases, this is where a branch evaluation can fall apart. Much time and energy is spent in defining what data will be needed and little or no time and energy in defining—in advance—how the data will be used.

This is the stage at which the researcher finds himself or herself buried in the numbers, flailing away in a futile attempt to make some sense of it all while the deadline inches closer and closer. The results can be disastrous—statistical tables so voluminous that the "truth" is unable to see the light of day.

Before you start, have a plan! Develop a clear idea of how the numbers are to be distilled to illustrate—not conceal—the basic truths about each branch being studied. In short, define, at the outset, a method for turning data into knowledge and knowledge into insights.

Here's a suggestion.

Step #1: Define Market Areas

- Each branch operates within a market area which has finite and definable geographical boundaries.

- Those boundaries are defined by characteristics that determine the potential retail and commercial business for which each branch can compete.

- Among the characteristics that define those boundaries are:

    Network of roads and highways that impact the ease with which customers can get to and from branches in a given area.

    Other topography (rivers, parks, government installations) that impact mobility patterns in and out of a given area.

    Demographics (of consumers and businesses) that determine who might (or might not) either choose or be able to bank in a given area.

    Special attractions (shopping malls, office buildings) that impact the drawing power of a given area.

    Historical neighborhood patterns.

- Call each of these defined areas "Market Areas."

Step #2: Define the Competitive Environment

- A branch system is, in fact, a distribution network through which products and services are delivered. You must, therefore, *ascertain the number of distribution points* (i.e., branches) within a defined "Market Area."

- You must include *all delivery points*, not just commercial bank and thrift branches. You must minimally include credit union offices and, if possible, other financial services provider points that compete for branch business (finance companies, mutual fund companies, investment companies).

- You must assign each and every distribution point (branch) to a "Market Area."

- You must *ensure the accuracy of the data* you're using to determine the number of branches. You will probably be relying upon FDIC branch call report data and Yellow Pages listings. Those sources are neither current nor accurate. Walk the turf. Check with your own branch managers. Make sure that what you say is there is, in fact, there. Make sure you've included all of the competitive distribution points. (Nothing is more embarrassing than evaluating your branch system against competition that is no longer there or failing to identify new competition that has made a significant impact.)

- You must *apply a weighting system* to each of the distribution points. Not all distribution points are equal. Here's an example (and only an *example*) of how you can develop a weighted number of competitors within a "Market Area."

Type of Delivery Point	Weight
Branch of commercial bank or thrift—full service	1.00
Branch of commercial bank or thrift—miniservice	0.75
Branch of commercial bank or thrift—electronic or convenience	0.10
Branch of credit union	0.25
Branch of finance company	0.10
Branch of mutual fund company	0.10
Branch of investment company	0.10

- Call the weight assigned to each branch the "Branch Weight."

- Sum up all of the weighted values *within each defined "Market Area."* (Call this the "Distribution Base" within the "Market Area.")

- While a weighting system might not be precise, it does represent a reasonable effort to accurately reflect differences in distribution points—and, first and foremost, accuracy is what you're after.

Step #3: Determine "Share of Distribution"

- You'll need some measure of what expected shares would be for each branch—all things being equal. Take the "Branch Weight" and divide it through by the "Distribution Base" for its "Market Area" as defined in Step #2.

- The result is, in effect, the branch's share of the "Distribution Base" in the "Market Area." Essentially, it is a measure of what a given branch can be expected to produce in the way of business—all things being equal.

- Call this the "Expected Share."

- Because all things are never equal, when you've determined actual branch market share (see Step #5), you'll be able to identify those crucial areas of inequality.

Step #4: Calculate a Market Share Base

- Determining market share is critical. Without doing it, *you cannot measure branch performance to any meaningful degree.* Unfortunately, it isn't easy.

- To determine market share, you'll need a reasonable measure of deposit and credit dollars in retail and in commercial accounts *in each "Market Area"*—i.e., a base on which to calculate the market share of deposits and credit in each "Market Area" captured by each of your branches within each "Market Area."

- Here's a suggested approach for calculating the deposit dollar base in each "Market Area":

  Sum up all of the FDIC-reported deposit dollars for all branches in each "Market Area."

  Multiply the savings component of that total for each "Market Area" by 0.15 and add the result to the total. (This will account for all mutual fund and investment company deposit dollars not picked up in the FDIC data.)

Call this the "Adjusted FDIC Total" in each "Market Area."

Model survey data on the retail market against Census demographics to project the total number of deposit dollars in the retail market in each "Market Area."

One way to do this is to acquire Census estimates (household counts) by Census Tract (preferable) or zip code broken out by combinations of household life cycle and income and assemble those estimates for each "Market Area."

Acquire survey data broken out by those same combinations that give you average deposit dollars per household in each life cycle and income combination. (The survey data need not be derived from each "Market Area." Survey data from a broader sampling universe are reasonable surrogates for data from each "Market Area.")

For each life cycle and income cell, multiply the estimated household count within the "Market Area" against the average deposit dollars per household figure.

Sum the results for all life cycle and income combinations and let this sum be the "Projected Dollars" in retail deposits in the "Market Area."

Subtract the "Projected Retail Deposit Dollars" from the "Adjusted FDIC Total." Let this remainder be the "Projected Dollars" in commercial deposits in the "Market Area."

- Now you'll need to find some way of determining a base of credit dollars for each "Market Area." Because of the complexity of commercial lending, it's advisable to concern yourself with only the retail credit side of the equation. The combination of Census estimates and survey data for life cycle and income combinations can be repeated on the credit side to yield "Projected Dollars" in retail credit in the "Market Area."

- As noted in the discussion about calculating the "Distribution Base" in each "Market Area," this method for calculating the market share base is not necessarily a precise one. It is, however, a reasonable methodology for producing something that is essential for the exercise—i.e., a base on which market share can be calculated.

Step #5: Calculate Branch Market Share

- It's time to call on your MCIF data for each branch.

- Allocate your MCIF-reported data among retail deposit dollars, commercial deposit dollars, and retail credit dollars.

- Call these figures "MCIF Dollars" for each branch in each category.

- For each branch, divide the "MCIF Dollars" in each category by the "Projected Dollars" in the "Market Area" for each category. Call the result the "Market Share" for the branch in the category within the "Market Area."

Step #6: Calculate the Performance Index

- You are now in a position to develop, for each branch, a series of highly focused performance measures that can then trigger the diagnostic process.

- Essentially, this measure is simply a comparison between the expected share for the branch and the actual share in each of the measurement categories.

- Here is how it is obtained:

  Divide the weight you assigned to your branch by the "Distribution Base" for the "Market Area." Call the result the "Expected Share."

  Divide the "Expected Share" value into the "Market Share" value for the branch.

  The result is referred to as the "Performance Index." A number above 1.000 indicates that the branch is performing above the expected level within its "Market Area"; a number below 1.000 indicates that the branch is performing below the expected level within its "Market Area"; a number equal to 1.000 indicates that the branch is performing at the expected level within the "Market Area."

- In effect, for each branch you will have *starting points* from which you can step off into the diagnostic process.

- Here's an example of how these "Performance Index" measures are developed. Let's assume we are analyzing three branches in one "Market Area." Two of the branches are full-service branches and one is a miniservice branch.

	MARKET AREA #1		
	BR #1	BR #2	BR #3
DISTRIBUTION			
Distribution Base	21.50	21.50	21.50
Branch Weight	1.00	0.75	1.00
Expected Share (%)	4.65	3.49	4.65
RETAIL DEPOSITS			
(In $MM)			
Projected Dollars	207.55	207.55	207.55
MCIF Dollars	12.22	8.28	8.41
Branch Share (%)	5.89	3.99	4.05
Performance Index	1.27	1.14	0.87
COMM'L DEPOSITS			
(In $MM)			
Projected Dollars	35.52	35.52	35.52
MCIF Dollars	1.66	1.02	1.93
Branch Share (%)	4.67	2.88	5.42
Performance Index	1.00	0.83	1.17
RETAIL CREDIT			
(In $MM)			
Projected Dollars	27.77	27.77	27.77
MCIF Dollars	1.39	0.98	1.15
Branch Share (%)	5.01	3.53	4.13
Performance Index	1.08	1.01	0.89
SUMMARY—SCORE ON PERFORMANCE INDEX			
Retail Deposits	1.27	1.14	0.87
Comm'l Deposits	1.00	0.83	1.17
Retail Credit	1.08	1.01	0.89

Before moving on, it is important to note how critical it is to evaluate each branch within the context of the "Market Area" to which you have assigned it. As you contemplate the logic of this approach, keep in mind that there are two separate and distinct evaluations going on in this process.

- Once you have defined your "Market Areas" and collected your data, you will then be able to answer these basic questions:

  How do these "Market Areas" compare to one another in terms of potential?

  In which "Market Areas" do I want to maintain my commitment of resources? In which do I want to increase my commitment? In which do I want to reduce my commitment?

- Until you can assess the "Market Areas" in which you operate (or do not yet operate), you have not yet defined a method for accurately and fairly evaluating your branches. To do so, you need to measure branch performance within the context of the "Market Area" in which it is situated. It is both unreasonable and misleading to simply analyze your branches one against the other and all within the entire marketplace. Why is that?

  Branches within your system can be outperforming other branches because they perform in "Market Areas" that hold greater potential. They might, in fact, be poor performers, given the high potential of their "Market Areas."

  Conversely, branches within your system can be underperforming other branches because they perform in "Market Areas" that hold lesser potential. They might, in fact, be superior performers, given the limited potential of their "Market Areas."

In short, picking winners, losers, and midpack performers must take into consideration the differences in the "Market Areas" in which your branches perform.

After the Performance Index, What Then?

The exercise to this point has met a number of impressive goals. Let's recap.

- You've accumulated the necessary numbers—internal and external, retail and commercial.

- You've located the necessary technology to work with those numbers in an integrated, flexible, user-friendly, and productive environment.

- You've defined a structure for analyzing and distilling the voluminous data into a set of highly focused measures that can start you on the diagnostic process. You've defined "Market Areas" and you've measured "Market Share" for each branch within those "Market Areas." You've produced "Performance Index" scores for each branch on three broad performance categories.

Although you have some sense of which branches are winning, which losing, and which performing as expected, you're going to have to answer two crucial questions:

- Why are they performing that way?

- So what? What does it mean to me?

Here's where the human factor enters the process. The numbers might point you in the right direction. They might serve as a scorecard. But that's all. You and your management (or client) will need to know how and why it got that way.

Tackle the Diagnosis at the "Market Area" Level First

You've done the hard part by defining "Market Areas." Now profile them using the numbers you've accumulated.

- Compare and contrast them in terms of what they're worth now and in the future in terms of product usage, dollar balances, and, if possible, profitability.

- Profile them in terms of who's competing against you. Measure branch growth (or lack of growth) within the "Market Area."

- Profile them in terms of demographic composition and relate those demographics to the value, now and in the future, of the "Market Area."

- Call the shot forcefully and conclusively. Go on the line by saying: "We ought to be here with more." Or by saying: "We ought to be here but with less." Or by saying: "We shouldn't be here at all." Let your analysis back you up.

- Hopefully, you will have walked the turf and acquired enough anecdotal information to support your conclusions beyond just the numbers. In each "Market Area" you should be able to point to new construction and development, or to competitive branches that have opened (or closed), or new roads and highways, or businesses entering or leaving.

Now Tackle the Branch Evaluation Process

With a full analysis of the "Market Areas" within which your branch system operates, you're now prepared to analyze the branches.

While the "Performance Index" on each of the three categories is a good starting point, that's all it is. You'll need to determine whether the starting point has, in fact, identified winners, losers, and midpack performers on an unqualified basis, or whether there's cause for qualification.

As any researcher who has grappled with this process knows, there's no standardized way of attacking this process. There are, however, some basic steps you ought to take to determine where your scorecard can stand as is and where you'll have to qualify your judgments. In no particular order of importance, you better be able to answer these questions.

- How long have the branch and its competitive branches been in place? Could the lack of "maturity" of the branch explain a poor performance? Can the lack of "maturity" of the branch's competitors explain its superior performance?

- Has a major competitor incurred a significant "trauma" which might explain your branch's performance?

- Are there service quality studies available on each branch's performance? Do those studies mirror your performance ratings?

- Are your branches competing with one another? Are they sharing primary trade areas of their own? Are they suffocating one another?

- Are your branches configured appropriately for the demographics of their "Market Areas" and primary trade areas?

There's really no fixed format for this process. If you've got a comprehensive database and the technology to query it, you're perfectly positioned to carry out this diagnostic process.

You'll know you've succeeded at this process when you can answer "yes" to this question: "Have I gathered the numbers and put them in a form that supports my conclusions?"

One final word—your diagnostic process should not be considered complete until and unless you have taken these last two steps:

- Gather enough anecdotal information on the branches you're evaluating to support your case. What do they look like? How are they maintained? How do they stack up against competition in terms of physical plant? What is access like? What kind of platform delivery exists? How about electronics? Have some specific examples to support the more controversial and/or forceful conclusions you'll be presenting. In short, add some drama to your case.

- Do your conclusions pass the "sanity check"? If you asked your management (or your client's management) to label branches as either winners, losers, or midpack performers, would you be at odds? If so, are you sure of your supporting data? In short, make certain you won't be "blind-sided" by a disbelieving management (or client) without the information to argue convincingly for your conclusions.

PART 7

Understanding Profitability and Pricing

20

CUSTOMER SEGMENT AND PRODUCT PROFITABILITY

UNLOCKING THE PROFIT POTENTIAL OF YOUR MCIF

Carla E. McEachern

Customer Insight Company

B*ottom Line Marketing* is a phrase often heard at financial industry conferences. A critical focus on the bottom line is also a hot topic in virtually every issue of the popular financial trade group periodicals. Both speakers and writers lecture about the need for financial services marketers to be accountable for the programs they initiate. In an environment where only the financially healthy organization can survive, marketing managers are challenged every day to justify their marketing budgets or strategies, and to develop tactics that promote profitable products and relationships.

The integrated profitability software in your Marketing Customer Information File (MCIF) can help you analyze the profitability of both your products and your customers. With this powerful information about product and customer profitability, you'll have an advantage you can use to develop and justify marketing strategies that achieve positive results. Profitability analysis can also help you avoid the sometimes costly mistake of blindly following competitors down the wrong path of rate or price wars.

Historically, organizations have addressed product profitability through their financial or accounting area. Lengthy studies are carried out and cost accounting software systems are installed. Generally, however, these studies and systems, based on averages, provide information about the product as a whole. The accountants are more interested in the big picture, not how an individual account of that product type might be profitable or unprofitable. For example, your institution's basic checking product might be a money-maker for the institution. However, obviously not all 10,000 of the basic checking accounts are profitable. All you'll probably know from the accounting study is that the average basic checking account makes money for the institution. What you need to know as a marketer, for new product development, pricing, and target marketing, are the characteristics of the money-making accounts, compared to those that result in a loss. The *simple* answer is "differences in account balances," but there are often other less obvious factors that contribute to the profitability of a product.

And there's no way for the accounting system to tell you the true value of an individual household or customer segment. As a marketer, you know the importance of relationships. You know that selling profitable products alone is not enough. It's just as important, if not more important, to capture and maintain profitable customers. Identifying, profiling, and tracking the profitable customer segments with your MCIF is critical to success.

Getting Started—Half the Battle

Many institutions talk about using profitability software with their MCIF, but never seem to get started. A marketing analyst at a midwestern organization said that even though she was charged with the responsibility of defining product and customer profitability, she wasn't making progress because she couldn't get anyone else in the organization to participate or agree on how the process should work. At another large organization one person spent 2 years gathering and arguing about the accuracy of pricing and cost data before they even began analysis. This type of one-man-band approach can sometimes get results, but is seldom as effective in the long term as a task force approach. If you go it alone, you won't have the benefits of a consensus, your case won't be built on mutual objectives, and you'll likely suffer through a longer implementation cycle.

Those institutions that are most successful in defining and using profitability analysis in their marketing strategies also have a management commitment to the process. From the top down, all departments know that defining and using the results of profitability is an important goal of the organization. This point is important because, as with most anything, a lack of management commitment will doom your process from the start.

When the top-down commitment is there, usually a task force is formed, with participation from key marketing, product management, operations, and financial staff. This task force works together to define objectives and initial assumptions, to gather pricing and cost data, and to agree on averages where data is not available. Because of their unified approach, they produce results faster and suffer fewer challenges from other departments.

Lindy Friedlander, Senior Vice President and Director of Research at Washington Mutual, a $6 billion institution, stresses the importance of participation by the finance and accounting staff. "We had a commitment from our Chief Financial Officer to the process of understanding customer profitability. He knew that as marketers, we were looking at profitability in a different way. Even though our numbers did not balance to the general ledger, they provided important measures of *relative* profitability of various customer subgroups to marketing. The financial area provided valuable input to our formulas with product costs from the cost accounting system."

Collecting Profitability Data

Before beginning to collect data to write your profitability formulas, most institutions define their goals and objectives for the process. For example, some institutions will start with the objective of defining simple initial formulas for assessing major product strengths and weaknesses. They also identify goals with longer term delivery dates, like understanding and tracking household profitability and product repricing. Differing departments may have different goals, but the task force can generally set priorities and make sure that both the short- and long-term goals of the group are communicated to the organization as a whole.

After agreeing on initial objectives, your next step in assessing profitability is to collect as much information as possible about income and expenses of each product offered by your organization. Sources for income and volume data include both your operations and marketing databases, along with input from product management and operations staff. Cost information is more difficult to collect by individual product, but some basic cost data can usually be provided by both operations and accounting. The types of cost data you'll want to gather include transaction costs (on a per unit basis if possible), data processing, postage and printing, and unique marketing or promotional costs. If your accounting department has implemented a cost accounting system, it may also be able to provide you with overhead cost data, allocated at the product level, like salaries, facilities, equipment, etc.

Creating a worksheet or checklist for each different product will help you identify all the unique income and expense components. On your list, you should consider including items like service charges with associated minimum balances, transaction fees, debit or credit card fees, interest rates (APRs) with associated balances, and other miscellaneous fees like those assessed for NSF transactions, late charges, dormancy, and inactivity.

At this point, it is easy to feel overwhelmed by the task. However, keep in mind that it's not necessary to have perfect formulas right from the beginning. Rather, profitability analysis is really an ongoing process that requires refinement and fine-tuning over time, as more information becomes available. Even if they are not totally comprehensive, your initial simple formulas can provide some valuable insights into relative profitability of various products.

Your MCIF database may not have been designed originally with profitability in mind. All the activity volumes and service charge information important to profitability analysis may not be part of the database. However, by working closely with your systems staff and your MCIF vendor, you should be able to easily modify your database to include all the information you need.

What if you don't have all the detailed information you'd like at the account level on your database? Or what if your organization hasn't implemented a cost accounting system? You can get around these hurdles by using averages. The Federal Reserve Bank conducts an annual study, the Functional Cost Analysis. This study, with results published separately for banks and thrift institutions for each Federal Reserve District, as well as nationally, provides average cost data for all major product categories.

The sample of institutions participating in the study is small, so it's important not to use the averages without some adjustment for your operating environment. Many institutions using these averages adjust the costs downward as much as 30% to 40% to account for differences in number of employees, number of branches, account activity volumes, and other variables. You may also want to get copies of both the bank and the thrift book, regardless of your regulatory affiliation. With both books, you can evaluate the data in each and decide which one most closely fits your operating environment for each product. Copies and pricing for the local and national studies can be obtained from your local Federal Reserve Bank district office.

Writing Profitability Formulas

Most profitability software that works in conjunction with an MCIF will allow you to specifically define individual product formulas, using the variable income and expense components you have collected for each product. The best software will be flexible enough for you to enter formulas in any format you choose, using individual account information, constants, and other calculated values. If possible, always account for differences in activity volumes (ATM, check, and branch transactions) on deposit accounts and for fees, acquisition costs, and loss reserves on loans. The software should also allow you to store the calculated results in a user-defined field on your database. Doing so will allow you to use these figures for in-depth database analysis and reporting. The best rule, when developing profitability formulas, is to *START SIMPLY* and then refine the formulas over time to add in more complex components.

Writing formulas for product profitability is different from writing formulas that let you examine the profitability or value of a customer or household relationship. For example, a formula for a product will use all variables, including fee income generated from NSF fees, late charges, or other *negative* income. However, if you're looking at the value of the household for targeting a new high balance CD account, you may not be as impressed if most of the profit from a household comes from NSF fees or late charges on loans. Most institutions try to set up and run two sets of formulas, one for product profitability and another set for household profitability.

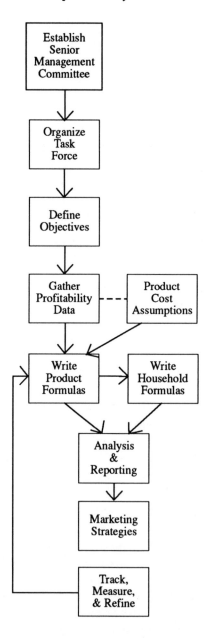

Analyzing and Using Profitability Results

Once you've defined your formulas and calculated the results, what do the profitability values tell you? You'll want to perform many types of analyses, but there are some issues you'll want to look at right away, including comparisons of products, customer segments, and branches. You may also want to look at using profitability results in designing incentive compensation programs.

Product Profitability

You should be able to use some of your standard reports, like Service Cross Sell, Detail PType/SType Summary, Balance Distribution, and Decile reports, to analyze the profitability of each product. With these reports, you'll want to examine average balances, activity volumes, and fees collected on both the profitable and unprofitable products.

If available, it will also be helpful to use the system's report writer capabilities to look at the contribution of each deposit product to overall deposit profitability. This type of report will allow you to compare both the profitable and unprofitable accounts for each product. A report like the following will help you quickly identify the high-achiever products. Which products contribute the greatest share? Are those the products your institution is targeting with promotional campaigns?

This type of report will also give you a quick picture of the numbers of accounts that are unprofitable. In the above example, DDA or checking accounts contribute almost 50% of total deposit account profitability, but 79% of the checking accounts are unprofitable! Some repricing for the unprofitable accounts could result in substantial changes to the institution's overall deposit product revenues.

When examining product profitability, also look at each product subtype, as well as the whole product. Some subtypes might not be pulling their weight. For each subtype, you should closely examine the set of accounts with negative profit values and compare them to those with positive values. What's different about the two sets? You should be able to identify specific repricing opportunities for those types of accounts with negative or marginal contribution to the

285

Matrix (prodcomp)	All Deposits	DDA	MMA	TCD	IRA	SAV
DEPOSIT PRODUCT PROFITABILITY						
All Deposit Accounts						
Total Households	3,755	2,832	330	228	278	1,255
Total Accounts	6,326	3,129	361	615	658	1,563
Percentage vs. Col	100.00%	100.00%	100.00%	100.00%	100.00%	100.00%
Total $ (000)	$557	$276	$106	$107	$10	$58
Percentage vs. Row	100.00%	49.57%	18.97%	19.29%	1.82%	10.36%
Profitable Accounts	1,311	601	190	185	207	397
	2,059	643	204	423	364	425
	32.55%	20.55%	56.51%	68.78%	55.32%	27.19%
	$759	$401	$112	$144	$22	$80
	100.00%	52.87%	14.76%	18.95%	2.89%	10.54%
Unprofitable Accounts	3,022	2,294	153	91	170	935
	4,267	2,486	157	192	294	1,138
	67.45%	79.45%	43.49%	31.22%	44.68%	72.81%
	-$203	-$126	-$7	-$37	-$12	-$22
	100.00%	61.94%	3.21%	18.02%	5.81%	11.03%

bottom line. Your MCIF should allow you to run *What If* scenarios against various balance segments to determine the impact of pricing changes on the profitability of the product.

Modeling various pricing scenarios with your MCIF is also a quick way to assess the potential impacts of your proposals. Producing graphs like the following can help illustrate the impacts of various strategies for each balance segment.

And, of course, don't forget to look at the potential impact of lost relationships. A price increase will generally result in a loss of some disgruntled customers. If a customer leaves due to a price increase, they take not just the unprofitable account but all of their accounts with them. You'll want to look closely at the relationships that will be impacted by a price increase.

DDA PRICING ANALYSIS
BY BALANCE SEGMENT

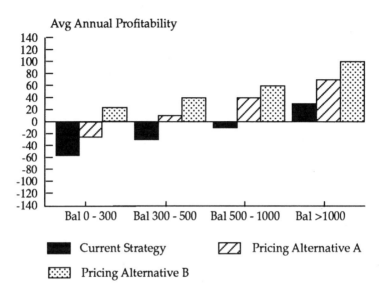

Avg Annual Profitability

| | Bal 0 - 300 | Bal 300 - 500 | Bal 500 - 1000 | Bal >1000 |

■ Current Strategy   ▨ Pricing Alternative A
▦ Pricing Alternative B

One approach to looking at the relationship impact of repricing is to create reports that show you how many of the customers in the lower balance segments, the ones usually affected by a price increase, are single-service customers. If more tend to be multiple-service customers, you'll also want to use your database to examine those relationships more closely. Package pricing may be a wiser strategy, in this case, than blind price increases. Packaging, or product bundling, will allow you to give credit to those customers with multiple relationships and provide an incentive for single-service customers to buy more of your products.

One midwestern thrift used its MCIF to determine that unprofitable checking account customers were actually writing far more than the anticipated 22 checks per month forecast when the product was originally conceived. It also found that almost one third of the bank's checking account customers did not have any other relationships with the bank. Equipped with this information, the bank began to charge for debits over 25 per month, unless the customers increased their relationships with the institution.

287

Colleen George, new Senior Vice President and Director of Marketing at $3-billion Bank Western, a Colorado thrift institution, easily justified the cost of profitability software by saying it was important to her to validate the use of media and direct marketing dollars in her budget. She plans to use profitability analysis to ensure that media dollars are spent on the most profitable products. Tracking the sales of profitable products will help her justify not only the expense but also the value of her marketing results to the institution's management.

It's also important, when looking at product profitability, to look at and account for the typical acquisition strategies used with each product. You can then determine if new strategies or different promotional methods might boost sales for the most profitable products. If you've coded your database to tell you whether an account was acquired through direct mail, telemarketing, a premium promotion, or personal selling, you can use the database to track and validate sales strategies for the most profitable products. Management will listen closely if you can demonstrate that your marketing budget is acquiring not just accounts but more profitable accounts for the organization.

Customer Segment Profitability

Comparing the profitability of one customer segment to another is where your MCIF can prove especially useful. Here, you're looking not just at individual product performance but at the total household relationship.

Classic marketing strategy says that 20% of your customers probably hold 80% of your balances. However, because of fee concessions made for large dollars, the high balance customers may not, in fact, be the most profitable. To prove this, compare the top 20% high balance households in your database to the top 20% in terms of profit. You may find some surprises. It's even possible that you'll find that only 4% to 5% of your customers contribute 80% of your institution's profitability. For example, high income households with large dollar time certificates are generally not the most profitable customers. This customer segment also often holds high balance credit card accounts, but because they tend to pay them off faster, these accounts may not be the most profitable. Looking at the profitability of the total customer relationship will provide the most accurate picture.

Once you've determined who your most profitable customers are, it's relatively easy to determine their profiles. What product combinations are most popular with this segment? What are their average balances in each product type? What kinds of fees are they paying? Are they primarily business or retail relationships? How long have they been doing business with you? Generally, answers to these types of questions will help you identify appropriate marketing strategies to this segment, as well as to other marginally profitable groups.

Chances are, you'll also have some single-service households in your most profitable customer segments. If so, assess the vulnerability of your organization to loss of these highly lucrative customers, based on product type and age of the relationship. Compare them with other more profitable customers and use the segmentation and modeling capabilities of your software to determine which of the most profitable products they're likely to buy. Then market to them.

You may also want to purchase demographic data to append to your database for these customers. How old are they? What is their average income? How many children do they have in each age group? Understanding the demographic profile of your profitable households and what products they are most interested in will allow you to develop the appropriate marketing strategies to buy look-alike prospect lists. You'll also have a better idea of how to target those current customers with the potential to become part of your profitable elite.

Another use for customer segment profitability analysis is to look at the marginally profitable households. Which of your most profitable products is this group most likely to buy? What marketing strategies will work best to sell this group, based on their demographic and purchasing profiles? Will package pricing or other incentives help boost their profitability? Using the *What If* capabilities of your software will help you to answer these types of questions and allow you to examine potential results of different strategies. Then after settling on the most appropriate promotion methods, you can use the tracking capabilities of your software to analyze shifts in profitability over time. You'll want to identify and track a control group as well. Creating graphs like the following can be very effective in demonstrating the results of your promotions to marginally profitable customer segments. The graph shows increases in profitability over time for a marginally profitable customer segment, compared to the control group.

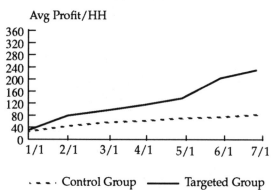

You may also want to look at the geographic distribution of your most profitable customer segments by creating maps that illustrate where profitable customers live. You may find that they're concentrated in one or two geographic areas, leaving your institution more vulnerable to the opening of a new branch by a competitor. This information will also be helpful both in direct marketing and in your own site selection for new branches. Maps highlighting the distribution of profitable customers have also been used by institutions to justify branch closings.

Additionally, many consulting and geodemographic vendors provide information on both product and profitability potential for custom market areas. Using census and other regulatory data, these firms can help you assess and compare the profitability of your products to the potential in your trade area.

Branch Profitability

Many institutions also use profitability analysis to compare one branch or region to another. At $8.9-billion Ameritrust Company,

N.A., Dick Harbke, Vice President of Retail Marketing, uses profitability software to help his branches identify profitable households for personal banking relationships. "After we calculate profitability, we accumulate the results across eight product types," explains Dick. "If profit for the household is greater than our profit goal, then that name is included on a report for inclusion in the branch's personal banker program." The objective, according to Dick, is to raise the service level and profitability of the household. "We see it as a way of focusing our efforts on those customers who have proven they deserve our special attention."

You may also wish to create reports like the following that examine the profit contribution of each product for the various branches within a region.

DEPOSIT PRODUCT PROFITABILITY CENTRAL REGION BRANCH COMPARISON						
Matrix (brchcomp)	All Deposits	DDA	MMA	TCD	IRA	SAV
Total Central Region						
Total Households	3,755	2,832	330	228	278	1,255
Total Accounts	6,326	3,129	361	615	658	1,563
Percentage vs. Col	100.00%	100.00%	100.00%	100.00%	100.00%	100.00%
Total $ (000)	$557	$276	$106	$107	$10	$58
Percentage vs. Col	100.00%	100.00%	100.00%	100.00%	100.00%	100.00%
Branch 209	1,349	1,046	135	50	93	399
	2,160	1,141	147	131	275	466
	34.14%	36.47%	40.72%	21.30%	41.79%	29.81%
	$226	$151	$47	$13	$3	$11
	40.63%	54.80%	44.41%	12.33%	34.49%	19.69%
Branch 210	2,406	1,786	195	178	185	856
	4,166	1,988	214	484	383	1,097
	65.86%	63.53%	59.28%	78.70%	58.21%	70.19%
	$331	$125	$59	$94	$7	$46
	59.37%	45.20%	55.59%	87.67%	65.51%	80.31%

In the preceding example, branch 209 has 21% of the region's time certificate (TCD) accounts, but they're only contributing 12% of the region's profitability for that product. Preparing these types of reports and closely examining product and customer differences will allow you to identify what causes one branch to be more profitable than another. The answer may be a concentration of more profitable products or a concentration of more profitable relationships. But the typical answers you may hear, "low balances" or "low income households," don't necessarily justify why one branch is less profitable than another. If you've examined product and customer profitability in depth, you can provide your branch managers with accurate data on the specific characteristics contributing to unprofitable products and customers. Armed with specific product and customer profitability information, you can help each branch to structure custom marketing programs that will boost their profitability.

Profitability and Incentive Compensation

Many institutions design incentive compensation programs for their employees that emphasize and reward cross-sell activity—any cross-sell activity. But, simple product sales alone don't guarantee valuable relationships. While adding relationships always helps assure retention of a customer, unprofitable customers adding more unprofitable accounts will not be effective for the institution.

Use the results of your profitability analysis in the design of your incentive systems. You may want to tier your compensation plans so that rewards are higher for sales of the most profitable products. For personal bankers, those assigned a specific set of clients, use the MCIF to track the changes in profitability over time in order to determine compensation.

What to Look for in Profitability Software

Most MCIF vendors provide profitability software with their products. In addition, there are many stand-alone profitability packages available in the software market. The best software will allow you to write and adjust profitability formulas in an interactive mode. Some systems provide only "canned" formulas or require that you submit formula changes to a remote programmer and then wait for results.

But standard or canned formulas limit your ability to make quick changes or refinements. Fine-tuning the formulas is an iterative process. Sometimes it's only after you view the results of your calculations that you'll know whether a formula is accurate. And, when you're looking at repricing strategies, you need the flexibility to make changes and immediately see the impact on your entire database. These kinds of changes are just not possible if you have to wait for a programmer to make the changes for you. With the right software, you should be able to accomplish the adjustments quickly while sitting at your computer.

Additionally, the most flexible software will let you assign user-defined names and values to variables that can be used over and over again in formulas. You should also be able to define conditional values for variables based on differences in account balances or transaction volumes. The software should also allow you to use data accumulated for the household in calculations. For example, you may wish to analyze the potential for a service charge on a checking account that is assessed based on the total of all certificate balances for any given household. This can only be accomplished if formulas can be written to accumulate balances within the household. Both simple and complex mathematical capabilities are important features, including calculation of compounding, present and future value, and amortization.

And, of course, profitability software should allow you to capitalize on the strengths of your MCIF software and database. Profitability values alone are not very effective unless you have the ability to easily report the results and then track shifts in profitability over time. These shifts will be important validations of your marketing promotions.

Many software vendors also will provide custom support and consulting on profitability analysis. They'll work with you to initially define formulas and adjust Federal Reserve averages to your operating environment.

Utilizing the profitability tools provided with your MCIF can give you an all-important edge in successful bottom line marketing. You'll achieve a better understanding of who your profitable customers are and learn more about your profitable products and where your most profitable branches are located. It will also be an important tool to use in strengthening unprofitable relationships, restructuring unprofitable branches, and repricing or eliminating unprofitable products. Profitability analysis will allow you to more closely track the performance of your marketing strategies, as well as justify your marketing expenditures. In an environment as volatile as this, understanding the fine line between profitable and unprofitable marketing strategies will determine whether you're a player in the coming decade.

21

HOW TO ADD SCIENCE TO THE ART OF REPRICING

Tom Rogers
OKRA Marketing

Charging fair prices for services rendered is regarded as a fundamental principle of the American economic system. Unfortunately, it is a principle that too many financial institutions have ignored—which means they have ignored opportunities to add hundreds of thousands of dollars to their bottom line, without adding a single new customer, a single new account, or a single new dollar of fixed cost.

In fairness to the industry, the technology and expertise to implement true household relationship pricing has not been readily available to most financial institutions. Until now, pricing has basically been set in one of two ways:

- Tracking competition
- Pricing to the common denominator

Tracking competition is probably the least reasonable approach to pricing. In effect, you are letting your competitors set your prices. There are two problems with that practice. First, your competitors probably don't know any more about pricing than you do, so why let them dictate to you? Second, their costs—if they can even identify them—are probably very different from yours, so the prices you set in response to a competitor's actions may be much higher than they need to be, or, more realistically, they are probably far lower than they should be.

Pricing to the common denominator, which means charging everyone in the same way regardless of the value of their relationship with your institution, isn't much better. True, it provides a predictable revenue stream, and it's easy on the data processing department, but it has some inherent problems.

First, it may or may not cover your true costs of providing the product or service. Second, and probably more important, it does not allow you to use pricing as a reward to your good customers or as an incentive for other customers to consolidate more of their financial dealings with your institution.

Partial Solutions Leave Big Problems

Many financial institutions have implemented minimum balance requirements as an attempt to recognize the "value" of a given customer. However, unless you have actually calculated whether the investment income you earn off these minimum balances even covers your costs, you can't be sure whether you are actually solving the problem of reasonable pricing or just hiding it.

Some progressive institutions have attempted to solve the pricing dilemma by hiring financial consultants and engaging in elaborate repricing exercises. Too often these exercises are both time consuming and costly, and often degenerate into turf battles over which department has the final say in determining official "costs." The results often don't justify the investment.

Other institutions, in an attempt to recognize valued customers, have gone to tiered pricing arrangements, where the higher the balances in the individual checking or savings accounts, the lower the fee that the customer pays. While this is a step in the right direction, it's just a step. Because of typical data processing limitations, tiered pricing can usually only be implemented at the individual account or customer level, so it does not motivate customers to consolidate all their household financial dealings with one institution.

MCIF Systems Make Relationship Pricing a Reality

The advent of powerful customer information database systems—commonly called marketing customer information files or MCIF technology—has given financial institutions a tool to take the guess-work out of repricing and given them tremendous opportunities to use repricing to gain both bottom line financial benefits and competitive marketing advantages.

Since MCIF systems provide a comprehensive picture of customer relationships at the household level, institutions can now set pricing based upon the value of the total household relationship. Rather than allowing the minimum balances in one or two accounts—or even the cumulative balances for one or two customers—to govern the pricing for the household, MCIF systems allow institutions to offer multiple pricing and service packages, and to implement those packages automatically, based on total household relationships.

Equally important, most MCIF systems give an institution the capability to create pricing models that incorporate either the institution's actual service delivery costs or the Federal Reserve Functional Costs, or both, to determine at least relative break-even costs. With that knowledge, you can still set pricing at whatever level you wish, but you can do so with the full knowledge of what impact your pricing strategy will have on the profitability of your institution.

This combination of capabilities allows you to set pricing that recognizes both the expense of providing the service and the overall value of the household as a *total customer relationship*. That means you can establish pricing programs that reward those customer households that maintain stable, profitable relationships with your institution and appropriately charge for services provided to those that don't.

Relationship pricing gives your customers a clear incentive to concentrate their banking affairs with you, but it also gives you a way to fairly—and regularly—recover the costs of providing services to those households that choose not to maintain an extensive relationship with you.

"Supermarket" Pricing vs. "Convenience Store" Pricing

During a time of declining margins and intense competition, many institutions are reluctant to implement any form of pricing changes, but true relationship pricing is a simple concept for them to understand and accept. After all, it's the same approach that they deal with every day when they decide where to stop for their grocery shopping. Let me explain.

Consumers have two choices for their grocery shopping. One of the choices is the supermarket. Everyone knows that supermarkets offer a wide selection of products priced at very low margins. The concept is that consumers will come in, fill their baskets, and the supermarket will make up on volume what it gives up by pricing with slim margins.

Consumers sacrifice a little convenience because they may have to drive a distance to the nearest location, and they may have to walk a distance through the parking lot to get to the door, but they sacrifice convenience to get lower prices.

The other shopping choice is the convenience store. By definition, these stores are located right in the neighborhoods, so they have convenient locations, and most are open 18 to 24 hours per day so consumers can shop "at their convenience." Consumers gladly pay higher prices so they can make a quick, convenient "bread and milk" stop.

Financial institutions need to recognize that they can begin to price the same way. Consumers who "fill up their carts" with a full range of products and services should be given the advantage of lower pricing since the volume and profitability of their total household relationship will be much higher. Consumers who shop for convenience—single-service checking or low balance savings—should either pay more for the convenience or should be motivated to shift more of their relationship to your institution, providing the mutual benefit of lower pricing to them and a more comprehensive, profitable relationship to you.

Tremendous Impact on the Bottom Line

The potential benefit to a financial institution is enormous. One $500-million institution in the southeast had been offering totally free checking, savings, and money market accounts. After profiling customer households, this institution discovered that 60% of all households were single service with total household balances less than $150.

The institution implemented a program of aggressive pricing not only for checking but also for savings and money market accounts as well. However, all service charges were waived for households with total balances exceeding a $5,000 minimum. This program produced an increase in fee income of nearly $223,000 in the first month. Over time, this increase stabilized at approximately $150,000 per month in additional income. Equally important, customers brought in nearly $2.5 million of new deposits in the first 3 months. Customer runoff was less than 5%, and was concentrated among those households with total balances of less than $500.

Obviously, when institutions that have been offering totally free services implement repricing, their initial gains will be dramatic. However, a $500 thrift in the midwest found that repricing also delivers significant bottom line impact, even when the institution already has fees and service charges in place.

This particular institution was earning approximately $23,000 per month in service fees from just over 44,500 checking, savings, and money market accounts. Using its MCIF, the institution discovered some disturbing facts about its transaction-oriented deposit base.

Eighty percent of these deposits were held by just 25% of the customer households; 64% of all transaction households had total balances under $2,600, and, most disturbing of all, 68% of all customer households were utilizing just one service. The institution launched a repricing program with the objective of reducing the number of low balance accounts and increasing overall household balances.

After determining its actual costs for providing products and services, the institution implemented three levels of pricing. Households with balances under $10,000 were charged for all products and services, item by item. Households with total relationship balances between $10,000 and $25,000 paid reduced fees for the basic transaction service, but also received a series of other services—check cashing, traveler's checks, ATM transactions—for free. Households with balances over $25,000 paid no service fees and received an even wider package of free services.

The results were far above expectations. In one year, monthly services fee income on just the transaction accounts rose to $57,000 per month, an increase of 161%, resulting in an income improvement of $408,000. There was a reduction of 26% in the number of savings accounts, an 18% reduction in checking accounts, and an 18% reduction in money markets. However, this was due in large part to consolidation of accounts and the overall household numbers dropped just 10%.

More important, of all savings accounts closed, 65% had balances of under $100. Among closed checking accounts, 57% had balances under $500. Total transaction deposits actually increased by 13% with average household balances increasing by 22%. Average savings balances increased 28%, average checking by 15%, and average money market by just 10%.

Must Be Carefully Planned and Executed

The results captured by these two institutions were not a happy accident. They were achieved through a series of carefully planned, carefully executed steps, and that's the key to any successful repricing effort. It should be a three-phase effort.

Phase I: Repricing Analysis

This is the "homework" phase where you must gather and analyze all the information that relates to your current pricing strategies. Your analysis should include:

- All current products and services offered by your institution.

- Current prices, fees, and charges that relate to those products, and the total income generated by product area.

- Current direct and marginal costs that relate to the delivery and processing of those products. If you do not have these costs exactly, it's far better to use Federal Reserve Functional Costs than to use no costs at all.

- Historical data showing trends in income, costs, and usage of those products.

- Competitive pricing within your market area.

- Current product usage and average balances of existing customers in each of the subject account areas.

This analysis sets your benchmark, and gives you the cost and income information needed to begin considering various pricing alternatives.

Phase II: Recommendations

This is the "alternatives" phase where you consider various pricing alternatives and then choose the one that meets your income and cost considerations. Critical factors to consider include:

- Types of checking, savings, and money market accounts that you intend to offer. Depending on your particular market situation, you may want to cull some products from your offering, you may want to consolidate some, or you may need to create new ones that will better support your pricing decisions.

- Various service charge levels and their income impact, based on the current number of users of each product type.

- Fees and charges for all ancillary services and their impact on income.

- Minimum household balance requirements to avoid service charges and the resultant reduction in projected fee income.

- Any other criteria for exempting accounts from service charges (employees, commercial accounts, etc.) and the impact that will have on projected income.

During this phase, you need to create a variety of "what-if" scenarios, changing charge and balance requirement variables to create projections of income improvements from increased service charge fees and increased average deposit balances and also the cost reductions due to account runoff. Finally, you identify one or two that meet your financial requirements and competitive market conditions. Because these conditions vary from institution to institution, there is no one scenario that will work for everyone.

Phase III: Implementation

Many institutions that launch repricing programs consider implementation to be nothing more than informing data processing, posting the new prices in the lobby, and perhaps sending a letter to the customer base.

And that's why many institutions that launch repricing run into a storm of staff resistance and customer protest. You need to be as meticulous in the implementation as you are in the planning. Elements to be sure to consider include:

- Determining the actual date for the implementation of the new pricing.

- Identifying all customer segments affected by the repricing, determining a strategy for announcing the repricing in a positive fashion, and scheduling the communications.

- Developing operation procedures to cover all aspects of the plan, including necessary interfaces and continuing communication with data processing so both the new fees and the waive procedures are properly implemented.

- Preparing and completing training for branch personnel, to give them a thorough understanding not only of the pricing strategy but also of how to handle customer comments, complaints, and problems.

- Making actual selections of affected households and establishing drop dates for announcement mailings and branch signage.

- Establishing a centralized customer comment center so that all customer complaints of any type can be analyzed and given appropriate response.

Announcement communications must be positive, but they must also be varied. Take a "bad news/good news" approach. For households that do not currently meet the minimum balance requirements, the communications should deliver the message that the bad news is that current conditions have forced your institution to reevaluate its product pricing. You're sorry, but it's a fact of economic life to maintain the health of the organization. Then state the new pricing.

However, the good news is that households can avoid all service charges by simply increasing their deposits to meet the minimum. Remind them that this pricing is based on the total household relationship, not just one or two individual accounts. You'll be surprised how many households will increase deposits to avoid service charges. Most consumers find it's easier to increase their deposit balance than to create an entirely new relationship with an entirely new institution.

For customers whose balances already qualify for a waive of charges, you can use the same "bad news/good news" approach, but with a twist. The bad news is that your institution has had to reevaluate pricing and increase the prices for most products and services. The good news is that this household will not have to pay the new charges because the household maintains a stable, valuable relationship with your institution. *Be sure to thank them for their business.*

Training for branch personnel must be positive and thorough. Explain the reasons for the repricing and expected income impact. Explain exactly how the program will be implemented, both at the data processing level and the branch level. Most important, explain exactly how any customer complaints are to be handled.

Phase IV: Measurement

During this phase, you measure and report actual income improvements and compare them with projections, making any adjustments that are necessary.

It's Work, but It's Worth It

Repricing is never easy, but the advent of MCIF technology has made it easier. Most important, it has taken much of the risk out of repricing because you can now create programs that protect and reward good customers while still recovering the costs of providing quality service to every customer.

22

A New Technology Model for Retail Banking for the 1990s

Clifford W. Potenza
Chemical Bank

Lately, it seems that all I've been hearing about is change . . . how rapidly it's happening . . . how much impact it has on our bank and on our industry . . . how it represents the catalyst for reevaluating our business . . . how change is the only constant! Yet, when I look at how we are addressing change, in the technology arena the bankers just haven't learned . . . the technologists just haven't learned . . . certainly, the vendors just haven't learned. Mike Hammer in a *Harvard Business Review* article was clearly right when he said "don't automate, obliterate," and I think we might start by obliterating some of the traditional ideas of how to support retail banking with automation.

Banking and Change . . . an Uncomfortable Alliance

Over the past decade there has been a proliferation of "solutions" that were going to change the way we did business, solutions that, through the magic of automation, were going to convert our transaction business into an efficient and effective sales, service, and marketing organization. Relationship banking, supported by cross-sell identification and management software running on high-powered colorful PC workstations, was going to transform our branch order takers and service people into super salespeople almost overnight and propel our banks to new heights in profitability. Plain paper forms created by laser printers driven by "desktop publishing" software were the answer to reducing printing costs, forms inventory maintenance, and stock obsolescence.

Credit bureau links combined with "statistically accurate credit scoring models" were to revolutionize the loan approval process and, when combined with the plain paper printing functions, would establish a new standard for loan documentation and, as a by-product, reduce losses. Database-driven telemarketing, centralized customer service facilities, and voice response technology were all going to change the telephone into our most important asset and provide us with differentiation through "superior service." I hate to be the bearer of the bad tidings, but for the most part all those great things have not happened. Ask almost any senior banking managers and they will tell you that there is clearly a gap between their expectations and the realities delivered by the technology.

Mismatch of Effort and Expectations

Perhaps the expectations haven't been met because we haven't given the technology enough time or because we have had economic problems that stood in the way of deploying enough workstations. Maybe we can blame the deregulated competitive environment. I suggest to you that maybe we have been led down a primrose path by technology suppliers who were more concerned with protecting the status quo, or protecting their installed customer base, than with offering real solutions. We've settled for hardware and software to automate processes we should have obliterated, we've been sold solutions to problems we don't have, we've accepted promises of futures that have been too long coming, and we've allowed vendors to tell us how our business should be run and what technology models we should use. Frankly, our customers don't recognize the model, they haven't asked for it, and they don't care about it.

Let me be more specific. How many of us have been told that the way to increase sales, deepen relationships through cross-selling and reduce expenses in our banks either is to integrate the systems that support the sales and service functions or to buy a Marketing Customer Information File (MCIF)? How many of us have been offered integration services by technologists that would provide the ability to use a myriad of software on a single workstation? Sounds great!! But, have you thought about the disastrous array of support and maintenance problems that accompany the integration solutions that create application program integration under windows or some other "integration umbrella"? Have you evaluated the training, support, and maintenance nightmares associated with multiple sets of keyboard, screen, and user interface standards deployed over a wide geographic area on hundreds of workstations? I don't think that an "integration program" or windowing technology that provides cut and paste will make a difference. I don't think that having to update all that software with an army of technicians using advanced "sneaker net" and pockets full of subway tokens is an efficient way to manage a branch network. I don't think the integration solutions being offered that tie together many pieces of disparate software on one terminal are the solutions that we need in our business. It may be right for the vendors but it is wrong for us, and I contend that we would be better served by the vendors' investing in "integrated systems" rather than "systems integration."

It's Time for a New Technology Model

I think we need a new technology model for our business. I think we need a model that recognizes that we are in the business of retailing bank services through multiple delivery channels that support effective sales and superior customer service. We need a model that recognizes, as Alan Silberstein, executive vice-president of Chemical Bank, has suggested, "branch layouts, furnishings, product offerings" and technology "tailored to the individual neighborhood and targeted segments." We need technology that supports each channel and channel variation, whether it is a physical branch, a telephone, a piece of mail, or something we haven't thought of yet. We need a technology that is capable of matching function and form to our customers' needs and capable of supporting levels of service that closely approximate the customers' economic value. Face to face sales, telemarketing, and direct mail all need the same information delivered from our MCIF and our application systems, albeit in different forms, about our customers, service, channel, and product preferences. Responding to customers problems and service inquiries requires consistency and reliability, whether it's delivered in a branch or on the phone or through the mail.

We need a model that separates the functions served from the method of delivery, the transaction processes, and the data presentation required to best serve them. We need an INTEGRATED SYSTEM, not SYSTEMS INTEGRATION. We need a system that can deliver the right information in the right form, at the proper time, and at realistic cost to the *customers' choice* of contact point. We need a technology that makes data location and form transparent, that maintains central control while providing extensive distributed access, and that presents information to both our customers and our employees in a form that is accurate, consistent, and self-evident. We need a technology that is scalable and flexible, that allows us to interchange hardware and software components as opportunity dictates, that reduces training across all user communities while providing staff interchangeability between functional areas. And finally, we need the technology that our customers ask for and one that we can AFFORD!

Technology as a Spiritual Experience

Look around the industry trade shows and you'll see some of the sexiest, most intriguing and fascinating hardware and software technologies ever assembled. It's a psychedelic experience of spiritual proportions. You'll see the integration of data, telephony, digitized photographs, and laser-disc-based motion pictures; you'll see a cacophony of light and sound that will astonish you and your customers. All of this technology, together with $1.15, will get you onto the New York City subway and most banks into the poorhouse.

Dr. Len Berry, the noted professor of marketing at Texas A & M who has spent so much time analyzing customer service talks about simple lessons like reliability, consistency, and fair play. Our customers want convenience, useful products, fair prices, and predictable service. They don't want and aren't asking for t-shirts, toasters, televisions, or cartoon characters on high-powered, "ultra-super-high-animated-graphics-capable-full-color PC workstations."

I would like to offer you a practical, affordable, yet state-of-the-art, architectural plan for the technology that we need to support what our customers expect from us. Such a technology that can gain us a competitive advantage throughout the next decade.

Where Are We Now?

I've always found that it's hard to figure out how to get someplace if I don't know where I am. So, with that in mind, I'd like to first explore where we are in the application of technology in the banking business.

First let's look at our technology strengths. We are great transaction processors! We can process electronic and paper transactions at lightning speeds. We are the envy of the product companies because we have such a wealth of customer, product, and usage data, however deeply buried in operationally oriented files and databases in the bank. We have a well-honed, efficient operations culture supported by a physical network of branches connected through some form of communications network. We also have a significant investment in a diverse set of hardware, homegrown or packaged, and highly modified packaged software, all of which is astronomically expensive to replace. Finally, we have a high level of computer expertise and literacy throughout the technical and business areas of the bank.

Let's look at the technology weaknesses. It is likely that very few of our mainframe application systems talk to each other, making it difficult to look across applications at customer relationships. If we have a customer information file (CIF), it is more than likely operationally oriented, with little behavioral data or information that is not required for actual account posting and statementing, which is fine for our accountants but makes it difficult to service the needs of our marketing and sales organizations. Our branch platform and teller systems were probably developed as administrative applications, requiring significant understanding of computer and transaction codes but having little sales and service functionality and even less ability to capture customer descriptive and behavior data.

On the people side, banks are asking all of us to be more customer focused and asking customer contact employees to be more sales and service focused. Yet, the information required to support these new demands is elusive at best. We are unable to deliver to our "knowledge workers" the information they need to be effective and, perhaps more importantly, we are unable to adequately measure the results. Our demands are for proactive, consultative selling from some employees, efficient order taking from others, and effective administration from still other employees without providing an adequate technology infrastructure.

Infrastructure

If there was ever a word more commonly used by bankers, it's infrastructure. I won't buck the trend, so in my context I'll define *infrastructure* as the most fundamental and simplistic level of business and technology support. The infrastructure is the foundation that supports our institution's ability to pay its employees' salaries.

The business infrastructure is simple: supporting sales and service to customers and prospects. We sell our products to prospects, they become customers, and we get to keep them by providing good service. In its broadest sense selling is the search for opportunities, the segmentation of prospects, the consultative dialogue, the order taking, the paperwork, and the follow-up, all of which contribute to the acquisition of business. And, again in the broadest sense, service is all the activities that retain the business, from the first "thank-you," to the statement rendering, to the handling of complaints.

The technology infrastructure is also fairly simple. Efficient transaction processing provides a level of reliability and consistency that we need to keep our service levels equal to our customers' expectations. Data storage or repository services provide us with the vast stores of information we need to decide who we want to do business with and how best to target them. Data distribution or network is simply the ability to get the transaction and stored data to the places they are needed. And, finally, there are the record processing, editing, and presentation services that change those mystical "data processing" hieroglyphics and codes into a form and language that are usable by our very human employees.

There is no magic to this technology business! Chemical Bank started to develop this model in 1986 and today has deployed it to more than

2000 of its employees. Chemical Bank's new Retail Delivery Technology Architecture is called *Genesys* and is defined as follows:

> gen-e-sys (gen-e-sis), n, pl 1. The Retail Delivery Technology of Chemical Bank which provides the ability to sell and service customers at their choice of contact point. 2. An Integrated Retail Banking sales and service support system providing self evident distributed access to centrally controlled and managed sales, service and transaction information. 3. The beginning of the future in Retail Banking.

Figure 1 depicts the typical financial institution's operating environment. It also depicts the environment in 1986 at Chemical Bank, when we had a series of "stovepipe" applications running in one or more central data centers on our mainframes supporting a myriad of files and databases using CICS, IMS, and VSAM written in COBOL, Assembler, and a vast array of other languages. Communications was supported through central communications controllers to branch controllers of many 3270 terminals or an occasional PC doing "emulation." At Chemical we also supported an ATM network through fault-tolerant, nonstop computers and had an independent and separate Marketing Information System.

Figure 2 depicts the model that I described earlier, which, I believe, is the business model for the banking business in the '90s. If you compare this model with Figure 1 you'll notice a mismatch between where functions are performed, where they are processed, and where and in what form information is needed. In the business model, the information is needed at various distribution channel endpoints, many of which are not even supported by the traditional technology. Telemarketing, teleservicing, automated voice response support, direct mail, nonbranch locational support, and nontraditional branches are not evident in the "solution."

Figure 3 depicts a typical solution to this mismatch. It is what we might call the first-generation delivery system. It basically establishes a need for technology support out of the central data center environment. The first-generation model creates a functionally driven solution based, I believe, on a very myopic view of the function. Yes, direct mail is important, telemarketing is a viable customer acquisition strategy,

FIGURE 1
TRADITIONAL SYSTEMS ENVIRONMENT

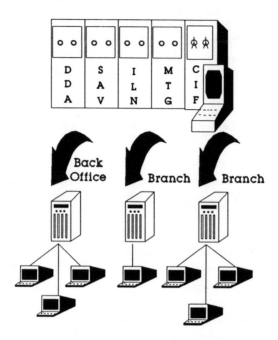

and voice response units can cut the expenses related to customer service. But as I look at this model, I see islands of technology that independently support each function. Each island looks suspiciously like the "stovepipes" of my mainframe environment of Figure 1, they don't support or integrate with each other.

Enter the creative genius of the technology vendors. We get Figure 4, representing the second-generation delivery system. In this model, our suppliers have created for us an "integration umbrella," which allows an intelligent PC workstation to support multiple applications and various emulation capabilities, such as 3270 and VT100. This approach is a quantum leap in the sense that it provides access to a multiple set of computers and application capabilities from a single PC workstation. Some of the "integration umbrellas," like Microsoft Windows and X-windows, extend the PC's capability from a single tasking device to one that can run multiple MS-DOS programs or

FIGURE 2

RETAIL BANKING BUSINESS MODEL

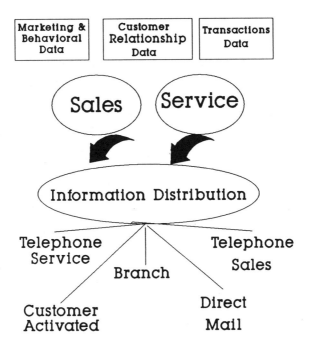

even, with some vendors, implementations, integrate multivendor, multiproduct environments including, PCs, MACs, PS/2s, VAXs, and RISC workstations. Of course, we still have those different user interfaces in each window, we still have to teach our employees a myriad of different key standards and functions for each application we need. And now, with this new, improved integration of applications, we also have to teach them how to use the "integration tool" itself so they become function-key literate and cut-and-paste proficient. What we still don't have is an integration of our MCIF.

Figure 5 represents the future of delivery system technology. It is known as a client-server-distributed architecture. It is the architecture employed by Chemical Bank in its support of its retail banking business. It is the architecture that supports sales and service excellence to Chemical's customers and provides consistency of informa-

315

FIGURE 3
FIRST GENERATION DELIVERY SYSTEMS

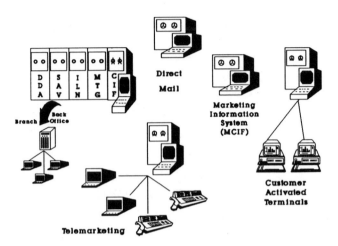

tion across a series of customer-selected delivery channels. It is the architecture called Genesys, and it provides a series of functions to support sales and service, whether they are face to face, through the mail, or on the phone with a single, easy to learn, self-evident user interface. It is composed of a series of mainframe, mid-range, and PC based applications capable of cooperatively processing requests for information from almost any source in the bank and delivering them to any location in the bank. It is a system that provides adherence to a set of open architectural principles providing inter-operability between disparate hardware and software. It is a system built and deployed using industry standard hardware, including IBM mainframes, Tandems, Wangs, a large Terradata Database Computer, a VAX cluster, small VAX processors, NCR and IBM PCs, Lundy Teller Terminals, Hewlett-Packard Printers, IBM printers, and miscellaneous other

devices. It is an architecture that allows the components to do what they do best, thereby maximizing their strengths and minimizing their weaknesses. It is the architecture that others will need to support sales and service in the upcoming decade. It is in use by 2000 of Chemical

FIGURE 4
SECOND GENERATION DELIVERY SYSTEMS

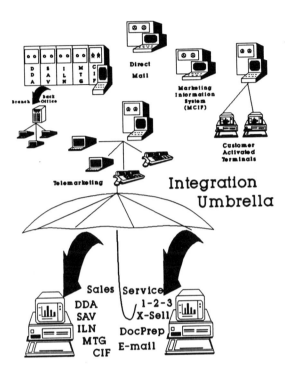

Bank's sales and service representatives in the support of its retail banking business.

Genesys ... Client Server Architectural Components

Separation of function is the key to client server architecture. Letting each component in the system service specific functions is a critical design element. Mainframes have been designed for high-speed processing of large amounts of data, while PCs have spoiled us with their ability to support a superior user interface.

FIGURE 5

THE GENESYS RETAIL DELIVERY SYSTEMS ARCHITECTURE

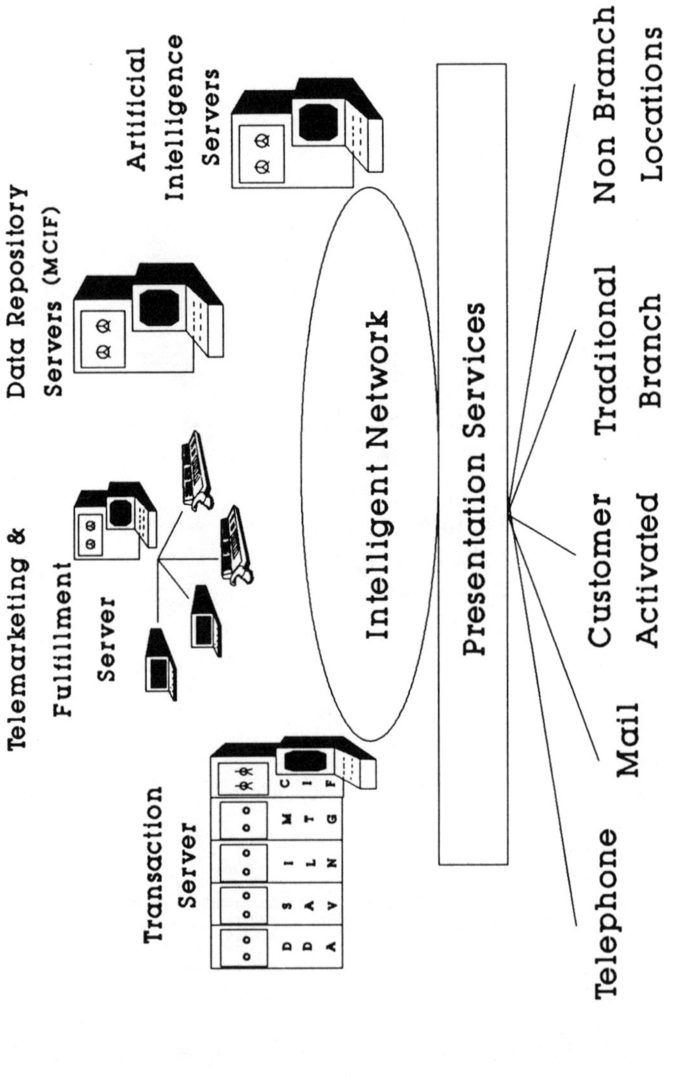
Transaction Server
DDA
SAV
ILN
MTG
CIF
Telemarketing & Fulfillment Server
Data Repository Servers (MCIF)
Artificial Intelligence Servers
Intelligent Network
Presentation Services
Telephone
Mail
Customer Activated
Traditonal Branch
Non Branch Locations

Mainframe Transaction Servers

As difficult as it might be for the traditional "mainframer" to accept, our mainframes will become large transaction servers providing high-speed, large-volume transaction processing services to client application requests. The CICS application programs that controlled terminals in our branches will give way to PC LANs that, over a wide area network, send transaction requests to our mainframe server programs, which will sort out the requests, access the appropriate database, capture the data, and send back a data stream of information to the requester. This critical "server program" at Chemical is called One-Stop and provides the intersystem communications link with different programs running in one or multiple mainframes as well as across different hardware machines.

Database Repository Servers

In the future, storage services for transaction information will continue to be provided by traditional mainframe IMS and VSAM databases, while a view of that information combined with a wealth of demographic, psychographic, usage, and preference data will be maintained relationally by large dedicated database machines or dedicated relational database systems. The use of a separate relational database provides the unique ability to maintain data that is not traditionally housed in or used by the operational aspect of our business. The architecture provides easy access to the information to support the marketing department, the sales and service functions, the direct mail and telemarketing activities, and the branches through an intelligent network.

Intelligent Network

The glue that holds this future together is intelligent networking facilities. On the branch level, local area networks (LANs) supporting as few as three work stations or as many as 300 will be interconnected to the mainframes. At Chemical this is currently performed using a Digital Equipment Corp. VAX backbone network running ethernet. DEC calls this backbone network and platform DecBank. Over this network we route data, rates, fee schedules, product descriptions, information bulletins, reports, security information, forms, etc., to or from each workstation. Over this network we distribute new software both to the VAXs that support each LAN and to every PC attached to those VAXs without any business user intervention. Our CSRs, our operations and business managers, are never asked to become technicians. I in fact our workstations, although standard IBM-compatible PCs, don't have any floppy disks, to prevent the information from leaving the bank. In the future the network and the processors that are a part of it will act as distributed file, print, communications, and network servers, providing utility but not application functions. More importantly, all the components of this distributed system must, and can be effectively managed remotely.

Presentation Services

Presentation of data, reports, single record processing such as editing, and "what if" calculations are the responsibility of the PCs. Built with a series of proprietary software tools, the applications at Chemical that support sales, cross-selling, loan approval processing, document preparation, telemarketing, fulfillment, customer service, currency exchange, and other operations execute on the PCs acting as clients that request service from other parts of the network. Using this concept, customer data, which may be anywhere in the network, can be accessed by any PC without compromising the central control and management over that data and without the worker's having to know anything about the data's location or format. Although the information is the same, the PC workstation will present the data in a form that is appropriate for the function. For example, in a branch we might use large print, color, bulleted displays appropriate for sharing with the customer in a face to face sales session. In telemarketing, the same data may be presented more concisely in recognition of the different need. In collections presentation may be different again, because the view is more administrative and operational than it is sales and service. In all cases, however, the keys, the screen interface, and the standards will be consistent.

Benefits of Client Server Architecture

The use of a client server architecture will, I believe, set a new standard in retail banking delivery systems technology. The benefits are significant.

Flexibility, the key to survival in this rapidly changing world, is truly supported by a distributed architecture like Genesys built with a set of application development tools. In fact, because of the flexibility of the system, Chemical has already started to deploy the technology to support other functional areas in the bank. For example, when the need for a new collection system was identified, the architecture provided the infrastructure, the platform, and the tools to shorten the development time and build a system integrated with the already existing data processing, MCIF, storage, and distribution facilities. When opportunities for the application of expert systems technology in the mortgage underwriting area were identified, the architecture provided for the development of an Expert Systems "engine," which was easily integrated into the network in a way that provided for the sharing of existing data and processes while leveraging the existing presentation services. This type of "server" implementation provides a cost-effective method for deploying expensive technology by providing for remotely distributed access to centrally managed functions. We don't need specialized functions like expert systems or MCIF running in every branch; rather, we need access to these functions and data from any branch. This flexibility provides Chemical with the unique ability to quickly deploy and integrate new technologies like videotex and image without major system rewrites or any significant training.

Scalability has been a major concern for some time. The difficulty of supporting a small branch with only a few workstations as well as a central service facility with several hundred has been the subject of many technical discussions and inventive solutions. Using the Genesys distributed architecture, Chemical can support any size operation, from a single dial-up workstation to a central teleservicing facility supporting over 400 workstations, without any software modifications. The ability to add PC workstations without concern for "controller capacity" is a significant strength of the architecture and the underlying software.

Although processing and storage costs have been steadily decreasing, the fact remains that mainframe costs still exceed $100,000 per MIP (million instructions per second), while PC costs are now at less than $1000 per MIP. The distributed, cooperative processing architecture provides the unique ability to contain, and even reduce, mainframe processing expenses by off-loading some processing to less expensive processors in the architecture. Screens, editing, and single record processing are more expensive using CICS and COBOL application programs on the mainframe than they are using tools on the PC. In addition, by using large data stream transfers between the workstations and the mainframe instead of 1920-byte screens, the network load is decreased, reducing the need for additional bandwidth or higher speed modems.

When change is rampant and rapid, any architecture that can extend software "shelf-life" becomes a critical success factor. An open distributed architecture, like Chemical's Genesys architecture, because of its flexibility, scalability, and adaptability, provides an extended shelf-life. It not only protects our investment in the delivery system, but it also protects the bank's investment in existing processing systems by extending their functionality, with the result of also extending their shelf-life.

Finally, I believe that in a business whose very foundation is based on technology, we can create a unique and significant competitive advantage through its creative application.

IBM is a trademark of and is owned by International Business Machines Corp. DEC, VAX, DecNet, and DecBank are trademarks of Digital Equipment Corp. Microsoft and Microsoft Windows are the trademarks of and are owned by Microsoft

Corporation.

About Financial Sourcebooks

Financial Sourcebooks specializes in books for financial professionals (bankers, accountants, financial planners) that are practical and results-oriented. Our goal is to help simplify for our readers complex, generally technical areas.

Among our recent Financial Sourcebooks titles are:

Building a Financial Services Marketing Plan: Working Plans for Product and Segment Marketing by Bank Marketing Association. "The most thumbed-through book on my bookshelf" as one banker recently told us. The book contains 18 actual financial marketing plans from institutions across the country.

376 pages, ISBN 0-942061-02-0 $49.95

Developing New Financial Products: From Needs Analysis to Profitable Rollout by Gary H. Raddon "...the most important thing a manager can do in a recession—and one of the most counterintuitive—is to fire off a broadside of new products." *Fortune* Magazine. "Four stars" *Bank Reading Review.* A step-by-step guide to developing successful new products for the financial services industry. "**A book that every serious finanical marketing practitioner will find invaluable** as a sourcebook for marketing success in the 1990s." *Credit Union Management.* "**Particularly useful are methods to translate marketing decisions into bank profitability.**" Senior Vice President, American National Bank.

288 pages, ISBN 0-942061-05-5 $69.95

Five-Star Service Solutions: Winning Ideas for Achieving Exceptional Service in Today's Financial Institutions by Barbara Sanfilippo. The key book on service for anyone working in financial services today. "...provides **a wealth of practical, ready-to-use ideas** for creating a customer service culture at any bank!" Robert J. Hutchinson, SVP, Manufacturers Hanover. "**Great!** Barbara Sanfilippo's Five Star Service Solutions takes the mystery out of the process of delivering terrific service with vivid examples and a simple but solid approach." Kenneth Blanchard, Co-author, *The One-Minute Manager.* "...**a must for the management team of every bank** in the service-driven society of the '90s." Wayne F. Miller, President, Orange National Bank. Provides over 100 detailed examples and tested ideas from banks, savings and loans and credit unions across the U.S.

288 pages, ISBN 0-942061-07-1 $39.95

The Electronic Future of Banking: Succeeding in the New Electronic Age for Tomorrow's Financial Institutions by Floyd E. Egner III, discusses the matching of technological capabilities with consumer needs. The book **addresses the major issues in electronic delivery of consumer financial services,** and details the experiences of major institutions who have attempted to provide these services—both successes and failures. Provides hands-on guidance and strategic research in developing new services. "This is **a gem of a book**—a treasure trove of electronic banking research translated by the author and placed in the perspective of a futures matrix from which electronic banking planners can develop product strategies for years to come." Dale Reistad, former President of the Electronic Funds Transfer Association.

255 pages, ISBN 0-942061-14-4 $49.95

Financial Services Direct Marketing: Tactics, Techniques and Strategies by James R. Rosenfield. For all those dissatisfied with their direct marketing results, this book is literally **crammed with how-to information**...exactly the kind financial providers (banks, saving and loans, credit unions, insurance companies, credit card companies, and stock brokerage houses) need to develop results-oriented, profitable direct marketing programs.Includes **detailed case histories** illustrating today's most innovative and successful direct marketing programs. Plus a collection of worksheets and checklists. **This is a practitioner's guide for developing marketing strategies that build profits.**

256 pages, ISBN 0-942061-13-6 $55.00

Attracting The Affluent: The First Guide to America's Changing Ultimate Market from the Editors of Research Alert. America's afluents are changing. Learn about this rapidly evolving market: Who they are; How they live; and Where to find them. Includes more than 150 tables and graphs substantiating key findings. Using the most current research available, this valuable book explores the different ways in which marketers can reach the different facets of this changing market.

272 pages, ISBN 0-942061-23-3 $49.95

Practical Marketing Ideas: 195 Profitable Tactics for Your Financial Institution from Bank Marketing Association. **The ultimate idea starter**, provides easy-to-implement ideas drawn from hundreds of financial institutions. "A treasure trove of ideas...**can be used as a springboard for [your] own marketing** efforts and used as 'experience' in developing products and programs." VP, Marketing, CCNB Bank. "This book **provides ideas which can be expanded upon, altered or used as they are.**" AVP/Marketing, Cleveland Bank & Trust.

300 pages, ISBN 0-942061-21-7 $49.95

American Banker's Banking Factbook 1991: The Comprehensive Guide to Banking in the U.S. and the World from*American Banker.* American Banker's annual ranking of America's leading banks **provides a convenient and comprehensive look at the American and international banking industry.** With over 100 tables covering every area of banking, this 1991 edition presents the key facts and vital statistics on the banking industry. **Plus a company index that enables readers to find institutions of interest quickly.**

152 pages ISBN 0-942061-37-3 $75.00

To order these books or any of our numerous other publications, **please contact your local bookseller.**

You can also obtain a copy of our catalog by writing:
Financial Sourcebooks
A Div. of Sourcebooks, Inc.
P.O. Box 313
Naperville, IL 60566
(708) 961-2161
FAX: 708-961-2168

Thank you for your interest in our publications.